T0134523

Springer Tracts in Electrical and Electronics Engineering

Series Editors

Brajesh Kumar Kaushik, Department of Electronics and Communication Engineering, Indian Institute of Technology Roorkee, Roorkee, Uttarakhand, India

Mohan Lal Kolhe, Department of Engineering and Science, University of Agder, Kristiansand, Norway

Springer Tracts in Electrical and Electronics Engineering (STEEE) publishes the latest developments in Electrical and Electronics Engineering - quickly, informally and with high quality. The intent is to cover all the main branches of electrical and electronics engineering, both theoretical and applied, including:

- Signal, Speech and Image Processing
- Speech and Audio Processing
- Image Processing
- Human-Machine Interfaces
- Digital and Analog Signal Processing
- Microwaves, RF Engineering and Optical Communications
- Electronics and Microelectronics, Instrumentation
- Electronic Circuits and Systems
- Embedded Systems
- Electronics Design and Verification
- Cyber-Physical Systems
- Electrical Power Engineering
- Power Electronics
- Photovoltaics
- Energy Grids and Networks
- Electrical Machines
- Control, Robotics, Automation
- Robotic Engineering
- Mechatronics
- Control and Systems Theory
- Automation
- Communications Engineering, Networks
- Wireless and Mobile Communication
- Internet of Things
- Computer Networks

Within the scope of the series are monographs, professional books or graduate textbooks, edited volumes as well as outstanding PhD theses and books purposely devoted to support education in electrical and electronics engineering at graduate and post-graduate levels.

Review Process

The proposal for each volume is reviewed by the main editor and/or the advisory board. The books of this series are reviewed in a single blind peer review process.

Ethics Statement for this series can be found in the Springer standard guidelines here https://www.springer.com/us/authors-editors/journal-author/journal-author-hel pdesk/before-you-start/before-you-start/1330#c14214

Devendra Kumar Sharma · Rohit Sharma ·
Gwanggil Jeon · Zdzislaw Polkowski
Editors

Low Power Architectures for IoT Applications

 Springer

Editors
Devendra Kumar Sharma
Department of Electronics
and Communication Engineering
SRM Institute of Science and Technology
Ghaziabad, India

Gwanggil Jeon
Department of Embedded Systems
Engineering, College of Information
Technology
Incheon National University
Incheon, Korea (Republic of)

Rohit Sharma
Department of Electronics
and Communication Engineering
SRM Institute of Science and Technology
Ghaziabad, India

Zdzislaw Polkowski
The Karkonosze University of Applied
Science
Jelenia Góra, Poland

Jan Wyzykowski University
Polkowice, Poland

ISSN 2731-4200 ISSN 2731-4219 (electronic)
Springer Tracts in Electrical and Electronics Engineering
ISBN 978-981-99-0641-3 ISBN 978-981-99-0639-0 (eBook)
https://doi.org/10.1007/978-981-99-0639-0

This Springer imprint is published by the registered company Springer Nature Singapore Pte Ltd.
The registered company address is: 152 Beach Road, #21-01/04 Gateway East, Singapore 189721,
Singapore

Preface

This book unites the experts in computer science, electrical engineering, intelligent systems, and very large-scale integration (VLSI) design. They review the latest theory, research, and practice in the design of low power architecture, with special emphasis on low power integrated circuit design for IoT applications. The book is intended for undergraduate and post-graduate students in integrated circuit design and low power equations who have a background in basic circuit design concepts and techniques for IoT applications.

Ghaziabad, India   Devendra Kumar Sharma
Ghaziabad, India   Rohit Sharma
Incheon, Korea (Republic of)   Gwanggil Jeon
Jelenia Góra, Poland   Zdzislaw Polkowski

Organization of the Book

The book is organized into 14 chapters. A brief description of each of the chapters follows:

Chapter 1 begins with a highlight on low-power IoT devices. The architectures for energy harvesting have been described in this chapter. The main energy harvesting sources have also been demonstrated. Following that, IoT energy storage was covered. This chapter also included some IoT system case studies that used energy harvesting.

Chapter 2 used Python and Verilog HDL for synthesis on the Artix 7 based Basys 3 dev kit to perform in two separate phases. The image data is first converted to grayscale for the Python implementation before being passed through the gradient-based edge detection (Sobel, Prewitt, and Robert) operator. The edges of the entire image are then determined using an edge detection technique. The resultant picture is then examined using various input parameters including PSNR and MSE.

Chapter 3 discusses combinational and sequential circuit design using various adiabatic approaches. Analysis of various parameters like transistor count, delay, power dissipation and power delay product is carried out. It has been analyzed that adiabatic circuits perform better than traditional methods.

Chapter 4 gives an insight into the methodologies of low-power which can be implemented for field-programmable gate arrays (FPGA). This insight includes design methodologies both at the level of system and device fostered on the commercial devices currently available in the market. It also enunciates the ongoing research on the design methodologies both at the level of circuit and architecture.

Chapter 5 enunciates the importance of IoT and its foster on the consumption of power and different techniques for reduction. Moreover, it focuses on the factor reliability in view of IoT devices. The discussion in the paper shall be a matter of importance for the persons who are keen in producing IoT devices energy-efficient to the level of maximum.

Chapter 6 illustrated various converter architectures for healthcare IoT, we can expect these topologies to continue pushing energy efficiency trends. A single system on a chip (SoC) will be used to implement many of these new IoT innovations, which will present challenges in terms of providing the highest level of integration and chip area reduction.

Chapter 7 proposed a IoT-based Efficient and Complete Management on-Street Parking. Here intelligent parking systems work in two modes i.e, online and offline; In offline mode, it acts as a conventional parking system just with a slight difference and that is it displays the number of empty and engaged slots on the LCD display at the entrance, in online mode, there is an addition i.e it sends this information to the customer via the internet so the customer can know beforehand about parking lots.

Chapter 8 proposed a high gain metal Fabry Perot antenna for deep space Cube-Sats. The constructed antenna is designed using High-Frequency Structure Simulator (HFSS) and optimized using the Quasi Newtonian method. The main feature of the proposed metallic antenna configuration is to significantly improve the antenna peak gain and to increase the lifetime for the target of deep orbit CubeSats.

Chapter 9 In this article, a noble compact two-port fractal antenna is designed for narrowband IoT applications. The patch is common between two feeds and the microstrip feed lines in orthogonal polarizations. The shared patch MIMO antenna is very small in size as compared to the conventional patch MIMO antenna in which two antenna is designed on a substrate. The proposed antenna is designed on an FR4 substrate of $\varepsilon r = 4.4$, and excitation is provided using a lumped port.

Chapter 10 proposed a system that uses a laser beam transmitter and receiver for detecting laps crossing. The ATMEGA 328 controller continuously triggers the laser transceiver. This system provides the solution for the time delay in lapse calculation for racing. The detection of vehicle is based on the beam cutting.

Chapter 11 proposes a long-term two-phase approach for purifying natural rainwater. Rainwater is collected and held in a tilted glasshouse where it absorbs the sun's rays and kills the most hazardous viruses once it reaches a certain temperature. An IoT-based temperature control sensor regulates the flow of water at the glasshouse's outflow based on the temperature of the water, which is signaled by an LED light.

Chapter 12 aims to illustrate the scope and importance of Blockchain technology in various sectors of Industry 4.0 as well as the risks associated with its use in parallel. Further, it intends to work as an initial point for future research to promote the application of Blockchain Technology.

Chapter 13 proverbs information about the contribution of blockchain in smart cities and the use of blockchain in the healthcare sector, enhancing the data securities and also how it can secure the online transaction between users. How services based on blockchain technology can be used in the upgradation and development of smart cities to improve their services and quality of life.

Chapter 14 discusses dimension identification, smart city evaluation techniques, and accessible technologies. Despite having multiple benefits, there are many failings in the deployment of blockchain technology. Further, it discussed the blockchain applications in different dimensions of smart cities. This article proposes a security framework that leverages blockchain technology in electronic devices to enable secure and reliable communications in smart cities.

Contents

Editors and Contributors

About the Editors

Devendra Kumar Sharma received his B.E. degree in Electronics Engineering from Motilal Nehru National Institute of Technology, Allahabad, in 1989, his M.E. degree from Indian Institute of Technology Roorkee, Roorkee, in 1992, and his Ph.D. degree from National Institute of Technology, Kurukshetra, India, in 2016. He is a Professor and Dean of SRM Institute of Science and Technology, Delhi-NCR Campus, Ghaziabad, India. Dr. Sharma has authored many papers in several international journals and conferences of repute. His research interests include VLSI interconnects, electronic circuits, digital design, testing, and signal processing.

Rohit Sharma is currently an Associate Professor and Head of the Department of Electronics and Communication Engineering, SRM Institute of Science and Technology, Delhi-NCR Campus, Ghaziabad, India. He is an Editorial Board Member and Reviewer of more than 12 international journals and conferences. He serves as Book Editor for 16 different titles His research interests are data networks, data security, data mining, environment and pollution trend analysis, Big Data, IoT, etc.

Prof. Gwanggil Jeon received the B.S., M.S., and Ph.D. (summa cum laude) degrees from the Department of Electronics and Computer Engineering, Hanyang University, Seoul, Korea, in 2003, 2005, and 2008, respectively. He is currently a Full Professor at Incheon National University, Incheon, Korea. He has published more than 65 papers in journals and 25 conference proceedings. He served as a Member of the Technical Program Committee at many international conferences in Poland, India, China, Iran, Romania, and Bulgaria. His area of interest includes IT in Business, IoT in Business, and Education Technology.

Zdzislaw Polkowski is a Professor of UJW at the Faculty of Technical Sciences and Rector's Representative for the International Cooperation and Erasmus+ Program at the Jan Wyzykowski University Polkowice. Since 2019, he is also Adjunct Professor in the Department of Business Intelligence in Management, at Wroclaw University of Economics and Business, Poland. He is the Former Dean of the Technical Sciences Faculty during the period 2009–2012 at UZZM in Lubin. He holds a Ph.D. degree in Computer Science and Management from the Wroclaw University of Technology, a postgraduate degree in Microcomputer Systems in Management from the University of Economics in Wroclaw and a postgraduate degree in IT in Education from Economics University in Katowice. He obtained his engineering degree in Computer Systems in Industry from the Technical University of Zielona Gora. He has published more than 65 papers in journals and 25 conference proceedings, including more than 19 papers in journals indexed in the Web of Science, Scopus, and IEEE. He served as a Member of the Technical Program Committee at many international conferences in Poland, India, China, Iran, Romania and Bulgaria. To date, he has delivered 20 invited talks at different international conferences across various countries. He is also a Member of the Board of Studies and an Expert Member of the doctoral research committee at many universities in India. He is also a Member of the editorial board of several journals and served as Reviewer in a wide range of international journals. His area of interest includes IT in Business, IoT in Business and Education Technology.

Contributors

Muhammad Afsar Department of Electronics and Telecommunication Engineering, BMS College of Engineering, Bengaluru, India;
VTU, Belagavi, India

Mustafa A. Al-Asadi Department of Computer Engineering, Selçuk University, Konyo, Turkey

Ahmed Alkhayyat College of Technical Engineering, The Islamic University, Najaf, Iraq

Sandeep Kumar Arora School of Electronics and Electrical Engineering, Lovely Professional University, Phagwara, Punjab, India

Amera Istiqlal Badran Department of Computer Sciences, Mosul University, Mosul, Iraq

Mohamed El Bakkali Faculty of Sciences, University Mohammed Five in Rabat (UM5R), Agdal, Rabat, Morocco

Boutaina Benhmimou Faculty of Sciences, University Mohammed Five in Rabat (UM5R), Agdal, Rabat, Morocco

N. Akash Bharadwaj Department of Electronics and Telecommunication Engineering, BMS College of Engineering, Bengaluru, India;
VTU, Belagavi, India

Surbhi Bhatia School of Engineering and Technology, Sharda University, Greater Noida, India;
College of Computer Science and Information Technology, King Faisal University, Hofuf, Saudi Arabia

Bharat Bhushan School of Engineering and Technology, Sharda University, Greater Noida, India;
College of Computer Science and Information Technology, King Faisal University, Hofuf, Saudi Arabia;
University of Kufa, Najaf, Iraq

Wasana Boonsong Department of EE, Rajamangala University of Technology, Songkhla, Thailand

S. Chandramohan Department of ECE, SCSVMV Deemed University, Kanchipuram, Chennai, India

Shrishti Choudhary School of Engineering and Technology, Sharda University, Greater Noida, India;
College of Computer Science and Information Technology, King Faisal University, Hofuf, Saudi Arabia

Hien Dang Department of Computer Science, University of Massachusetts Boston, Boston, MA, USA;
Faculty of Computer Science and Engineering, Thuyloi University, Hanoi, Vietnam

E. Ganasri Department of ECE, Sona College of Technology, Salem, Tamilnadu, India

Josep M. Guerrero Center for Research on Microgrids (CROM), Department of Energy Technology, Aalborg University, Aalborg East, Denmark

Anu Gupta Department of EEE, Birla Institute of Technology and Science, Pilani, India

C. Gururaj Department of Electronics and Telecommunication Engineering, BMS College of Engineering, Bengaluru, India;
VTU, Belagavi, India

A. H. Hariharasudan Department of ECE, Sona College of Technology, Salem, Tamilnadu, India

Balqees Talal Hasan Department of Computer and Information Engineering, Nineveh University, Mosul, Iraq

Niamat Hussain Department of Smart Device Engineering, Sejong University, Seoul, South Korea

Pratik Jadon School of Engineering and Technology, Sharda University, Greater Noida, India;
University of Kufa, Najaf, Iraq

Oliver James Institute of Basic Sciences, Centre for Cognition & Sociality, Seoul, South Korea

Kapish Kumar Khaitan Department of Electronics and Telecommunication Engineering, BMS College of Engineering, Bengaluru, India;
VTU, Belagavi, India

Abhik Kumar De School of Engineering and Technology, Sharda University, Greater Noida, India;
College of Computer Science and Information Technology, King Faisal University, Hofuf, Saudi Arabia

Akash Kumar School of Engineering and Technology, Sharda University, Greater Noida, India

Shashank Kumar School of Engineering and Technology, Sharda University, Greater Noida, India;
University of Kufa, Najaf, Iraq

S. Kumarganesh Department of ECE, Knowledge Institute of Technology, Salem, Tamilnadu, India

Rachid Ahl Laamara Faculty of Sciences, University Mohammed Five in Rabat (UM5R), Agdal, Rabat, Morocco

Praveen Kumar Malik Department of Electronics and Communication, Lovely Professional University, Phagwara, India

Milan Mitra School of Engineering and Technology, Sharda University, Greater Noida, India

D. Muthukumaran Department of ECE, SCSVMV Deemed University, Kanchipuram, Chennai, India

Ahmed J. Obaid School of Engineering and Technology, Sharda University, Greater Noida, India;
University of Kufa, Najaf, Iraq

Fouad Omari Faculty of Sciences, University Mohammed Five in Rabat (UM5R), Agdal, Rabat, Morocco

S. Omkumar Department of ECE, SCSVMV Deemed University, Kanchipuram, India

Ramesh Chandra Panda Research Development Cell, Synergy Institute of Engineering and Technology, Dhenkanal, Orissa, India

Shraiyash Pandey School of Engineering and Technology, Sharda University, Greater Noida, India;
College of Computer Science and Information Technology, King Faisal University, Hofuf, Saudi Arabia

Rahul Department of Electronics and Telecommunication Engineering, BMS College of Engineering, Bengaluru, India;
VTU, Belagavi, India

Md. Safikul Islam Dr. Ambedkar International Centre (DAIC), Ministry of Social Justice and Empowerment, New Delhi, India;
Department of Geography, Jamia Millia Islamia, New Delhi, India

K. Martin Sagayam Department of ECE, Karunya Institute of Technology and Sciences, Coimbatore, Tamilnadu, India

Minakshi Sanadhya Department of Electronics and Communication Engineering, Faculty of Engineering and Technology, Delhi-NCR Campus, SRM Institute of Science and Technology, NCR Campus, Modinagar, Ghaziabad, UP, India

Buddhi Prakash Sharma Department of EEE, Birla Institute of Technology and Science, Pilani, India

Devendra Kumar Sharma Department of Electronics and Communication Engineering, Faculty of Engineering and Technology, Delhi-NCR Campus, SRM Institute of Science and Technology, NCR Campus, Modinagar, Ghaziabad, UP, India

Lakshya Sharma School of Engineering and Technology, Sharda University, Greater Noida, India;
University of Kufa, Najaf, Iraq

Chandra Shekhar Department of EEE, Birla Institute of Technology and Science, Pilani, India

M. Sivakumar Department of ECE, Mohamed Sathak AJ College of Engineering, Chennai, India

Sneha Department of Electronics and Communication, Lovely Professional University, Phagwara, India

B. Thiyaneswaran Department of ECE, Sona College of Technology, Salem, Tamilnadu, India

K. Umapathy Department of ECE, SCSVMV Deemed University, Kanchipuram, Chennai, India

Lokesh Yadav School of Engineering and Technology, Sharda University, Greater Noida, India

Ranjeeta Yadav ABES Engineering College, Ghaziabad, Uttar Pradesh, India

Sachin Yadav G L Bajaj Institute of Technology and Management, Greater Noida, India

Chapter 1
A Study on Energy Management for Low-Power IoT Devices

Balqees Talal Hasan and Amera Istiqlal Badran

Introduction

The first report on IoT was released by the International Telecommunications Union (ITU) more than fifteen years ago. The IoT paradigm was initially described as a new dimension added to the field of information and communication technologies that enables connections for everyone and anything, anytime, and anywhere to create a new dynamic network of networks. The IoT is not a new trend anymore. With applications in numerous areas, including civil infrastructure, environment monitoring, energy, transportation, smart buildings, healthcare, defense, manufacturing, and production, it has emerged as one of the most significant technologies of the current century. IoT is still expanding (Sanislav et al. 2021). According to the State of IoT Q4/2020 and Outlook 2021 reports, there will be over 30 billion IoT connections by 2025, which equates to nearly four IoT devices per person (Hameed 2022).

One of the biggest challenges for IoT is smart energy management. Every active IoT network component needs to consume a certain amount of energy to operate. Despite using few energy resources, the amount of data produced by IoT has significantly increased recently. As a result, wireless communication devices' batteries quickly discharge and regularly need to be replaced (Zeadally et al. 2020).

Batteries have historically been the most practical option for powering electronic devices, but when combined with tiny sensors that are used in a variety of environments, their disadvantages become more apparent. These disadvantages include the difficulty of replacement and recharging, biological incompatibility with the human body, and high environmental contamination. These limitations severely restrict the growth of wireless sensor nodes and IoT systems, which prompts new

B. T. Hasan (✉)
Department of Computer and Information Engineering, Nineveh University, Mosul, Iraq
e-mail: Balqeestalal.cs@gmail.com

A. I. Badran
Department of Computer Sciences, Mosul University, Mosul, Iraq

research approaches toward self-sustainability that are being attained through energy harvesting and self-powered sensing technology (Liu et al. 2021a).

Energy harvesting is a process for obtaining and converting energy from outside sources, such as temperature gradients, vibrations, mechanical load, or light, and delivering it to electronic equipment in the form of electricity. An environmentally friendly way to power wireless devices is by the use of a green energy source that absorbs energy from the environment and can either charge secondary cells or take the place of primary batteries (Sanislav et al. 2021). By eliminating the need for battery replacement and upkeep, the energy harvesting technology will produce more dependable and durable solutions (Elahi et al. 2020).

The most difficult and demanding study area in IoT is energy management, which is in charge of ensuring that gathered electricity is used efficiently and offering methods to manage energy so that there is only a small amount of loss. Making the element in charge of power management while keeping the harvesting principle in mind is the finest method for harvest transformation (Elahi et al. 2020). IoT platforms focus their efforts mostly on energy conservation. An enormous quantity of energy is required to run the IoT system and transport the massive amount of data produced by IoT devices. As a result, a major challenge is still the energy consumption of IoT systems. To lower the power consumption of IoT systems, many strategies have been tried (Motlagh et al. 2020).

The remaining chapter has been organized as follows: Sect. 1.2 presents Low-power IoT devices. Section 1.3 goes into detail about energy harvesting technology, with subsections like energy harvesting architectures, sources of energy harvesting, energy storage in IoT, and energy harvesting-based IoT system: case studies. Section 1.4 provides a new proposed categorization for energy conservation technologies that is based on four levels: hardware, communication, operating system, and software, with the essential energy conservation technologies covered in each level. Section 1.5 explores the roles of cloud computing and fog computing in energy management. Finally, Sect. 1.6 provides a summary of the chapter.

Low-Power IoT Devices

IoT devices are intelligent devices made up of numerous sensors that are in charge of transmitting sensed data to the base station, where it is utilized for a variety of purposes in the medical field, home automation, environmental monitoring, and surveillance (Hameed 2022). As a result, The IoT manages a vast network of web-enabled smart devices, which are small devices that collect, transmit, and elaborate on environmental data using embedded systems including processors, sensors, and communication equipment. Therefore, these devices consist of scalable, light-weight, power-efficient storage nodes that run on batteries and energy (Elahi et al. 2020).

Battery maintenance has become a crucial limiting element for the IoT infrastructure's long-term survival with the rise in deployments of that infrastructure for numerous applications. Batteries have significant limits, for example, they can only hold a fixed amount of energy, therefore they must either be replaced or recharged, which is not only expensive but also impractical in some deployments. Batteries may also represent significant safety issues in some deployments. Finally, it is not environmentally friendly to dispose of billions of harmful batteries. These factors have led to the IoT revolution's grand challenges (Ma et al. 2020). Use of low-power battery-less IoT devices that use energy harvesting techniques to transform ambient energy into electrical energy which can be used to power these devices are a promising solution for eliminating battery dependency and thus accelerating IoT deployments. Figure 1.1 depicts the components of a battery and a battery-less IoT device. The three major parts of a battery-less IoT device are a transducer, which transforms environmental energy into electricity which can then be utilized to power IoT devices, a storage unit, which keeps the energy, and a load, which consists of an MCU, radio, and sensors (Hameed 2022; Ma et al. 2020). Energy can be harvested from various sources using a variety of transduction methods and materials. There are four primary ambient energy sources that are appropriate for IoTs. They are thermal, solar, radio frequency (RF), and kinetic (also known as mechanical, vibration, and motion) (Ma et al. 2020). Supercapacitors are commonly utilized as storage units in these devices because they can be charged and drained considerably quicker than batteries and have nearly infinite charge–discharge cycles. However, based on the sensor node's application and energy needs, a system comprised of numerous supercapacitors or a combination of rechargeable batteries and supercapacitors can be utilized (Hameed 2022).

An IoT device's operation consists mostly of four stages: data sensing, processing, storage, and communication. All of these stages must consider low-power and energy-efficient technologies, which necessitate low-power and compressed sensors, low-power microcontrollers, new low-power memory technologies, and revolutionary low-power wireless technologies. In addition to energy-efficient hardware, software optimization for reduced power usage offers enormous promise. In reality,

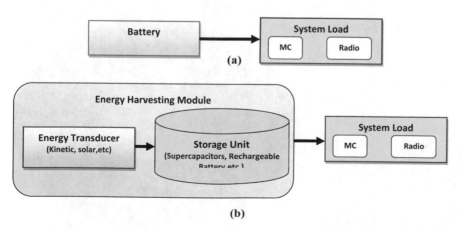

Fig. 1.1 Generic Low-Power IoT device Components for **a** Simple Battery IoT Device and **b** Simple Battery-less IoT

studies revealed and concluded that when energy efficiency is taken into account in software design, significant energy savings can be realized (Henkel et al. 2017).

Energy Harvesting

Since the 1900s, energy harvesters have been proposed and investigated as an alternative to batteries because they can convert a variety of available energy sources in the surroundings into electricity (Liu et al. 2021a).

Generally, energy harvesting aims to transform energy from one form into a form that may be utilized to power electronic equipment. It may immediately capture ambient energy from the environment being monitored when used in environmental monitoring nodes and utilize it to power the nodes of environmental wireless sensor networks, enhancing their performance and/or increasing their lifespan. Outdoor areas provide numerous chances to take advantage of natural forces like the sun and wind. The nodes can, however, be powered by other sources of energy, such as radio frequency signals produced by human activity (Prauzek et al. 2018).

A sensor node can run continuously if the energy supply is significant and available on a regular basis. The periodicity and magnitude of the harvestable energy can also be used to modify a node's system parameters in order to enhance network and node performance. A node can use energy efficiently to maximize performance while waiting for the next harvesting cycle, as it is only restricted by energy at that time (Sudevalayam and Kulkarni 2011).

Power generation plays a crucial function in an energy harvesting system, which is made up of numerous parallel subsystems and is in charge of powering IoT devices (Prauzek et al. 2018). As illustrated in Fig. 1.2, the energy harvesting process is divided into four phases (Zeadally et al. 2020):

Fig. 1.2 Energy harvesting process

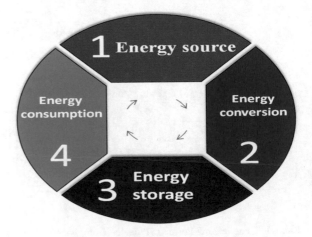

(1) Energy source: The first phase is the availability of energy sources. It is critical to select an adequate and abundantly available energy source in the surroundings of the installed system.
(2) Energy conversion: Mechanisms for energy conversion are included in the second phase. The harvester or transducer detects and transforms the energy. A converter circuit is also employed in this phase to achieve rectification.
(3) Energy storage: The third phase stores energy using batteries or supercapacitors. This phase also includes the control and power management unit. Based on the power supply, the power management unit has regulators to deal with the power demand.
(4) Energy consumption: The final step involves using the harvested energy in a device that is suitable for the job.

Energy Harvesting Architectures

Battery life for IoT devices is significantly impacted by continuous sources of energy. The technique of energy harvesting helps IoT devices become more self-sustaining and extend their useful lives (Mohd and Hayajneh 2018). Energy harvesting can be categorized into two architectures: (1) Harvest–Store–Use: When possible, energy is harvested and kept for future utilization and (2) Harvest–Use: Energy is harvested only when it is needed (Sudevalayam and Kulkarni 2011).

(1) **Harvest–Store–Use**
This architecture includes a storage component that serves to both power the sensor node and store energy that is harvested, as shown in Fig. 1.3a. When available harvested energy is greater than what is being used at the moment, energy storage becomes advantageous (Sudevalayam and Kulkarni 2011). Depending on the application and the surrounding conditions, the storage could be a capacitor, rechargeable battery, or a mix of the two. To keep the system working in the event that the primary storage is exhausted, a secondary storage component is occasionally also introduced. Only after a particular amount of energy has been accumulated can the harvested energy be used. This architecture has the advantage of supplying the device with power even when energy harvesting is not feasible (Hameed 2022). A Harvest–Store–Use system, as an example, can utilize energy sources like solar energy. Energy is used for labor during the day and is also saved for use at a later time. The sensor node is powered during the night by the energy that has been stored (Sudevalayam and Kulkarni 2011).
(2) **Harvest–Use**
The energy harvested in this architecture is used immediately to power the device; the harvesting system does not have an energy storage component as shown in Fig. 1.3b. Only when the harvester's output power exceeds the device's minimum operating power demand does the device remain on. The device won't turn on if there is not enough energy present. This architecture has the consequence of causing the device to oscillate between the on and off states if the

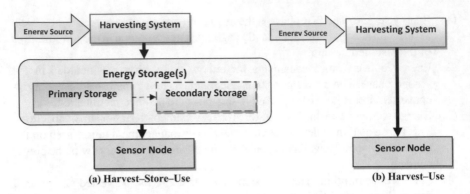

Fig. 1.3 Energy harvesting architectures

gathered power swings close to the minimal working power of the device. If the collected power exceeds the load demand or remains below the minimum operational power, energy is also wasted in this scenario (Hameed 2022). This architecture can be designed to employ mechanical energy sources like walking, pedaling, pressing buttons, etc. For instance, pressing a key or button can cause a piezoelectric material to deform and produce electrical energy, which can then be utilized to send a brief wireless message (Sudevalayam and Kulkarni 2011).

Sources of Energy Harvesting

Energy harvesting, often known as energy scavenging, is the process of transforming readily accessible environmental energy into electrical energy. This offers an effective way to power varied loads continuously. The environment is full of sources that we may employ to generate energy, both natural and man-made (Zeadally et al. 2020). The few sources of energy harvesting from the environment for WSNs are thermal, solar, water energy, vibrational, wind, and electromagnetic sources, as shown in Fig. 1.4 (Sherazi et al. 2018). This section addresses effective and popular energy harvesting sources.

(1) *Solar Energy*

According to the International Renewable Energy Agency's 2018 report, solar energy is one of the most common and utilized green energy sources. It is a cheap source of green energy that is abundantly present in nature and can lower the IoT sector's energy needs (Mishu et al. 2020). Despite the unpredictability of solar energy, it can be forecasted using seasonal and daily patterns. Photovoltaic cells convert solar energy into electrical electricity. The photovoltaic principle states that the amount of output power a cell produces depends on the amount of light present, the size, and the efficiency of the cell (Prauzek et al. 2018).

Fig. 1.4 Sources of energy harvesting (Sherazi et al. 2018)

(2) *Wind Energy*

The second-best renewable energy source in the world, after solar energy, is wind energy. Wind flow is a naturally occurring source of vibrational energy. The speed of the wind flow determines the wind's vibrations (Mishu et al. 2020). Applications for outdoor WSN can make use of wind energy. To convert kinetic energy into electricity, this type of energy harvesting employs turbines, rotors, and the electromagnetic induction principle (Prauzek et al. 2018). Due to the wind's variable and unexpected behavior, which makes it impossible to always harvest an equal amount of energy, wind energy's main drawback is its unreliability (Sherazi et al. 2018).

(3) *Acoustic Energy*

A new technological invention known as "acoustic energy harvesting" or "sound energy harvesting technology" has been researched due to the available quantity of pure sound waves. Most sound waves are semi-permanent, making them a valuable alternative energy source for Internet of Things-based wireless sensor networks (WSNs) (Mishu et al. 2020).

(4) *Thermal Energy*

Both indoor and outdoor environments are filled with thermal energy, often known as heat energy. It can be obtained from human bodies (body heat or skin heat), electrical appliances (engine heat), or temperature gradients. Different types of thermal energy exist, including heat from sunshine, heat from exhaust gases, heat from internal resistance, and heat flux (Zeadally et al. 2020). Thermo-electric transducers, which use temperature differences in space, and pyroelectric transducers, which use temperature variations in time, may both transform thermal energy into electricity (Prauzek et al. 2018).

(5) *Radio Frequency (RF)*

Radiofrequency (RF) energy is the most widely used and reliable sort of energy when compared to other energy sources. Due to signal radiation from different common transmitters, such as frequency modulation (FM)/amplitude modulation (AM) transmitters, TV broadcasts, cellular transceiver stations, and wireless fidelity (Wi-Fi), RF is an ambient source of energy. In contrast to rural areas, where RF energy is scarce, urban areas have tremendous RF energy (Zeadally et al. 2020). RFID tags—also referred to as RF tags—are widely used devices that run by RF propagation. The RF energy harvesting technique is a viable energy source because it generates less power. Given that IoT nodes consume less power, these tags are useful for IoT sensors (Mishu et al. 2020).

(6) *Vibrational*

Faraday's law of electromagnetic induction states that vibration is a mechanical source of ambient energy harvesting. Many sophisticated WSN applications, from button presses to shoe sensors, are increasingly using this form of energy scavenging. The shoe sensor is powered by energy that has been harvested from the force of human movement and is utilized to power various WSN applications, satisfying the energy needs of data packets of a particular size. Similar to this, the energy generated when a car goes over a traffic sensor causes it to become operational for a reading (Sherazi et al. 2018).

(7) *Microbial Fuel Cells (MFCs)*

MFCs are recognized as a significant energy harvester in addition to the various energy sources. Barnet Cohen used the MFC in his initial research in 1931. The MFC is regarded as a bio-electrochemical transducer that is typically utilized in biosensors, for the synthesis of hydrogen fuel, and for the treatment of wastewater. Potential anaerobic bacteria are used in MFCs, which respire, oxidize, and conduct electrons (Mishu et al. 2020).

Energy Storage in IoT

Energy storage is the process of transforming energy from a form that is difficult to store (such as electrical energy) to a form that is easy to store (such as electrochemical). It is possible to transform this stored energy back into a usable form. Energy storage devices come in a variety of ranges with various features including charge/discharge rates, capacity, and power (Prauzek et al. 2018).

(1) **Primary Batteries**

The terms conventional and non-chargeable batteries are also used to describe primary batteries (Zeadally et al. 2020). The benefits of this type of energy storage are temperature stability and large capacity. Their primary drawback is that they must be replaced after their useful lives are up; another drawback is that they demand regular maintenance. Alkaline and acidic batteries are two different subgroups. Acidic batteries are more reliable and less expensive than alkaline batteries, yet the latter perform better (Elahi et al. 2020). With the exception of lithium-ion batteries, most batteries struggle to function properly in cold weather due to an increase in internal resistance that reduces capacity. For their operation at high temperatures, the contrary is true, but at the cost of a major reduction in their service life or possibly irreversible damage. Depending on the operational cycle and the battery's type of electrochemistry, the projected range for battery storage efficiency is between 60 and 80% (Prauzek et al. 2018).

Primary batteries are the most practical and cost-effective power source for a small IoT network that is installed in a low-demand area. However, primary batteries can't be used to power such systems when the network size expands. Long-term operation of the IoT network is required, or when battery replacements cannot be done at the deployment site (such as in military applications). Therefore, primary battery utilization is constrained by network size, node count, and application type. Conventional batteries in this situation become a bottleneck for ongoing operation and network life (Zeadally et al. 2020).

(2) **Rechargeable Batteries**

Rechargeable batteries can be employed to effectively power a network. The issue of battery replacement is reduced with rechargeable batteries. To provide continuous network power, a recharging method is required in addition to a rechargeable battery, even when a battery or power supply unit needs to be replaced. Rechargeable batteries also improve the economics of an IoT system since they reduce the expense of purchasing more batteries regularly over time. There are various rechargeable batteries (with varying efficiency) on the market (Zeadally et al. 2020).

(3) **Supercapacitors**

Supercapacitors have a higher power density than conventional capacitors and batteries. Either pseudocapacitors or electrochemical double-layer capacitors are used in their fabrication (Elahi et al. 2020). Supercapacitors benefit from having a high number of charge and discharge cycles. A super capacitor's charging process is straightforward and doesn't call for any additional equipment. Occasionally, additional circuitry can be employed to transmit energy effectively (based on the energy input type). However, under typical circumstances, a simple voltage connection is sufficient to charge the capacitor. Super capacitors effectively buffer energy from various harvesting resources, such as solar energy. They quickly recharge since their super capacitor charging efficiency is 98%. As a result, super capacitors are the finest energy storage option for the IoTs (Zeadally et al. 2020). With supercapacitors, there is a self-discharge issue (Elahi et al. 2020). The severity of the issue varies between manufacturers and even within specific production batches in addition to being dependent on device capacity (Prauzek et al. 2018).

Energy Harvesting-Based IoT System: Case Studies

With the continuing advancement of energy harvesting and sensor technologies, various self-powered sensors and IoT applications with self-sustaining features are being promoted to support smart cities (Liu et al. 2021a). This section provides numerous case studies of self-power devices that harvest energy from multiple sources.

(1) **Smart Homes**

In order to build an integrated and energy-efficient smart home system, the power consumption of sensor nodes can be reduced using energy sources from both the internal environment and the exterior environment (Liu et al. 2021a).

Wang et al. reported a hybridized nanogenerator made up of Si-based solar cells (SC) and triboelectric nanogenerators (TENG) that can scavenge solar and wind energies separately or simultaneously, as illustrated in Fig. 1.5a. The SC can generate an output power of 8 mW in a device area of roughly 120 mm 22 mm, but the TENG can deliver an output power of up to 24 mW (Wang et al. 2016).

Kim et al. (2018) developed a human-mechanical piezoelectric energy harvester system. The proposed system suggests using a floor tile, such as the one seen in Fig. 1.5b, which generates enough energy when someone steps on it to wirelessly send data to an electrical device. The developed system had good stability for 30 days with an output voltage and current of 42 V and 52 A. Additionally, the floor tile responded to an average person's weight (50–80 kg). The primary electrical appliance's receiver switch module and wireless transmitter sensor node were successfully operated by the output voltage derived from a person's footsteps. The wireless signal transmission to the switch module served as a demonstration of the self-powered real-time floor tile system.

(2) **Smart Shoe**

Jeong et al. created a self-powered wireless communication system using a shoe-mounted piezoelectric energy harvester (PEH). The PEH was created with a straightforward design and affixed to the bottom of a shoe. Using a pushing

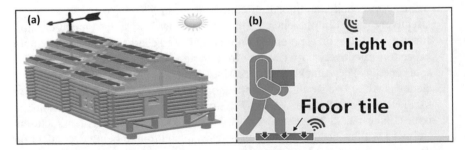

Fig. 1.5 Smart home. **a** Harvesting solar and wind energies on the roof of a smart house model (Wang et al. 2016), **b** the lights are activated by means of the floor tile (Kim et al. 2018)

tester, the PEH's durability was tested, and its suitability for use in shoes was investigated. After 24 steps, the transmitter can be used for the first time. The PEH, which is included into a shoe's sole, produces electricity in reaction to human movement. As a self-powered wearable device, the electrical energy accumulated is subsequently used to power a wireless communication system. If the user keeps moving, the wireless transmitter is powered by PEH power by sending a periodic signal to a receiver in a control room. On the other hand, if the user is involved in an accident and does not move, the PEH will not produce electricity or operate the wireless transmitter. When a worker's signal is lost from the receiver for a considerable amount of time, it is deemed a risky circumstance and the administrator is alerted to the risk, as illustrated in Fig. 1.6. The potential uses for this technology are unlimited because it is directly tied to the security of vulnerable workers (Jeong et al. 2022).

(3) **Smart Vehicle**

Driver fatigue is one of the main causes of traffic accidents, thus identifying it is crucial for improving car safety. Xu et al. designed a self-powered steering-wheel angle sensor (SSAS) based on TENG technology that can detect driver tiredness and provide real-time driver status monitoring, as shown in Fig. 1.7. The SSAS records the turning angle of the driver's steering wheel, and the signal processing unit analyzes the average angle, number of rotations, and other factors in the driver's recorded data to generate a warning level for each

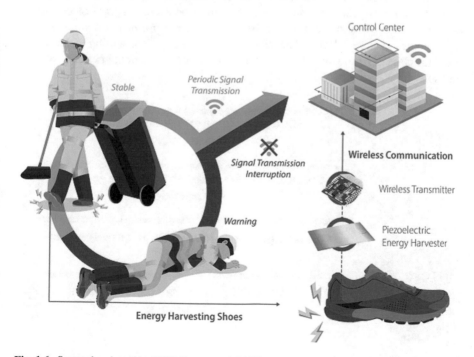

Fig. 1.6 Smart shoe based on PEH (Jeong et al. 2022)

Fig. 7. Self-powered steering-wheel angle sensor (SSAS) (Xu, et al. 2021)

parameter. By comparing these characteristics and threshold values, the system determines the driver's condition in real time, and experimental findings show that the driver's status is correctly determined (Xu et al. 2021).

Energy Conservation

Integration of energy harvesting and conservation are critical enablers of IoT device energy efficiency. Designing low-power IoT devices does not have a single solution. At all design abstraction layers, including hardware system components, OS, and software, low-power design technologies must be used. An order of magnitude decrease in energy consumption can be achieved by a promising combination of technologies at several levels. This chapter divides energy-conserving technologies into four classes, as shown in Fig. 1.8: hardware, communication, operating system, and software.

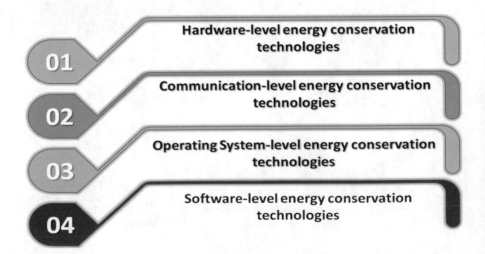

Fig. 1.8 Levels of energy conservation technologies in low-power IoT devices

Hardware-Level Energy Conservation Technologies

One of the main factors driving research in the area of low-power system design is the ever-growing number of battery-powered devices with frequently complex functionality. The slower rate of battery technology development makes it natural to search for methods to improve hardware architectures' power usage (Qadri et al. 2009).

IoT applications must be developed using a complicated stack of technologies that includes hardware elements for instance, CPUs, controllers, sensors, communication tools, and so on. Processors are employed in IoT at several points, including end nodes and coordinators, as well as PCs that serve as servers. Energy efficiency and low-power consumption are crucial features of IoT CPUs (Banday 2018).

The power consumption of the majority of commercial processors is expressed as two values: active power and static power consumption. When discussing continuing data processing, active power consumption is used to describe the energy used for transistor switching. When there is small or no data processing going on and non-essential modules are turned off, the CPU employs static power. The majority of low-power CPUs have a peak operational power of under 400 mW and a standby power of 15 mW or less (Maheepala et al. 2021).

Energy utilization per unit of time is referred to as power consumption. Processor energy consumers include (Banday 2018):

(1) Clock Frequency: higher frequencies require more energy.
(2) Supply Voltage: higher supply voltage requires the use of more energy.
(3) Register File Size: the chip uses more energy when the register file is larger.
(4) Execution: orderly or disorganized execution may have an impact on energy use.
(5) Multi-core: more cores could mean higher energy usage.

IoT processors may employ the following low-power techniques to offer extended device battery life (Banday 2018; Cheour et al. 2020; Maheepala et al. 2021; Qadri et al. 2009):

A. *Clock Gating*
   A simple way for lowering dynamic power consumption is to reduce gate toggling, either by minimizing the number of gates in a device or by minimizing the number of times each gate toggles. This technique sacrifices computing speed in order to reduce power by lowering switching capacitance. The clock often contributes 20–40% of total energy usage.
B. *Small Silicon Area*
   Small Silicon Area lowers the effective capacitance and hence reduces the energy used.
C. *Low Supply Voltage*
   The majority of microcontrollers run at the conventional +5 V logic voltage. However, operating at lower voltages is preferred for IoT CPUs to maximize battery life.

D. *High Performance*

Frequency scaling is an option for processors. The CPU's frequency can be changed to reduce energy consumption significantly, dependent on the workload. Consequently, energy wastage occurs when a CPU is used at its maximum frequency without taking the variability in workload into account.

E. *Smart Peripherals*

These peripherals can function even when the processor is still in sleep state and can wake it up using interrupt-driven techniques.

F. *Use Multiple Clocks*

It is possible for a microcontroller to use only one clock source that runs at a specific frequency, however several clock sources are preferred for IoT processors. For instance, it is preferable for IoT CPUs to have secondary clock-operated units that can run at much lower clock frequencies than the main clock and are powered by tiny coin-cell backup batteries to enable deep sleep modes where the processor's primary energy-consuming units can be put into sleep modes when not in use. Therefore, the power consumption was decreased by using a clock source with a very low frequency for sleep modes.

G. *System on Chip*

Because it requires a lot of power to transfer data between chips via data buses, it is possible to decrease the energy used by integrating the required peripherals directly into the processing chip rather than having them externally attached.

H. *Power-mode variation*

The system stays in sleep mode and can utilize the slowest clock speed possible to conserve energy when no requests need to be processed. It is also possible to set up the wake-up interrupt controller to support asynchronous operation, which would enable it to operate without a clock signal.

Communication-Level Energy Conservation Technologies

The IoT's overall vision revolves around the idea of communication between intelligent objects, allowing them to act, hear, see, think, and communicate with one another in order to make savvy decisions. It effectively embeds intelligence into the objects using ubiquitous computing, networking technology, and applications. As the number of connected IoT devices grows, challenging connectivity requirements such as scalability, low latency, low-power operation, and high reliability are imposed. The requirement for low-power operation assists nodes in conserving power and avoiding undue communication attempts, hence preventing premature death and increasing network lifetime (Nikoukar et al. 2018).

Wireless sensor networks (WSNs) represent the IoT's backbone. WSNs are networks of distributed sensors that aggregate data from the surrounding environment. It is used to monitor environmental variables like pressure, temperature, and moisture and send this data to the target node. WSN has demonstrated its value in numerous applications, including military use, landslide detection, traffic monitoring, weather forecasting, fire detection, etc. (Jadhav and Satao 2016). Since IoT nodes are powered by batteries or energy harvesting sources, energy efficiency is an essential component in the implementation of IoT. It is therefore crucial to increase the network's lifespan. WSN energy-conserving techniques can be used to accomplish this (Haimour and Abu-Sharkh 2019).

IoT communication solutions should be able to interact with nodes in a way that satisfies their demands for low data rates, varying ranges based on the application's requirements, dependability, and low energy consumption. Given the significance of WSN in implementing the IoTs, the sources of energy consumption in WSN are shown in Fig. 1.9 and can be summed up as follows (Haimour and Abu-Sharkh 2019):

(1) The primary inefficient cause of power consumption in sensor nodes is idle listening, which is when a node continues to listen to the channel even when there isn't any communication.
(2) The main sources of power consumption are RF transmission and reception.
(3) Collisions, when two or more nodes send their packets simultaneously.
(4) overhead in control packets.
(5) Receiving packets intended for another node.
(6) when transmitting to a node that is not yet ready.

This section describes numerous energy-conserving solutions for WSN.

A. *Duty Cycle Technique*
With this technique, nodes can live up to 5–10 years longer due to the fact that they sleep the majority of the time and only wake up at certain times. Scheduled duty-cycling, in which nodes awaken at the predetermined time so that transmission can only take place when the active time arrives, is the technique that is most frequently used. The on-demand duty-cycling method, which is predicated on the notion that the node can be awakened as needed, offers an alternative strategy (Kozłowski and Sosnowski 2019). The most energy-conserving protocols are those that employ duty-cycling methods, but they also suffer from delays because one node must wait for another to wake up. The transmitter node is also

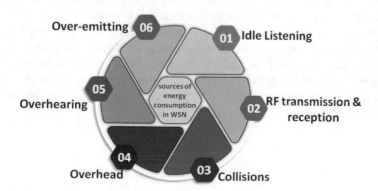

Fig. 1.9 Sources of energy consumption in WSN

unable to broadcast messages. Therefore, the fundamental component of duty-cycling systems is modifying and managing the active periods (Haimour and Abu-Sharkh 2019).

B. *Wake-Up Radio Technique*

The system's overall power consumption can be greatly decreased by using a low-power wake-up radio. But more importantly, it enables faster frame transmission to target nodes, which is essential for delay-sensitive applications, particularly those found in Industry 4.0. The idea is to employ a second receiver that consumes so little power that it can always be on. When communication is required, the additional receiver will wake up a particular node using a low-power signal, and this node will then begin sending at its maximum transmission power (Haimour and Abu-Sharkh 2019; Kozłowski and Sosnowski 2019).

C. *Low-Energy Adaptive Clustering Hierarchy (LEACH)Protocol*

Since communication between sensor nodes in WSN consumes the majority of their energy, finding a solution to the issue of a routing protocol that is energy-efficient is essential for extending the lifespan of sensor networks (Chen et al. 2012). To increase the network's lifespan, various routing protocols are available. The routing protocols that use hierarchies are more energy-efficient. The first energy-efficient clustering routing protocol is called LEACH (Kaur and Grover 2015). LEACH, which Wendi Rabiner Heinzelman of MIT developed in 2000, is where cluster-separated thought first appeared in WSN. LEACH uses rounds to divide how sensor networks operate. Each round, all sensor nodes select a cluster-head node to transmit data from other nodes, which reduces energy consumption through data-fusion and lengthens the network's lifespan(Chen et al. 2012).

D. *Energy-Efficient Opportunistic Routing*

Based on a predetermined criteria, conventional fixed path routing systems over wireless networks choose which nodes will transport data. The intended relay nodes might not be able to receive data across unreliable wireless channels, even if the most reliable wireless link is chosen. As a result, the sender is required to resend the packets to the relay nodes. Due to the wireless channel's broadcast nature, any nearby nodes within the sender's transmission range can hear the relayed packets (Xu et al. 2015). The main idea of OR is to make use of wireless networks' broadcasting capabilities, which enable transmission from one node to be overheard by several nodes. The OR chooses the next forwarder node dynamically throughout transmission as opposed to making a predetermined choice. The forwarding is done by the node that is closest to the destination. Energy-Efficient OR provides a strategy for selecting the forwarding list in a wireless sensor network using least energy depletion as a cost criterion (Jadhav and Satao 2016).

OS-Level Energy Conservation Technologies

Despite the fact that hardware selection largely determines how much power is utilized, OSs that include power management technologies are able to effectively manage apps to extend battery life and permit as many long sleep cycles as feasible. The conventional OSs are developed for personal computers and powerful workstations. This makes them unsuitable for IoT devices with limited resources. IoT devices require special kind of OSs due to their constrained resources. A variety of factors can be used to classify IoT OSs. For example, they might be classified as having open or closed source code. Another distinction to make is between Linux-based and non-Linux-based OSs. Finally, OSs are classified as high-end or low-end IoT devices based on the devices for which they are developed. Single-board computers, such as the Raspberry Pi, are examples of high-end IoT devices, whereas Arduino, which are resource-constrained, are examples of low-end IoT devices (Hasan and Abdullah 2022; Qutqut et al. 2018).

A long chain of IoT OSs with a wide range of features is always growing (Gaur and Tahiliani 2015). Table 1.1 provides an overview of the most widely used modern IoT OSs. This section investigates several energy conservation technologies that have been adopted for various IoT OS.

A. *Rate Harmonized Scheduling (RHS)*
    Nano-RK OS implements RHS for energy savings. Most current CPUs provide capability for numerous modes of operation, each of which consumes a different amount of energy. There are three modes available: active, idle, and sleep. Sleep mode, in which no processing is performed, uses the least amount of energy. Any idle duration on a CPU using energy-saving RHS can be transitioned into sleep mode. As a result, energy savings are maximized (Randhawa et al. 2018; Rowe et al. 2008).
B. *Tickless Scheduler*
    RIOT OS has an energy-saving Tickless scheduler. The RIOT scheduler changes to the idle thread when there are no pending tasks. The only function of the idle thread is to determine the deepest sleep state based on the peripheral devices being used. This technique ensures that the amount of time spent in sleep mode is maximized, reducing the system's overall energy consumption (Baccelli et al. 2012).
C. *Software Thread Integration (STI)*
    TinyOS uses STI technique to save energy. Motes, the nodes of typical WSNs, frequently undergo busy-waiting times while communicating with radios, A/D converters, flash memory, sensors, etc. Due to the short wait durations in these cases, switching to another task would be cost-prohibitive. During those times, useful work could be done via STI. STI can regain CPU idle time that context switches cannot use. The mote can now execute valuable tasks during what was formerly busy-wait time, earlier completion of its active cycle, returning to a low-power mode earlier, and using less energy as a result (Purvis and Dean 2008).

Table 1.1 IoT OSs overview

IoT OS	IoT devices type	Hardware requirements		CPU	Scheduler	Real time	Development language
		Min-RAM (KB)	Min-ROM (KB)				
TinyOS	Low-end devices	1	4	8 Bit	Non-preemptive FIFO	Not supported	NesC
Contiki	Low-end devices	2	30	8 Bit	Preemptive FIFO	Partially supported	C
RIOT	Low-end devices	1.5	5	16–32 bit	Preemptive priority, tickless	Supported	C, C++
Nano-RK	Low-end devices	2	64	8-Bit	Preemptive, Fixed Priority-based	Supported	C
Raspbian	High-end devices	512–256	–	ARM Cortex-A53	Preemptive	Supported	C, Ruby, Python, Java, PHP, C++, Node.js
Android Things	High-end devices	128	32	ARM, Intelx86, MIPS	Preemptive	Supported	C, C++

D. *Application-Specific Management*
    Contiki's power management support is provided via API rather than through an
    explicit power-saving feature in the kernel. The applications in execution are in
    charge of conserving energy by keeping track of the size of the task queue. When
    no tasks are scheduled, the CPU can be put into sleep mode by the application
    until an interrupt wakes it up (Gaur and Tahiliani 2015; Randhawa et al. 2018).
E. *Integrated Concurrency and Energy Management (ICEM)*
    ICEM has been designed and implemented as a significant component of
    TinyOS's second generation. Peripheral energy management, which switches off
    each peripheral when it is not in use, necessitates knowledge of the application
    utilization model. Applications can easily control the power states of dedicated
    devices, but for virtualized and shared devices, the OS is in charge of system-
    wide power management. The power locks method proposed by ICEM takes
    advantage of the concurrent nature of application I/Os to automatically reduce
    energy consumption without further specifics from the application (Klues, et al.
    2007; Dong et al. 2010).

Software-Level Energy Conservation Technologies

While designers and researchers at the hardware level pay close attention to energy
efficiency, software developers sometimes overlook it because they are uninformed
of how energy-efficient software is developed (Uelschen and Schaarschmidt 2022).
According to recent studies, even more energy can be saved by motivating software developers to participate in the process (Lewis et al. 2017). Sometimes, energy
optimization is frequently replaced with performance optimization because a more
speedy system uses less energy. Even though this is a positive step, it is by no
means enough and occasionally even inaccurate. For instance, performance may be
improved through parallel processing by cutting down on processing time. On the
other hand, saving and restoring the execution context, and allocating threads could
end up consuming more resources than sequential processing (Pang et al. 2015). The
interaction of the system's software and hardware is responsible for up to 80% of
the system's overall energy consumption, hence energy consumption from the software perspective needs to be carefully considered. Software is crucial in addressing
IoT device's energy efficiency. Software-level optimization technologies can lower
the overall energy consumption, extend operational lifetimes, and affect the entire
hardware design, which lowers costs (Uelschen and Schaarschmidt 2022).

Energy consumption is a widespread issue, and in the next years, developers
will need to be even more attentive of it. However, developers now lack a thorough
understanding of how to develop, maintain, and evolve energy-efficient software
systems (Lewis et al. 2017).

This section provides examples of some of the aspects that programmers should
consider when developing software for low-power IoT devices.

A. *Efficient Computation offloading Approach*

The technology of computation offloading is crucial for the development of edge computing and IoT. By offloading tasks to other devices or servers, it is thought to provide a solution to the restricted resources of IoT devices. It can provide a variety of advantages, including extended battery life, less latency, and improved application performance. Numerous factors influence the effect of computation offloading in practice, which prevents many offloading from accomplishing their intended goals (Liu et al. 2021b). For example, in a client–server architecture, portable device apps can offload processing to the server to save energy. It is expected that the server is grid-powered. This uses the server's energy to extend the portable client's battery life. Computation offloading reduces the load on the client's CPU, but it must send and receive data via the client's network interface. Therefore, energy conservings via computation offloading are only possible if communication energy is smaller than processing energy. As a result, to decide whether to offload and which part of the computation to offload, it is required to evaluate the energy consumption prior to execution (Xian et al. 2007).

B. *Convenient Data structure*

During the recent years, one of the essential components of computer programming, data structures, have been the subject of extensive research regarding how they behave in terms of energy use (Lewis et al. 2017). Pinto et al. (2016) looked at how much energy various Java programming language thread management primitives used. For example, they discovered in one of their implementations that while ConcurrentHashMap outperforms Hashtable by 1.46 times, it consumes 1.51 times the power. In light of their findings, it is advised to use caution while deciding whether or not to utilize ConcurrentHashMap, especially in situations where energy consumption is more crucial than performance.

C. *Powerful Parallel Programming*

Gaining a detailed grasp of the energy behaviors of concurrent apps is the first step toward optimizing their energy usage. Pinto et al. presented an empirical study to clarify and comprehend the energy characteristics of Java concurrent programs on multicore platforms. Their experiments have produced a variety of findings, including the fact that various thread management constructs have varying effects on energy usage. For programs that require I/O, the Threadstyle uses the least energy, while the ForkJoinstyle uses the most. The opposite is true for embarrassingly parallel benchmarks (Pinto et al. 2014).

Cloud and Fog Computing Roles in IoT Energy Management

With the continued development of IoT applications, a new computing termed fog computing is being created in addition to cloud computing to fulfill requirements such as bandwidth, latency, and location awareness. The cloud is not replaced by fog computing in the IoTs; rather, they work best together as complements (Jalali et al. 2017). Fog computing is essentially an extension of the cloud that is closer to the devices that function with IoT data. Fog computing functions as a bridge between the cloud and end devices, bringing processing, storage, and networking resources closer to the end devices (Atlam et al. 2018). Therefore, the data reduction at the fog computing layer can result in a quick response from the smart end devices as well as a reduction in the amount of uploaded data to the cloud platform, which saves network bandwidth (Idrees and Idrees 2022). When contrasting the relative power consumption of fog versus cloud computing, there are a number of significant distinctions. The power consumption of the transport network will be higher when using the cloud than when using the fog since cloud data centers are usually situated further away from the IoT device network than fog data centers are. The power used by the transport network may, in some circumstances, account for a considerable fraction of the total power needed by the IoT service, and as such, it should not be disregarded (Jalali et al. 2017).

Numerous IoT applications will gain from the integration of fog computing with the IoT. In particular for time-sensitive IoT applications, the fog facilitates real-time interactions between IoT devices to reduce latency. Fog computing also has the ability to support large-scale sensor networks, which is a major issue with the IoT's exponentially increasing number of devices, which will eventually number in the billions (Atlam et al. 2018).

Once effective method to preserve the power of any IoT device is to request assistance from other devices that are represented by fog nodes to carry out tasks on that IoT device's behalf. Task offloading is the practice of sharing resources among devices to accomplish tasks. The tasks are divided into local and offloaded components; the IoT device itself completes local tasks, while fog nodes complete offloaded tasks. Different sorts of resource allocation approaches are used to control the job offloading choice. Offloading a job allows an IoT device to conserve computing power at the expense of the energy needed to communicate data between the IoT device and the task assistance fog nodes. Offloading tasks saves energy. The amount of energy saved can be increased if work offloading is combined with energy-conserving approaches based on device control. These approaches govern certain features or functions of devices to improve efficiency and performance. Local IoT devices and fog nodes can adjust characteristics including transmission power, on/off switching duration, battery supply voltage, frequency, and modulation method via device control (Malik et al. 2021).

Conclusions

IoT is currently making headlines around the world, playing a significant part in our daily lives, and opening up several new opportunities. The idea of networking devices, where the range of communications between devices expands yearly, is exciting. However, when more IoT devices are installed, the need for energy increases as a result. Since many IoT devices are powered by batteries or rely on energy harvesters with restricted energy sources, low-power consumption and effective energy management are essential design objectives in hardware, communication systems, operating systems, and software applications. The energy harvesting technology has been discussed from a variety of aspects, including energy harvesting architectures, sources of energy in IoT, energy storage in IoT, and several energy harvesting-based IoT systems have been introduced. The essential energy conservation technologies have been discussed in each of the four layers of this chapter's proposed categorization for technologies that save energy: hardware, communication, operating system, and software.

References

Atlam HF, Walters RJ, Wills GB (2018) Fog computing and the internet of things: a review. Big Data Cogn Comput 2(2):1–18. https://doi.org/10.3390/bdcc2020010

Baccelli E, Hahm O, Wahlisch M, Gunes M, Schmidt T (2012) RIOT: one os to rule them all in the IoT. pp. 1–16, [Online]. Available: http://hal.inria.fr/hal-00768685

Banday MT (2018) A study of current trends in the design of processors for the Internet of Things. ACM Int Conf Proc Ser. https://doi.org/10.1145/3231053.3231074

Chen Y, Zhu YL, An J, and Liu Q (2012) An energy-saving routing protocol based on LEACH. Proc. - 2012 4th Int. Conf. Multimed. Secur. MINES 608–611. doi: https://doi.org/10.1109/MINES.2012.62

Cheour R, Khriji S, Abid M, Kanoun O (2020) Microcontrollers for IoT: optimizations, computing paradigms, and future directions. IEEE World Forum Internet Things, WF-IoT 2020 - Symp. Proc. 1–7. doi: https://doi.org/10.1109/WF-IoT48130.2020.9221219

Dong W, Chen C, Liu X, Bu J (2010) Providing OS support for wireless sensor networks: challenges and approaches. IEEE Commun. Surv. Tutorials 12(4):519–530. https://doi.org/10.1109/SURV.2010.032610.00045

Elahi H, Munir K, Eugeni M, Atek S (2020) Energy harvesting towards self-powered IoT devices. pp. 1–31. doi: https://doi.org/10.3390/en13215528

Gaur P, Tahiliani MP (2015) Operating systems for IoT devices: a critical survey. Proc. - 2015 IEEE Reg. 10 Symp. TENSYMP 2015 33–36. doi: https://doi.org/10.1109/TENSYMP.2015.17

Haimour J, Abu-Sharkh O (2019) Energy efficient sleep/wake-up techniques for IOT: A survey. 2019 IEEE Jordan Int. Jt. Conf. Electr. Eng. Inf. Technol. JEEIT 2019 - Proc., 459–464. doi: https://doi.org/10.1109/JEEIT.2019.8717372

Hameed A, Battery-less IoT devices: energy source manipulation attacks, April, 2022.

Hasan BT, Abdullah DB (2022) Real-time resource monitoring framework in a heterogeneous kubernetes cluster. IEEE 184–189. doi: https://doi.org/10.1109/micest54286.2022.9790264

Henkel J, Pagani S, Amrouch H, Bauer L, Samie F (2017) Ultra-low power and dependability for IoT devices (Invited paper for IoT technologies). Proc 2017 Des Autom Test Eur 954–959. doi: https://doi.org/10.23919/DATE.2017.7927129

Idrees SK, Idrees AK (2022) New fog computing enabled lossless EEG data compression scheme in IoT networks. J Ambient Intell Humaniz Comput 13(6):3257–3270. https://doi.org/10.1007/s12652-021-03161-5

Jadhav P, Satao R (2016) A survey on opportunistic routing protocols for wireless sensor networks. Proc Comput Sci 79(020):603–609. https://doi.org/10.1016/j.procs.2016.03.076

Jalali F, Khodadustan S, Gray C, Hinton K, Suits F (2017) Greening IoT with fog: a survey. In: Proc. – 2017 IEEE 1st Int. Conf. Edge Comput. EDGE 2017, pp. 25–31. doi: https://doi.org/10.1109/IEEE.EDGE.2017.13

Jeong SY, Xu LL, Ryu CH, Kumar A, Do Hong S, Jeon DH (2022) Wearable shoe-mounted piezoelectric energy harvester for a self-powered wireless communication system. MDPI

Kaur A, Grover A (2015) LEACH and extended LEACH protocols in wireless sensor network-a survey. Int J Comput Appl 116(10):1–5. https://doi.org/10.5120/20369-2576

Kim KB et al (2018) Optimized composite piezoelectric energy harvesting floor tile for smart home energy management. Energy Convers Manag 171(May):31–37. https://doi.org/10.1016/j.enconman.2018.05.031

Klues K, et al., Integrating concurrency control and energy management in device drivers. In: SOSP'07 – Proc. 21st ACM SIGOPS Symp. Oper. Syst. Princ. pp. 251–263, 2007. doi: https://doi.org/10.1145/1323293.1294286

Kozłowski A, Sosnowski J (2019) Energy efficiency trade-off between duty-cycling and wake-up radio techniques in IoT networks. Wirel Pers Commun 107(4):1951–1971. https://doi.org/10.1007/s11277-019-06368-0

Lewis B, Smith I, Fowler M, Licato J (2017) Energy efficiency: a new concern for application software developers. In: 28th Mod. Artif. Intell. Cogn. Sci. Conf. MAICS, pp. 189–190. doi: https://doi.org/10.1145/1235

Liu L, Chen C, Feng J, Xiao TT, Pci QQ (2021b) A survey of computation offloading in vehicular edge computing networks. Tien Tzu Hsueh Pao/acta Electron Sin 49(5):861–871. https://doi.org/10.12263/DZXB.20200936

Liu L, Guo X, Liu W, Lee C (2021a) Recent progress in the energy harvesting technology—from self-powered sensors to self-sustained iot, and new applications. Nanomaterials 11(11). doi: https://doi.org/10.3390/nano11112975

Ma D, Lan G, Hassan M, Hu W, Das SK (2020) Sensing, computing, and communications for energy harvesting IoTs: a survey. IEEE Commun Surv Tutorials 22(2):1222–1250. https://doi.org/10.1109/COMST.2019.2962526

Maheepala M, Joordens MA, Kouzani AZ (2021) Low power processors and image sensors for vision-based IoT devices: a review. IEEE Sens J 21(2):1172–1186. https://doi.org/10.1109/JSEN.2020.3015932

Malik UM, Javed MA, Zeadally S, ul Islam S (2021) Energy efficient fog computing for 6G enabled massive IoT: recent trends and future opportunities. IEEE Internet Things J 4662(c),1–22. doi: https://doi.org/10.1109/JIOT.2021.3068056

Mishu MK et al (2020) Prospective efficient ambient energy harvesting sources for IoT-equipped sensor applications. Electron 9(9):1–22. https://doi.org/10.3390/electronics9091345

Mohd BJ, Hayajneh T (2018) Lightweight block ciphers for IoT: energy optimization and survivability techniques. IEEE Access 6:35966–35978. https://doi.org/10.1109/ACCESS.2018.2848586

Motlagh NH, Mohammadrezaei M, Hunt J, Zakeri B (2020) Internet of things (IoT) and the energy sector. Energies 13(2):1–27. https://doi.org/10.3390/en13020494

Nikoukar ALI, Raza S, Poole A, Güneş M., Dezfouli B (2018) Low-power wireless for the internet of things : standards and applications, 67893–67926. doi: https://doi.org/10.1109/ACCESS.2018.2879189

Pang C, Hindle A, Adams B, Hassan AE (2015) What do programmers know about the, pp. 1–11

Pinto G, Castor F, Liu YD (2014) Understanding energy behaviors of thread management constructs. ACM SIGPLAN Not 49(10):345–360. https://doi.org/10.1145/2660193.2660235

Pinto G, Liu K, Castor F, Liu YD (2017) Artifacts for 'a comprehensive study on the energy efficiency of Java's thread-safe collections,'" In: Proc. – 2016 IEEE Int. Conf. Softw. Maint. Evol. ICSME 2016, pp. 614–615. doi: https://doi.org/10.1109/ICSME.2016.86

Prauzek M, Konecny J, Borova M, Janosova K, Hlavica J, Musilek P (2018) Energy harvesting sources, storage devices and system topologies for environmental wireless sensor networks: a review. Sensors (Switzerland) 18(8). doi: https://doi.org/10.3390/s18082446

Purvis ZD, Dean AG (2008) TOSSTI: Saving time and energy in TinyOS with software thread integration. In: Proc. IEEE Real-Time Embed. Technol. Appl. Symp. RTAS,354–363. doi: https://doi.org/10.1109/RTAS.2008.38

Qadri MY, Gujarathi HS, McDonald-Maier KD (2009) Low power processor architectures and contemporary techniques for power optimization – A review. J Comput 4(10):927–942. https://doi.org/10.4304/jcp.4.10.927-942

Qutqut MH, Al-Sakran A, Almasalha F, Hassanein HS (2018) Comprehensive survey of the IoT opensource OSs. IET Wirel Sens Syst 8(6):323–339. https://doi.org/10.1049/iet-wss.2018.5033

Randhawa RH, Ahmed A, Siddiqui MI (2019) Power management techniques in popular operating systems for IoT devices. In: Proc. - 2018 Int. Conf. Front. Inf. Technol. FIT 309–314. doi: https://doi.org/10.1109/FIT.2018.00061

Rowe A, Lakshmanan K, Zhu H, Rajkumar R (2008) "Rate-harmonized scheduling for saving energy," In: Proc. Real-Time Syst. Symp. 113–122. doi: https://doi.org/10.1109/RTSS.2008.50

Sanislav T, Mois GD, Zeadally S, Folea SC (2021) Energy harvesting techniques for internet of things (IoT). IEEE Access 9:39530–39549. https://doi.org/10.1109/ACCESS.2021.3064066

Sherazi HHR, Grieco LA, Boggia G (2018) A comprehensive review on energy harvesting MAC protocols in WSNs: challenges and tradeoffs. Ad Hoc Netw 71:117–134. https://doi.org/10.1016/j.adhoc.2018.01.004

Sudevalayam S, Kulkarni P (2011) Energy harvesting sensor nodes: survey and implications. IEEE Commun Surv Tutor 13(3):443–461. https://doi.org/10.1109/SURV.2011.060710.00094

Uelschen M, Schaarschmidt M (2022) Software design of energy-aware peripheral control for sustainable internet-of-things devices. In: Proc. 55th Hawaii Int. Conf. Syst. Sci., vol. 7, pp. 7762–7771. doi: https://doi.org/10.24251/hicss.2022.933

Wang S, Wang X, Wang ZL, Yang Y (2016) Efficient scavenging of solar and wind energies in a smart city. ACS Nano 10(6):5696–5700. https://doi.org/10.1021/acsnano.6b02575

Xian C, Lu YH, Li Z (2007) Adaptive computation offloading for energy conservation on battery-powered systems. In: Proc. Int. Conf. Parallel Distrib. Syst. - ICPADS, vol. 1. doi: https://doi.org/10.1109/ICPADS.2007.4447724

Xu W, Wu D, Liu (2015) A data privacy protective mechanism for WBAN. Wirel Commun Mob Comput 421–430. doi: https://doi.org/10.1002/wcm

Xu Y. et al. (2021) Real-time monitoring system of automobile driver status and intelligent fatigue warning based on triboelectric nanogenerator, ACS Nano 2021. doi: https://doi.org/10.1021/acsnano.1c00536

Zeadally S, Shaikh FK, Talpur A, Sheng QZ (2020) Design architectures for energy harvesting in the Internet of Things. Renew Sustain Energy Rev 128(May):109901. doi: https://doi.org/10.1016/j.rser.2020.109901

Chapter 2
Efficient FPGA-Based Implementation of Image Segmentation Algorithms for IoT Applications

N. Akash Bharadwaj, Muhammad Afsar, Kapish Kumar Khaitan, Rahul, and C. Gururaj

Introduction

Image processing is the term used to describe the process of enhancing or extracting valuable features or information from an image. Numerous engineering professions use image processing in their routine work. Image segmentation is one of the methods used in image processing. The technique of segmenting a picture involves breaking it up into its component parts, such as regions and objects.

Edge pixels, or more specifically the edges of the picture where the pixel's intensity rapidly changes, are found via edge detection methods. The Sobel, Prewitt, and Robert approaches, which work in the X and Y axis with 3×3 or 2×2 kernels, are well-known gradient-based edge detection algorithms. Filtering, Differentiation, and Detection are the three components of every edge detection method.

Real-time processing of the images is an important aspect of image processing. The hardware implementation with minimum resource utilization of the edge detection algorithms is a challenging task. FPGAs, or Field Programmable Gate Arrays, are well renowned for their low power consumption, adaptability, and effective data processing (Wang and Zhu 2015).

The FPGA is very well popular in disciplines requiring greater calculations, such as image processing, computer vision, and machine learning, because of its parallel processing design. Semiconductor hardware realization of these algorithms proves to be the stepping stone toward implementing optimized AI and ML algorithms.

N. A. Bharadwaj · M. Afsar · K. K. Khaitan · Rahul · C. Gururaj (✉)
Department of Electronics and Telecommunication Engineering, BMS College of Engineering, Bengaluru, India
e-mail: gururaj.tce@bmsce.ac.in

VTU, Belagavi, India

© The Author(s), under exclusive license to Springer Nature Singapore Pte Ltd. 2023
D. K. Sharma et al. (eds.), *Low Power Architectures for IoT Applications*, Springer Tracts in Electrical and Electronics Engineering, https://doi.org/10.1007/978-981-99-0639-0_2

Literature Review

A. *The Design of FPGA-Based Digital Image Processing System and Research on Algorithms*

High speed, high resolution, high integration, and reliability are all characteristics of the evolving image processing system (Gururaj et al. 2015). Because of its benefits for real-time image processing, FPGA becomes the preferred option (Gururaj and Tunga 2019). The system employs edge recognition and rapid median filtering algorithms that can digitize and sample data streams from cameras (Gururaj et al. 2016). When it comes to high speed performance and cost effectiveness, the suggested method is more effective than conventional median algorithms (Lu et al. 2017).

B. *Analysis and Implementation FPGA Implementation for Image Processing Algorithm*

Real-time image processing can be executed with the help of FPGAs. Xilinx ISE is used to synthesize the modules which are based on HDL design. Simulation is carried out by an ISIM simulator. The Xilinx XC6VCX75T chip based on Virtex 6 is used to implement the design. The control medium filter theory employs a feedback signal for each feedback to distinguish between neighboring stimuli (Fatma and Garg, 2020).

C. *Demonstration of Quantum Image Edge Extraction Enhancement Through Improved Sobel Operator*

The quantum image of the Sobel operator serves as the foundation for the edge detection approach. The edge detection method of a quantum picture is implemented using the optimum Sobel operator in the quantum circuit, and the gray gradient is generated using an improved eight-direction Sobel operator (Ma et al. 2020).

D. *Novel VLSI Architectures for Image Segmentation and Edge Detection Algorithm*

The method employs edge detection and thresholding on still grayscale photos taken from a distance of around 50 m. The Spartan-3E FPGA runs the model at a 100 MHz clock speed (Dewan et al. 2016).

E. *Real-Time Edge Detection via Ip-Core-Based Sobel Filter on FPGA*

The Sobel operator is one of the most popular edge detection filters that can be applied to a video stream. Thus, despite utilizing minimal FPGA resources, edges of objects may be easily viewed online on a VGA screen (Yaman et al. 2019).

F. *Comparing Energy Efficiency of CPU, GPU, and FPGA Implementations for Vision Kernels*

Embedded vision requires high performance with energy constraints. For complicated vision pipelines FPGAs outperform others with better energy/frame. And as the complexity grows, FPGAs results are increasingly better (Qasaimeh et al. 2019).

G. *Parallelism to Reduce Power Consumption on FPGA Spatiotemporal Image Processing*

Parallel processing techniques can help in reducing power consumption and help in faster processing. Observed that there is 45% reduction in power with shorter processing time (Atabany and Degenaar 2008).

Implementation

A. *Edge Detection Algorithms*

An edge detection is an algorithm which produces a list of edges of a particular image. This list of edges can also be termed as the contour or the boundary or simply an outline of the image. This outline of the image finds its application in many domains such as automotive industry, manufacturing sector, and medical image processing.

(1) *Sobel Operator*

The Sobel operator is a discrete differential operator which was proposed by Sobel & Feldman in 1968. Hence it is also known as the Sobel-Feldman operator. It calculates a rough estimate of the image intensity function gradient. It works by convolutionally transforming the image in the horizontal (Gx) and vertical (Gy) directions with a tiny, separable, integer-valued filter. For high-frequency fluctuations in the image, the gradient approximation it generates is particularly rudimentary.

(2) *Prewitt Operator*

Similar to the Sobel operator, the Prewitt operator likewise uses gradient detection but changes the gradient matrix that is convolved with the source picture. It calculates a rough estimate of the gradient of the picture intensity function. Its foundation is the horizontal (Gx) and vertical (Gy) convolution of the picture using a small, separable, integer-valued filter. It creates a relatively elementary gradient approximation, especially for high-frequency fluctuations in the picture.

(3) *Robert Operator*

It was one of the original edge detectors, and Lawrence Roberts first suggested it in 1963. Additionally, the operator is based on gradient detection. The Robert operator uses discrete differentiation to estimate an image's gradient, and it does so by computing the sum of the squares of the differences between diagonally adjacent pixels. This operation's output will show fluctuations in intensity that are diagonal. This operation's simplicity is in the kernel being compact and comprises only integers and it is one of its most appealing features. The operator however, suffers considerably from sensitivity to noise and this benefit is minimal given the speed of today's computers.

B. *Implementation of first phase*

The research was first done in Python without the usage of built-in methods to better grasp the aforementioned Edge detection algorithms. 'For' loops were used to implement the operations (Gonzalez and Woods 2009). Input image was transformed into grayscale image which then was processed for edge detection. The edge converted image later is subjected to image quality parameter analysis.

(1) *Numpy Library*

One of the essential libraries for Python programming, NumPy, supports arrays. In essence, an image is a regular NumPy array with pixels for the data points. Therefore, you can change the pixel values in a picture by using fundamental NumPy operations like slicing, masking, and clever indexing.

(2) *Matplot Library*

Python's Matplotlib toolkit provides a complete tool for building static, animated, and interactive visualizations. Matplotlib.pyplot can operate like MATLAB thanks to the functions in pyplot. Each pyplot function modifies a figure in some way, such as by creating a figure, a plotting region within a figure, some lines within a plotting area, labeling the plot, etc.

(3) *Math Library*

We have access to certain common arithmetic functions and constants in Python due to the Python Math Library, which we may use throughout our code to perform more intricate mathematical operations. You don't need to install the library to use it because it is a built-in Python module. The most popular functions and constants from the Python Math Libraries will be utilized in examples throughout this tutorial.

C. *Implementation of second phase*

The Vivado Design Suite 2018 from Xilinx is used to create the Verilog design. In order to make it simple to instantiate each Verilog module with the top module, hierarchical design flow is maintained (Chaple et al. 2015). The algorithm receives an input picture in the grayscale format. Pixel by pixel, the input picture is read and stored in the line buffer. Line buffer serves as an intermediary storage for the values of the pixels. Four line buffers are started for the Sobel and Prewitt operators. Only three of the four line buffers are operational at any given moment. In order to reduce the time required to read the pixels, a fourth line buffer is used. Three line buffers, of which two are active at once for the Robert operator, are started (Afsar et al. 2021). The edge detection method receives pixel values from the line buffer and feeds them into the convolution process, which either utilizes 3×3 kernels or 2×2 kernels. The output buffer, which serves as another component of memory storage, is where the convoluted output is stored. The edge detected pixel values are read from the output buffer, and then the picture is produced using the edges. The picture generated by edge detection is then utilized to evaluate the various aspects of image quality.

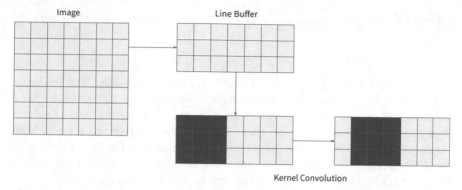

Fig. 2.1 Use of buffers

(1) *Handling incoming pixels—Line Buffer*

The storage component used as an intermediary step to hold the incoming pixel data is a line buffer. Four buffers are started out of which only three are used at any given moment for the 3 × 3 kernel-based operators of Prewitt and Sobel. In order to reduce the time required to read the pixels, the unused empty line buffer is used. Three buffers are started out of which only two are used at any given time for the Robert Operator. The line buffer has a capacity of 8 bits wide, which is the number of bits utilized to hold each pixel. Read pointer and write pointer is used to read and write onto the line buffer. The size of the read and write pointer is $\log_2$(number of columns). Whenever there is a request to read the pixel data, a read pointer is used to fetch the data for further processing. The added advantage of the line buffer is that instead of sending only pixel values, three or two pixel values are sent at a given time depending on the operator, which is basically the number of pixels required for the convolution process. 24 bits of data can be sent at once with the use of these buffers (Fig. 2.1).

(2) *Control of data flow*

Based on the operator, the number of buffers active at a time is handled by the image controller. Meanwhile in order to reduce the read time, one more row of pixel data is written to the extra buffer which is being used. Once all the pixels from all the active line buffers are sent, the process of writing the pixel data again starts. This time the extra line buffer and others are used for the processing. The first buffer will be used to store the next set of pixel values and won't contribute to the convolution process. The process, controlling, filling the buffers, and pushing the pixels from the buffers are controlled by a module named Image Controller. The image controller controls the pixels' data flow from the input image to the convolution process. The buffer is created by the image controller. The image controller receives the incoming pixel data before sending it to the buffer. The empty buffer receives the received pixel data and writes it there. Based on the selected edge detecting operator, the image controller delivers 32 bits or 72 bits for the corresponding convolution operation, only after all the active buffers have been completely written with the incoming pixel values.

(3) *Detection of Edges*

The algorithm for the edge detection receives the input pixel value from the image controller. 32 bits are convoluted for the Robert operation and 72 bits for the Sobel and Prewitt. The convolution kernel is declared as the 2 dimensional array. The input pixel data and the kernels are convolved to get the convolved output. The convolved output is then compared with the threshold. If the convolved value is greater than the threshold then a white pixel value is sent to the output buffer, indicating there is an edge or else a black pixel value is sent indicating no edge detected.

Tables 2.1, 2.2, 2.3, 2.4, 2.5 through 2.6 represent the kernel values used for convolution. These kernel values are standard kernels used for the respective operations.

(4) *Final Edge Detected Output*

Once the valid data is received from the convolution section, the convolved data is written to the FIFO. The final image is reconstructed by reading the values from the FIFO. The FIFO used is configured as an IP from the Xilinx with width and depth of 8 and 16 bits respectively.

(5) *Testing*

The input image is taken from the function $fopen in the binary mode. The function $fscanf is used to read the image pixel data and $fwrite to write the output edge detected data in the binary form. An interrupt is raised whenever all the line buffers are full, to momentarily stop the write operation onto the line buffers. The process will stop once all the pixels are read and the pixels are convolved. The timing diagram will be generated which shows the flow of input and output data with respect to the clock values. The input image and the edge detected image will be stored in the simulation files of the Vivado Design Suite.

Table 2.1 Gx kernel for Sobel operation

1	0	−1
2	0	−2
1	0	−1

Table 2.2 Gy kernel for Sobel operation

1	2	1
0	0	0
−1	−2	−1

Table 2.3 Gx kernel for Prewitt operation

1	0	−1
1	0	−1
1	0	−1

Table 2.4 Gy kernel for Prewitt operation

1	1	1
0	0	0
−1	−1	−1

Table 2.5 Gx kernel for Robert operation

1	0
0	−1

Table 2.6 Gy kernel for Robert operation

0	1
−1	0

D. Basys 3 Artix 7 FPGA Trainer board

The basic FPGA board used primarily for educational purposes is the Basys 3 trainer board. The Artix 7 FPGA family is present on the Basys 3 board in the XC7A35T-1CPG236C package. The board comes with the four 12-pin PMOD connector, VGA output of 12 bits and a USB JTAG port for the FPGA communication and programming. The Artix 7 FPGA contains 5200 slices of 33,280 logic cells. Each logic cell has upto four, 6 input LUTs and 8 Flip Flops. The internal clock can reach upto 450 MHz, however 100 MHz is most popular. 1,800 Kbits of Block RAM is present to store the data. FPGA also comes with 90 digital signal processing slices known as DSP.

E. Parameters

By assessing the variables that can define overall performance, the implemented algorithms can be analyzed. FPGA power consumption is also one of the parameters which describes the performance of FPGA.

(1) Mean Squared Error (MSE)

The average squared difference between the estimated and original values is measured by the mean squared error, which is a parameter used in image analysis.

(2) Peak Signal to Noise Ratio (PSNR)

Peak signal to noise ratio (PSNR) is a measure of how well a signal may be represented while taking into account the influence of corrupting noise. The inverse of mean squared error is used to calculate PSNR.

(3) *FPGA Power Consumption*

The power consumption of the FPGA determines the total on-chip power estimated by the FPGA in the synthesis and implementation phase.

(4) *Clock Frequency versus Processing Speed*

The Basys 3 board can be clocked upto 450 MHz. Typically the operating clock frequency would be 100 MHz. For our experimentation, the edge detection process was carried out with three clock frequencies of 50 MHz, 100 MHz, and 200 MHz. Higher clock frequency would provide less processing time and slower the frequency higher the processing time. Processing time would be the total time taken to complete the verilog simulation.

Results

The outcomes attained are summarized in this section. Screenshots of Edge identified photos have been included for the readers to visualize. The metrics for measuring image quality are tabulated and thoroughly discussed in the following discussion.

A. *Test Images*

'Butterfly' and 'Abstract' images are used for testing the algorithm shown in Fig. 2.2.

B. *Experimental Results*

In this part, the tabulated findings are recorded in Tables 2.7 and 2.8. The mean squared error (MSE) and peak signal to noise ratio (PSNR) are displayed in relation to the aforementioned function.

Fig. 2.2 Input images used for testing

Table 2.7 Analysis of 'Butterfly' image

Butterfly	PSNR	MSE
Python Sobel	27.83	107.04
Python Prewitt	27.89	105.66
Python Robert	27.95	104.11
Verilog Sobel	28.17	99.04
Verilog Prewitt	28.18	98.73
Verilog Robert	28.19	98.64

Table 2.8 Analysis of 'Abstract' image

Abstract	PSNR	MSE
Python Sobel	28.03	102.33
Python Prewitt	28.47	92.36
Python Robert	28.23	97.72
Verilog Sobel	28.38	94.37
Verilog Prewitt	28.41	93.76
Verilog Robert	28.40	93.95

C. *Power Consumption*

On-chip power consumption provides the information on how much power FPGA typically will be consuming.

Figures 2.3 and 2.4 depict the power consumption during synthesis and implementation phase. In the synthesis phase a total of 20.453 W is consumed. And in the implementation phase a total of 22.44 W is consumed. In both the cases the majority of the power is consumed by the internal signals. The power consumption by the signals can also be reduced with more optimization in the implementation logic. The I/Os, BRAM, DSP, and the Logical blocks contribute less than 40% of the total power consumed.

D. *RTL Design*

This section provides the RTL design obtained by the Verilog description of each edge detection operator implemented as shown in Fig. 2.5.

From the RTL design, Sobel operator uses 17 standard cells, 23 I/O ports with 119 Nets.

From the RTL design in Fig. 2.6, Prewitt operator uses 17 standard cells, 23 I/O ports with 119 Nets which is similar when compared with Sobel operator as both of the operators work on 3 × 3 kernels.

From the RTL design in Fig. 2.7, Robert operator uses 17 standard cells, 23 I/O ports, and 79 Nets. The number of Nets for Robert operator is less when compared to Sobel and Prewitt, as Robert works on 2 × 2 kernels.

Fig. 2.3 Synthesis power consumption

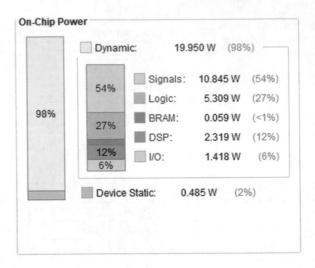

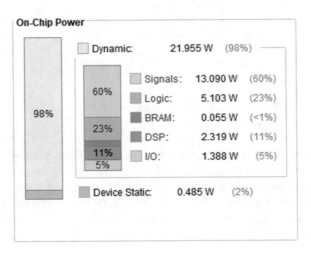

Fig. 2.4 Implementation power consumption

E. *Clock frequency versus Processing time*

(1) *For 50 MHz clock frequency*

For the 50 MHz clock the clock period is set to 20 ns and the clock toggles every 10 ns seen in Figs. 2.8, 2.9 through 2.10.

From the simulation timing diagrams, the Sobel, Prewitt, and Robert operation takes roughly the same time. The simulation time for all the three operations is 5,284 µs.

(2) *For 100 MHz clock frequency*

For the 100 MHz clock, the clock period is set to 10 ns and the clock toggles every 5 ns seen in Figs. 2.11, 2.12 through 2.13.

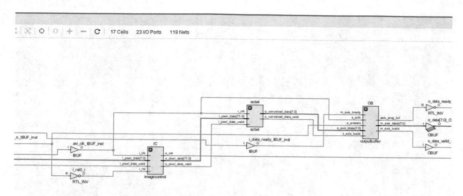

Fig. 2.5 RTL design of Sobel Operator

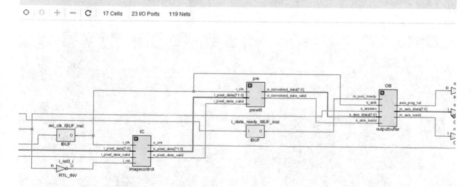

Fig. 2.6 RTL design of Prewitt Operator

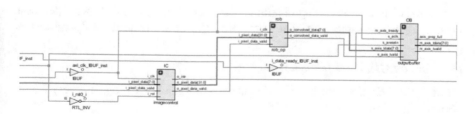

Fig. 2.7 RTL design of Robert Operator

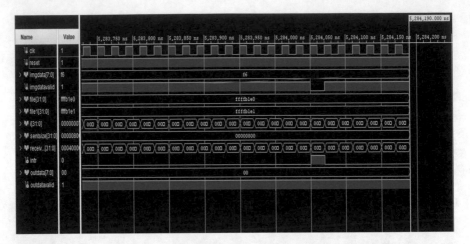

Fig. 2.8 Processing time for the Sobel operator considering 50 MHz clock

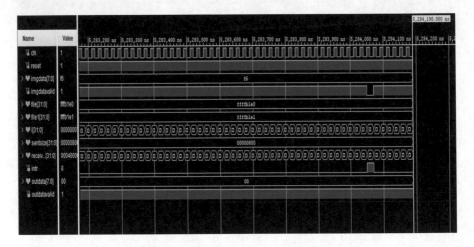

Fig. 2.9 Processing time for the Prewitt Operator considering 50 MHz clock

From the simulation timing diagrams, the Sobel, Prewitt, and Robert operation takes roughly the same time. The simulation time for all the three operations is 2,642 μs.

(3) *For 200 MHz clock frequency*

For the 200 MHz clock the clock period is set to 5 ns and clock toggles every 2.5 ns seen in Figs. 2.14, 2.15 through 2.16.

From the simulation timing diagrams, the Sobel, Prewitt, and Robert operation takes roughly the same time. The simulation time for all the three operations is 1,321 μs.

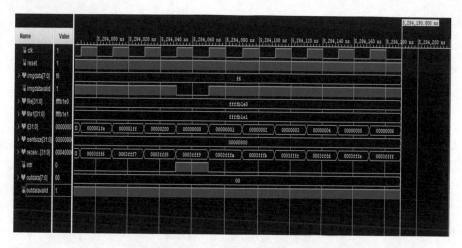

Fig. 2.10 Processing time for the Robert Operator considering 50 MHz clock

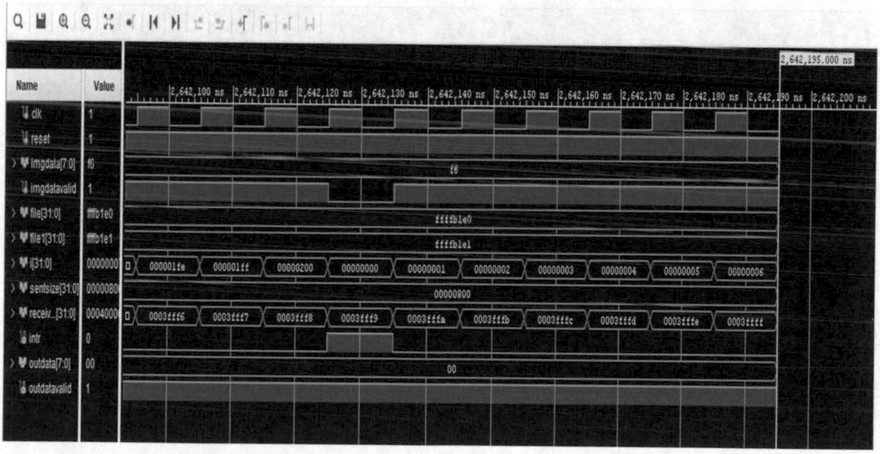

Fig. 2.11 Processing time for the Sobel Operator considering 100 MHz clock

Analyzing the above results suggests that with higher clock rates, the number of operations carried out increases which results in less processing time, when compared to the slow clock rate.

(4)   *Comparison of the processing times*

This section would compare results of all the processing time obtained based on the different clock frequencies. This can be seen in Table 2.9 and Figs. 2.17, 2.18 through 2.19.

38

N. A. Bharadwaj et al.

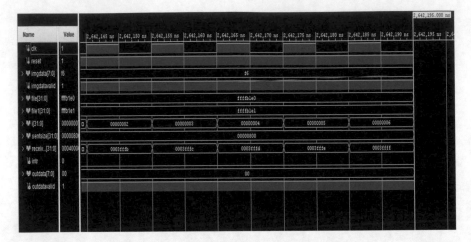

Fig. 2.12 Processing time for the Prewitt Operator considering 100 MHz clock

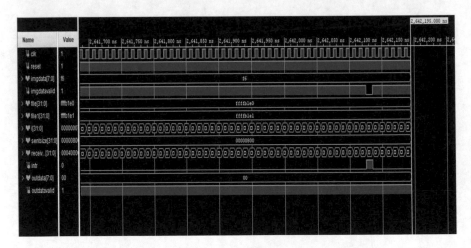

Fig. 2.13 Processing time for the Robert Operator considering 100 MHz clock

F. *Results Analysis*

Result analysis is done through snapshots which are means to illustrate the outcomes attained. Snapshots offer a way to compare the outcomes visually. Sobel, Prewitt, and Robert are seen in the pictures from left to right. This is observed in Figs. 2.20 and 2.21 for Python implementation and Figs. 2.22 and 2.23 for Verilog implementation. The parameter comparison images can be verified through Figs. 2.24 and 2.25.

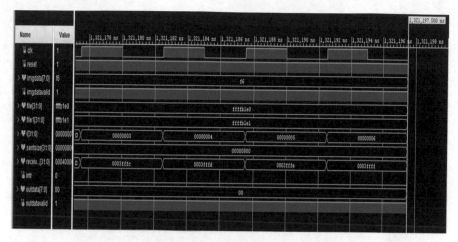

Fig. 2.14 Processing time for the Sobel Operator considering 200 MHz clock

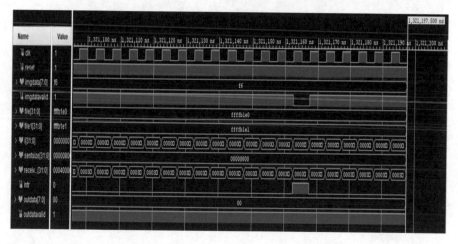

Fig. 2.15 Processing time for the Prewitt Operator considering 200 MHz clock

(1) *Comparison from Python implementation*

(2) *Comparison from Verilog implementation*

(3) *Parameters comparison charts*

Conclusion

The Sobel, Prewitt, and Robert edge detection algorithms are designed, implemented, and are evaluated in this study. The concept was put into practice using Python and

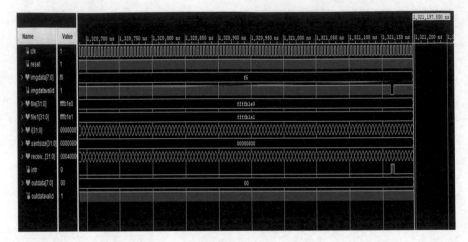

Fig. 2.16 Processing time for the Robert Operator considering 200 MHz clock

Table 2.9 Comparison of clock frequencies versus processing time

Clock frequency (MHz)	Time (μs) Sobel	Time (μs) Prewitt	Time (μs) Robert
50	5284	5284	5284
100	2642	2642	2642
200	1321	1321	1321

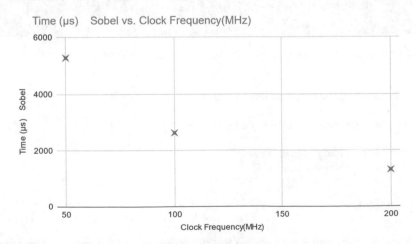

Fig. 2.17 Sobel processing time versus clock frequencies

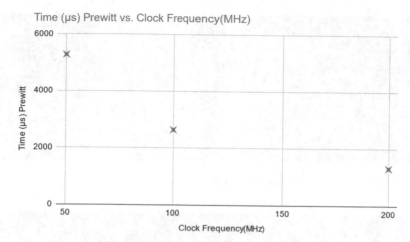

Fig. 2.18 Prewitt processing time versus clock frequencies

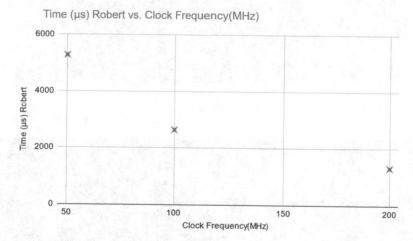

Fig. 2.19 Robert processing time versus clock frequencies

Fig. 2.20 Python—Edge detected butterfly images

Fig. 2.21 Python—Edge detected abstract images

Fig. 2.22 Verilog—Edge detected butterfly images

Fig. 2.23 Verilog—Edge detected abstract images

Verilog, and the outcomes of the two comparisons were made. The Sobel operator has a higher edge detection efficiency than the Prewitt and Robert operators. The Sobel operator-based edge detection technique finds thick edges. Robert's operator-based edge detection method can be used for applications like road lane detection in smart automobiles where quick processing is necessary. Sobel operator-based edge detection systems can be utilized to obtain sharp edges for systems like barcode readers. For applications that need quicker calculation times, FPGA can be employed as a

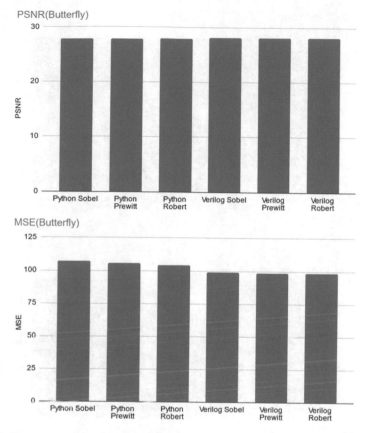

Fig. 2.24 Parameters results chart for Butterfly Image

hardware accelerator. Affordable, re-configurable solutions would be made possible by FPGA-based hardware acceleration. From the power analysis, one can use FPGA-based systems which offer low power solutions compared to the traditional CPU- or GPU-based solutions. The increase in the clock frequency would decrease the processing time without the compromise in power. FPGA realization of these algorithms paves way for the better implementation of AI and ML algorithms. AI and ML projects based on image processing and computer vision can be accelerated with the help of FPGA along with the added advantage of less power consumption.

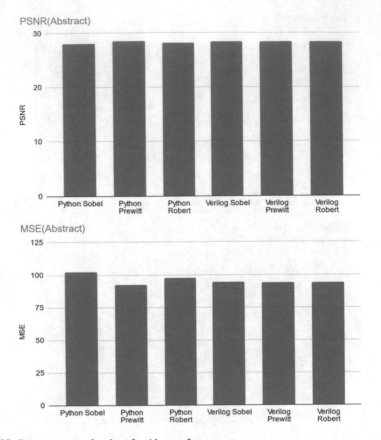

Fig. 2.25 Parameters results chart for Abstract Image

References

Afsar M, Khaitan KK, Rahul, Gururaj C (2021) Optimized FPGA implementation and synthesis of image segmentation techniques. In: 2021 IEEE mysore sub section international conference (MysuruCon), pp. 191–196. https://doi.org/10.1109/MysuruCon52639.2021.9641613

Atabany W, Degenaar P (2008)Parallelism to reduce power consumption on FPGA spatiotemporal image processing. In: 2008 IEEE international symposium on circuits and systems (ISCAS), pp. 1476–1479. https://doi.org/10.1109/ISCAS.2008.4541708

Chaple GN, Daruwala RD, Gofane MS (2015)Comparisions of Robert, Prewitt, Sobel operator based edge detection methods for real time uses on FPGA. In: 2015 international conference on technologies for sustainable development (ICTSD), 2015, pp. 1–4. https://doi.org/10.1109/ICTSD.2015.7095920

Dewan P, Vig R, Shukla N (2016) Novel VLSI architectures for image segmentation and edge detection algorithm. Int J Comput Appl 149:32–36. https://doi.org/10.5120/ijca2016911577

Fatma A, Garg S. (2020) Analysis and implementation FPGA implementation for image processing algorithm. J CritAl Rev 7(14), 2637–2645. https://doi.org/10.31838/jcr.07.14.514

Gonzalez R, Woods R (2009), Digital Image Processing, 3rd edn. Pearson International Edition, Pearson Education

Gururaj C, Jayadevappa D, Tunga S (2015) An effective implementation of exudate extraction from fundus images of the eye for a content based image retrieval system through hardware description language. In: Third International Conference on Emerging Research in Computing, Information, Communication and Applications, Springer, pp. 279–290, Bengaluru, India. ISBN 978-81-322-2552-2

Gururaj C, Tunga S (2019) AI based Feature extraction through content based image retrieval. J Comput Theor Nanosci 17(9–10):4097–4101. ISSN: 1546-1955

Gururaj C, Jayadevappa D, Tunga S (2016) Content based image retrieval system implementation through neural network. IOSR J VLSI Signal Process (IOSR-JVSP) 6(3), Ver. 3 (May–June 2016), pp 42–47. e-ISSN: 2319–4200, p-ISSN No.: 2319–4197

Gururaj C (2018) Proficient algorithm for features mining in fundus images through content based image retrieval. In: IEEE international conference on intelligent and innovative computing applications (ICONIC – 2018). Plaine Magnien, Mauritius, pp 108–113. ISBN 978-1-5386-6476-6

Jingcheng S, Zhengyan W, Zenggang L (2019)Implementation of sobel edge detection algorithm and VGA display based on FPGA. In: 2019 IEEE 4th advanced information technology, electronic and automation control conference (IAEAC), pp. 2305–2310. https://doi.org/10.1109/IAEAC4 7372.2019.8997533

Lu R, Liu X, Wang X, Pan J, Sun K, Waynes H (2017) The design of FPGA-based digital image processing system and research on algorithms. (2017)

Ma Y, Ma H, Chu P (2020) Demonstration of quantum image edge extration enhancement through improved sobel operator. IEEE Access 8:210277–210285. https://doi.org/10.1109/ACCESS. 2020.3038891

Mathur N, Mathur S, Mathur D (2016) A novel approach to improve sobel edge detector. Procedia Comput Sci 93:431–438. https://doi.org/10.1016/j.procs.2016.07.230. ISSN 1877-0509

Qasaimeh M, Denol K, Lo J, Vissers K, & Zambreno J, Jones P (2019) Comparing energy efficiency of CPU, GPU and FPGA implementations for vision kernels. https://doi.org/10.1109/ICESS. 2019.8782524

Upadhyaya BK, Chakraborty D (2018) FPGA implementation of gradient based edge detection algorithms for real time image. In: 2018 2nd international conference on trends in electronics and informatics (ICOEI), pp 1227–1233. https://doi.org/10.1109/ICOEI.2018.8553820

Wang C, Zhu SM (2015) A design of FPGA-based system for image processing. Rev Comput Eng Stud 2(1), 25–30. https://doi.org/10.18280/rccs.020104

Yaman S, Karakaya B, Erol Y (2019) Real time edge detection via IP-core based Sobel filter on FPGA. In: 2019 international conference on applied automation and industrial diagnostics (ICAAID), pp 1–4. https://doi.org/10.1109/ICAAID.2019.8934964

Chapter 3
Study of Adiabatic Logic-Based Combinational and Sequential Circuits for Low-Power Applications

Minakshi Sanadhya and Devendra Kumar Sharma

Introduction

The number of transistors on a single chip has grown significantly since the late 1960s, from a few hundred to over one billion. In 1965, Gordon Moore published article (Ito 2003), which predicted that the number of transistors per integrated circuit would double yearly at the possibly lowest cost. Moore's Law indicated that transistors would be doubled every two years. These projections have driven the microelectronic industry's pursuit of increasing integrated circuit complexity and lowering fabrication costs. Moore's predictions have proven to be very accurate upto this point, that is, from the first Intel microprocessor 4004 to the current gold Pentium CPU. The internet, portable computers, and mobile phones would not have been feasible without the tremendous growth of integrated circuits, and they will undoubtedly continue to expand their importance in the high-tech world.

CMOS will undoubtedly continue to be the core technology (Ito 2003). In the modern microelectronics industry, CMOS technology is the most significant breakthrough. In the age of information technology, it has emerged as the most critical source of innovation (Panda et al. 2014; Manikandan et al. 2015). The CMOS process is a well-defined and integrated set of processing steps that enables innovative materials and structures to produce electronic devices (Zhou 2001).

Due to the rising need for moveable and compact devices, integrated circuits require efficient techniques to develop circuits with less power consumption (Sundar 2016). Semiconductor technologies are becoming increasingly important, and the market for semiconductor products has increased. So far, two products, microprocessors and dynamic random-access memories have been the main drivers of the needs,

M. Sanadhya (✉) · D. K. Sharma
Department of Electronics and Communication Engineering, Faculty of Engineering and Technology, Delhi-NCR Campus, SRM Institute of Science and Technology, NCR Campus, Delhi-Meerut Road, Modinagar, Ghaziabad, UP, India
e-mail: minakshisanadhya@gmail.com

© The Author(s), under exclusive license to Springer Nature Singapore Pte Ltd. 2023
D. K. Sharma et al. (eds.), *Low Power Architectures for IoT Applications*, Springer Tracts in Electrical and Electronics Engineering, https://doi.org/10.1007/978-981-99-0639-0_3

and mobile and digital products have been the secondary drivers. In recent decades, the fast rise in transistor density on integrated circuits and the fast-switching speed of transistors have enabled computer systems to enhance their performance by several orders of magnitude. Unfortunately, such remarkable advances in interpretation have increased system power and energy dissipation.

The main barrier to portability is power dissipation. In a typical CMOS circuit, the types of energy dissipation are dynamic and static. Dynamic power dissipation is the amount of energy a device uses when switching. Static power dissipation occurs when a system is unplugged or in standby mode.

Various approaches are available in the VLSI design process to optimize energy consumption. The scaling of supply voltage is essential for power reduction. Device performance deteriorates when the supply voltage is minimized, such as increased leakage issues and reduced circuit speed. So, the adiabatic approaches are explored to reduce dynamic power dissipation (Ishwarya 2018). For optimized circuit design, to get the best outcomes, the sources of power dissipation and the factors that influence them must be thoroughly understood. Low-power circuit designs are possible at multiple levels, including architecture, gate, and technology. As a result, one of the most critical aspects of modern digital circuit design is low power consumption.

This chapter analyzes combinational and sequential circuit designs using various adiabatic approaches. Results are compared exhaustively. The chapter consists of six sections. In Sect. 3.2, preliminaries are discussed. Section 3.3 includes the adiabatic techniques-based combinational circuits. In Sect. 3.4, adiabatic techniques-based sequential circuits are discussed. The analysis of performance parameters is carried out in Sect. 3.5. Section 3.6 concludes the chapter.

Preliminaries

Adiabatic means no exchange of energy from the environment. A slow-varying AC power source is used in adiabatic logic instead of a constant one. It also allows for energy recycling, which decreases the overall amount of energy drawn from the source. The adiabatic logic technique is superior to other circuit design techniques in terms of less energy consumption. The adiabatic charging and discharging circuit are shown in Fig. 3.1.

Power-Clock Generation

The constant DC power supply refills the dissipated energy by restoring the maximum voltage. However, there may be some hitch in several existing styles since various logic charging and discharging alters from period to period during the execution process, eliminating the stable load condition. The power supply generation for adiabatic techniques is the most crucial part of driving the circuit (Rao 2017).

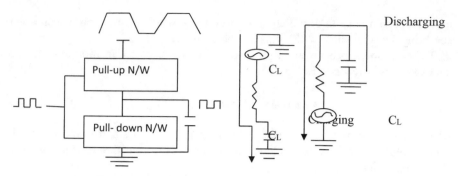

Fig. 3.1 Adiabatic charging and discharging

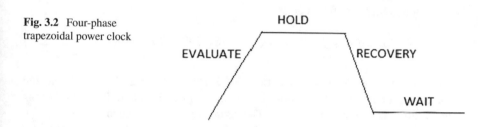

Fig. 3.2 Four-phase trapezoidal power clock

The trapezoidal power clock has four phases: evaluation, ideal, hold, and recovery. The power-clock operation is illustrated in Fig. 3.2. The circuit accepts no inputs when the clock is at the ideal phase. The input provided at minimum voltage logic "0" or maximum voltage logic "1" will be evaluated during the evaluation phase. The logic output will be enabled and held concerning the power clock at the hold phase. In the recovery phase, the power stored in the load capacitance will be discharged to the ground.

Adiabatic and Non-adiabatic Losses

While implementing the adiabatic circuits, three major concerns are there which need to be taken care of -

(i)   Never turn on a transistor when its two terminals are potentially different.
(ii)   When a current flows through a switch, never turn off the switch.
(iii) Current should never be passed through a diode.

If the above-said conditions are not followed while designing the adiabatic circuits, power dissipation may occur in the circuit. This power dissipation can be of two categories: adiabatic and non-adiabatic. Even once the conditions mentioned above are fully met, adiabatic power loss is an implicit energy loss. Non-adiabatic power loss is a certain amount of violation of these laws, which causes power loss when accessing the adiabatic loss (Sharma and Noor 2015).

The adiabatic loss is inversely proportional to the clock's transition time T. The adiabatic loss is given by Eq. (3.1).

$$E_{\text{Adiabatic}} = (R_{ON}C_L/T)\, C_L V_{DD}^2 \tag{3.1}$$

where, R_{ON} is the switch on-resistance, load capacitance (C_L), and V_{DD} is the clock supply voltage. Adiabatic loss is lowered by making the transition time much more significant than $R_{ON}C_L$.

The non-adiabatic losses represented by Eq. (3.2) are caused by the potential differential across the terminals of the switch when it is on. Non-adiabatic losses become apparent at low frequencies.

$$E_{\text{Non-Adiabatic}} = 1/2((C_1 C_2)\,/\,(C_1 + C_2))\,(V_1 - V_2)^2 \tag{3.2}$$

V_1 and V_2 are the voltages across the switch terminals, and C_1 and C_2 are the capacitances across them. Non-adiabatic losses are proportional to the square of the voltage difference across the switch. Therefore, zero-voltage switching should be achieved. To prevent non-adiabatic losses, the transistor should not be turned on when there is a potential difference between the drain and the source. A separate charge recovery path is required to recycle the power, and the output must be used to construct the input, which is possible only with reversible logic (Shari Jahan and Kayalvizhi 2012a).

Adiabatic Logic Circuits

There are two different forms of adiabatic logic circuits:

- Fully adiabatic circuits
- Partially/Quasi-adiabatic circuits

Fully Adiabatic Circuits

In contrast to quasi-adiabatic circuits, fully adiabatic circuits contain no non-adiabatic loss but are significantly extra complex. The power supply fully recovers all charges on the load capacitance. Fully adiabatic circuits experience numerous issues with operating speed and input power-clock synchronization (Samanta et al. 2019). A brief of the well-known, fully adiabatic approaches is given in the subsequent sub-sections.

PAL (Pass Transistor Adiabatic Logic)

PAL is a dual-rail logic with two cross-coupled PMOS devices in each phase by *out* and *out⁻* pass transistor NMOS functional blocks. A PC sinusoidal power clock is used in the PAL gate (Pindoo et al. 2015). Oklobdzija et al. presented a 2:1 Multiplexer based on innovative pass transistor adiabatic logic that utilizes a single power-clock supply and has less energy consumption than partially adiabatic logic approaches. Dual-rail logic called PAL has significantly fewer gates complexity of complementary and true NMOS functional blocks (Oklobdzija et al. 1997).

SCRL (Split-Rail Charge Recovery Logic)

SCRL logic requires fewer transistors and minimizes power dissipation compared to the quasi-adiabatic technique. It is shown in Fig. 3.3. This approach uses split level power clock. Therefore, clock synchronization is more complex (Sundar 2016). Rani et al. presented the design and circuit simulation of a carry look-ahead adder using split-level charge recovery logic. Every change in output level causes a loss of bits in conventional circuits, and the energy associated with those bits is transformed to heat. This directly affects computing costs by raising the system overhead required to remove the heat, leading to weight issues, short battery life, etc. (Rani and Kadam 2013). Hänninen et al. described the adiabatic CMOS of restricted reversible energy recovery and the initial stages of design automation. Adiabatic complementary transistor circuits design using these "steep" devices at the system level. Proposed circuit design is achieving switching energy improvements of 2 to 4 orders of magnitude over standard CMOS (Hänninen et al. 2014).

Partially/Quasi-Adiabatic Circuits

Partially adiabatic circuits have a straightforward design and power-clock system. Adiabatic loss occurs when current passes via a non-ideal switch (Sharma and Noor 2015). The non-adiabatic energy loss in some operating regions of partially adiabatic logic family circuits is typically proportional to the square of the threshold voltage and the capacitance driven (Bindal 2016). For low-power applications, adiabatic logic circuits have been presented by Nandal et al. and low-power VLSI circuits are used to create power-efficient systems. Due to its ability to recirculate energy rather than letting it dissipate, the adiabatic operation offers significant power reduction (Nandal and Kumar 2017). The following are the partially adiabatic approaches that the researchers in the literature have employed:

Fig. 3.3 SCRL circuit

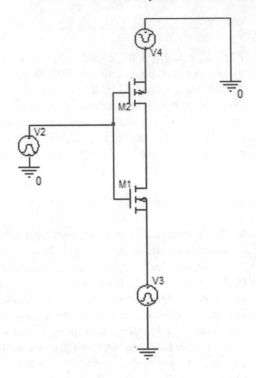

ECRL (Efficient Charge Recovery Logic)

Two cross-coupled PMOS transistors are used for the ECRL pull-up block section and
it is used for pre-charge and evaluation, while a tree of NMOS transistors is employed
for the pull-down section. It is depicted in Fig. 3.4. Only NMOS transistors are used
in the pull-down region to implement the functional block of the logic function
(Swaroop 2013). The charge delivered by the power clock is recovered by ECRL
using a 4-phase power clock. Each clock had a 90° phase leg before the subsequent
clock (Zhang and Hu 2011). Ng et al. had presented a low-power flip-flop design
based on the ECRL technique. While designing adiabatic energy recovery systems,
the ECRL-based flip-flops provide essential building blocks (Ng and Lau 2000).

2N-2P Adiabatic Logic

The 2N-2P adiabatic logic circuit, which uses differential logic and contains two
NMOS devices and two PMOS devices, provides a logic function and its complement. Figure 3.5 depicts the 2N-2P basic circuit. Cross-coupled PMOS devices are
linked to the power-clock supply, and each NMOS device receives inputs with the
corresponding negative and positive polarity. The outputs are complimentary when
the power-clock supply ramps down during the reset phase, and the inputs are low.

Fig. 3.4 ECRL circuit

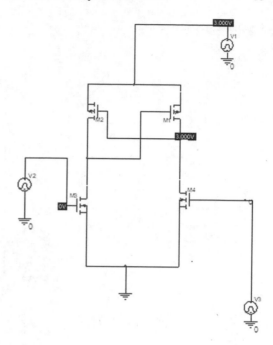

As a result of the low power supply during the waiting phase, the inputs and outputs remain low. The power supply ramps up when the outputs are evaluated and the results are complemented. During the hold state, the power supply clock remains high while the inputs ramp down to low. This logic provides low power consumption, but it has floating output problem (Sanadhya and Kumar 2015).

2N-2N-2P Adiabatic Logic

The 2N-2N-2P adiabatic approach is derived from ECRL to diminish the coupling effect and 2N-2P floating output problem. Figure 3.6 depicts the 2N-2N-2P basic circuit. Its fundamental advantage over ECRL is the cross-coupling of NMOS transistor switches, resulting in non-floating outputs during a significant recovery state (Kramer et al. 1999). The power loss of 2N-2N-2P is made up of adiabatic and non-adiabatic power losses. The following reasons lead to the formulation of non-adiabatic power loss models for 2N-2N-2P, consisting of leakage current, dissipation through latch formation, and insufficient charge recovery. Most diode-based adiabatic logic includes floating pulse-mode outputs, similar to dynamic logic. Pulse-mode outputs are also available in 2N-2N2P. They do not float while the output is valid for the whole HOLD period (Kramer et al. 1999).

Fig. 3.5 2N-2P basic circuit

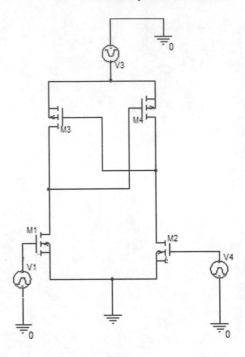

NERL (NMOS Energy Recovery Logic)

NERL uses NMOS transistors only and a more straightforward 6-phase clocked power, which uses effective energy transfer and recovery via adiabatic and bootstrapping approaches NMOS switches to alter the NERL circuits. It is offering excellent throughput with low energy consumption. NERL provide full output voltage swing, less dependence on the power-clock frequency, output load capacitance insensitivity, and complementary outputs for balanced capacitance load to the power clock (Kim et al. 1999). Its power dissipation and area overhead measure smaller than the existing adiabatic approach. NERL is most appropriate compared to the other adiabatic circuit approaches for applications with low energy consumption but compromising other performance parameters (Fazal and Ahmer 2015). NERL is the best low-power digital logic technique in mixed-signal IC as well as in digital IC design.

CAL (Clocked Adiabatic Logic)

CAL functions in non-adiabatic mode as well as adiabatic mode. When CAL is operated in non-adiabatic mode, it has DC power supply and in adiabatic mode, it has single-phase power-clock supply. Figure 3.7 illustrates a basic CAL circuit. Core of the CAL is similar to an SRAM cell. Consequently, this can be used in adiabatic and non-adiabatic methods (Sanadhya and Kumar 2015). The two NMOS control transistors placed among the input pull-down network and the output nodes, which

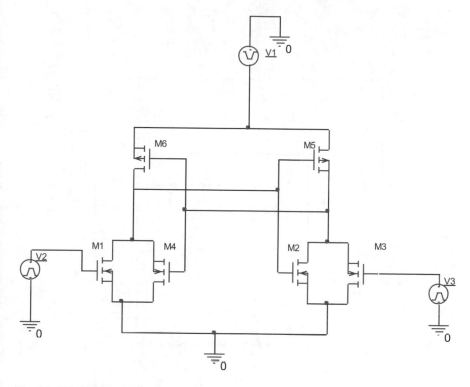

Fig. 3.6 2N-2N-2P basic circuit

are controlled by two complementary square-wave auxiliary signals, distinguish CAL from other adiabatic families. Although the circuit can operate as a single-phase PC with just two signals, it can only do so at half the frequency of a trapezoidal PC. An essential key benefit of using a single-phase PC is to simplify chip synchronization. The biggest drawback is the auxiliary signals. New inputs can only be accepted at half the PC frequency (Cutitaru and Belfore 2013).

TSEL (True Single-Phase Adiabatic Logic)

In TSEL logic, a sinusoidal single-phase power clock is used. PMOS and NMOS gates are connected in cascades. Two DC reference voltages ensure a high rate of operation. Additionally, it allowed to connect TSEL gates which is cascaded in an NP-domino fashion. TSEL performs better at 100 MHz frequency at all temperatures, and at frequencies beyond 100 MHz, performance of TSEL is degraded (Kim and Papaefthymiou 2001). Manjurathi et al. had presented true single-phase energy recovery logic-based multiplier for low-power application (Manjurathi 2009). A source-coupled TSEL variation that uses a tunable current source to regulate the

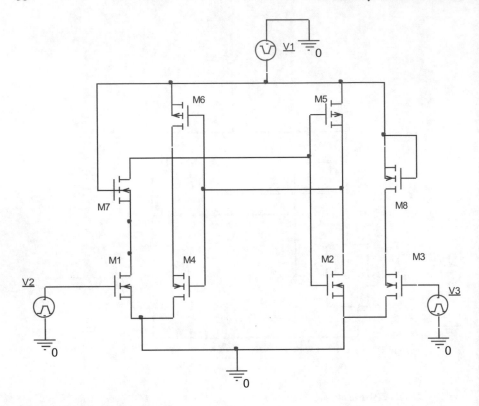

Fig. 3.7 CAL basic circuit

rate of charge flow into or out of each gate to maximize energy efficiency. Our adiabatic circuitry addresses various issues with multiple power-clock systems, including layout complexity in clock distribution, increased energy dissipation, and clock skew.

.

SCAL (Source-Coupled Adiabatic Logic)

SCAL logic used a single-phase power-clock logic for its operation Adjusting a current source connected to each gate makes low-power operation possible across a wide range. It eliminates many issues with multiple stages, more energy efficient, such as multiple AC power supplies, clock skew, and layout complexity in the clock distribution network. Its effective operation is based on a current source that may be adjusted to control the rate of charge flow into or out of the gate while evaluation phase occurs (Kim and Papaefthymiou 1999).

QSERL (Quasi-Static Energy Recovery Logic)

A conventional CMOS gate with two extra diodes forms the QSERL gate. The PMOS block top diode controls the charging path, while the NMOS block bottom diode controls the discharging path. Low-threshold voltage MOSFETs devices are used in their implementation (Pindoo et al. 2015). The presented QSERL is similar to static CMOS in behavior and uses two complimentary sinusoidal supply clocks. As a result, switching activity is much lower than dynamic logic. In addition, static CMOS circuits can be used to design QSERL circuits. QSERL approach are compatible with two complimentary sinusoidal clocks and it produces a high-efficiency clock generation circuitry (Ye and Roy 2001). This technique minimizes energy dissipation, but the output is floating, which is undesirable (Upadhyay et al. 2013a).

CEPAL (Complementary Energy Path Adiabatic Logic)

CEPAL is a combination of pull-up and pull-down network. The power clock and the complementary sinusoidal power clocks are used in CEPAL logic. The static logic QSERL is replaced with CEPAL, which inherits all of its benefits and eliminates the hold phases, improving throughput and robustness.

When the clock ramps down, this makes the Vout to follow it and generate a floating node. This condition is avoided, the complementary clock, which swings high, avoids the floating node and the weak high signal problem by removing both the hold state seen in two-phase clock-operated circuits. The complementary clock similarly eliminates the weak low signal (Turaga et al. 2014).

2PASCL (Two-Phase Adiabatic Static CMOS Logic)

Two complementary split-level sinusoidal power supply clocks with a height equal to V_{dd} are used in the low-power 2PASCL circuit. It comprises two MOSFET diodes that increase the discharge rate of internal signal nodes and recycle charges from the output node. One diode is connected between the power clock and the output node, while another is connected between the NMOS and the alternative power source. Sometimes, discharging of the circuit nodes happens during each clock cycle because of these MOSFET diode connections. As a result, node switching activities are significantly decreased and it reduces the energy consumption and gives high fan out. Its main drawback is floating outputs, connected to alternate hold phases, throughout the circuit operation (Suguna and Rani 2020).

DFAL (Diode Free Adiabatic Logic Circuits)

Two power supplies producing symmetrical and asymmetrical power clocks are used in the DFAL circuit. Figure 3.8 depicts the basic DFAL circuit. With one clock pulse being in phase and the next being out of phase, the evaluation and hold state is divided into a circuit's functioning according to the timing of the clock pulses. Also,

Fig. 3.8 DFAL basic circuit

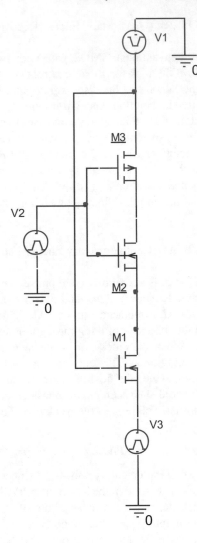

the charging and discharging path in the circuit do not contain diode connected MOSFETs. This technique overcomes the constraints such as delay, complexing, and degradation of output amplitude problems. The proposed DFAL inverter will therefore be an excellent option even at greater frequencies than the existing adiabatic inverters (Upadhyay et al. 2013b).

CPAL (Complementary Pass Transistor Adiabatic Logic)

CPAL logic comprises two parts: one is the load drive circuit, combined with two transmission gates, and the other part is the logic function circuit, composed of complementary pass transistor logic function blocks and four NMOS transistors. The

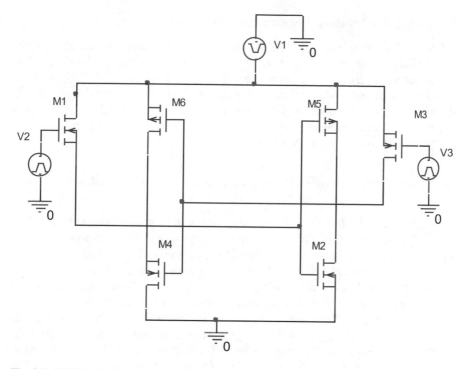

Fig. 3.9 PFAL basic circuit

clamp transistors maintain stable operation by preventing output nodes from floating. Complementary pass transistor logic for evaluation and transmission gates for energy recovery make CPAL circuits more effective at transferring and recovering energy due to eliminating non-adiabatic energy loss of output loads (Maheshwari et al. 2017). Because complementary pass transistor logic has eliminated non-adiabatic energy loss of output loads, CPAL circuits are more effective at transferring and recovering energy. CPAL circuits have significantly fewer transistors than other adiabatic logic design approaches. The complementary pass transistor logic approach reduces the complication of the circuit (Patpatia et al. 2011).

PFAL (Positive Feedback Adiabatic Logic)

PFAL is employed as a partial energy recovery circuit due to its low power consumption compared to other well-known approaches. Figure 3.9 depicts the basic PFAL circuit. The core component of the PFAL is an adiabatic amplifier, a latch with 2-PMOS and 2-NMOS transistors. This prevents the logic level at the output nodes out and out from degrading. To implement the logic functions, it additionally includes two n-trees. Also, it has good durability against technological parameter variations (Swathi et al. 2018).

MPFAL (Modified Positive Feedback Adiabatic Logic)

MPFAL is the upgrade design of PFAL. Figure 3.10 illustrates the basic structure of the MPFAL circuit. In MPFAL, between the source and ground terminal of PFAL cross-coupled inverters, it uses an additional drain gate connected NMOS transistor to reduce the power dissipation more than the PFAL inverter design (Sundar 2016). Kushawaha et al. had presented the design of ultra-low-power full adder. Compared to positive feedback adiabatic logic, the proposed circuit's average power is lower in the MPFAL (Kushawaha and Sasamal 2016).

DC-DB PFAL (Direct Current Diode-Based Positive Feedback Adiabatic Logic)

The latch of the DC-DB PFAL circuit uses two NMOS transistors and two PMOS transistors, similar to the PFAL logic circuit (Agrawal et al. 2017). Similar to PFAL logic, the transmission gates are formed by connecting the functional blocks of NMOS logic in parallel with the PMOS transistors of the latch. The difference lies in the pull-down block with an NMOS diode and a DC voltage source connected between the pull-down NMOS transistors and the grounded-DB PFAL Basic Circuit as shown in Fig. 3.11. The use of a diode at the bottom of the NMOS tree is intended to control the discharging path by slowing the rate at which internal nodes in the logic circuit discharge, and an additional positive DC voltage source is placed between the diode and the ground to utilize the benefits of level shifting technology better. The level shifting technique lowers the output transistors gate to source voltage and also lowering the gate current and leakage current.

Adiabatic Technique-Based Combinational Circuits

Various adiabatic logic-based combinational circuits are discussed in this section. A design whose output depends on the current set of inputs and is independent of previous information is called combinational design.

Adiabatic Logic-Based Inverter

In the adiabatic logic inverter, the circuit pull-up and pull-down networks charge and discharge the output node capacitance. It ensures that the power supply can retrieve the energy stored at the output node at the end of each cycle. Wang et al. presented a low-power switched adiabatic output logic. The circuit uses only one NMOS for pre-charge instead of two diodes (Agrawal et al. 2017; Wang and Lau 1998). A CMOS combinational logic circuit has been described by Chaudhary et al. (Chaudhary and Girdhar 2013), and power analyses are done at 180 nm technology using the adiabatic

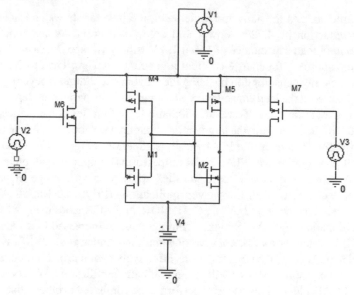

Fig. 3.10 MPFAL basic circuit

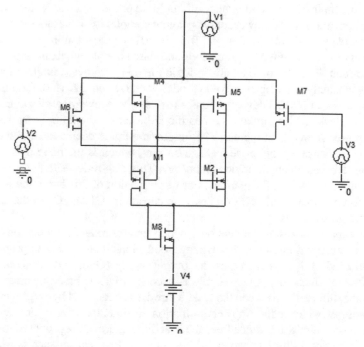

Fig. 3.11 DC—DB PFAL basic circuit

reduction method. At the adiabatic logic level, the inverter shows an improvement in power reduction by 4.72%. Power and delay measurements are done using a constant output load capacitance of 1pf at 1.8 V supply voltage. Priya et al. reported an adiabatic approach for energy-efficient logic circuit design. The PMOS networks show lesser energy consumption by using the adiabatic technique, recycling some of the energy stored at the load capacitance. The changes in its parameter depend greatly on adiabatic logic families. However, adiabatic logic families consume less energy than CMOS logic throughout the large range of parameter variations. At the high load capacitance and frequency, the PFAL exhibits superior energy savings than ECRL. In terms of power efficiency, PFAL NOR outperforms compared to all other existing circuits. As a result, adiabatic logic families apply to a wide range of parameter variations. It can be used in low-power applications (Priya and Rai 2014). Anuar et al. presented the design of NAND, NOT, NOR, and XOR gates using a two-phase clocked adiabatic static CMOS logic technique. Due to increased load capacitance, a 2PASCL inverter shows low energy consumption (Anuar et al. 2010). Kim et al. presented a SCAL approach that functions effectively over a broad frequency range. Comparing the proposed design with other adiabatic families, it is observed that the proposed SCAL adders show superior performance compared to other adiabatic logic families in energy consumption. Adiabatic logic only needs one power-clock phase to function, eliminating several issues with multiple phases, such as increased power consumption, multiple AC power sources, layout complexity in the clock distribution network, and clock skew (Cutitaru and Belfore 2013). Garg et al. had presented the implementation of a GFCAL (glitch-free and cascade-able adiabatic logic) based inverter circuit. The proposed adiabatic logic method employs a single trapezoidal pulse power supply. There are two MOS diodes here, D1 and D2. The charging path's D1 transistor is an NMOS device, whereas the energy recovery path's D2 transistor is a PMOS device. This circuit modifies diode-based adiabatic logic by assuming that the power source is triangular. The output amplitude decreases, and there is a lot of noise because of the diode leakage current, which is the main disadvantage of the diode-based adiabatic logic technology. This also reduces the noise margin, output swing, and output fluctuations. For minimization of this issue, the proposed design has combination of MOS diodes with capacitors C1 and C2 in the charging and discharging circuits.

These capacitors absorb fluctuations, which greatly reduces fluctuations. Additionally, in charging circuitry, the dynamic body bias technique was proposed in the MOS diode D1 so it increases the output swing (Garg and Niranjan 2016). The split-level sinusoidal power supply is used in a DFAL-based inverter design. The voltage differential between the two electrodes is decreased by employing these power supplies, which reduces power dissipation. In either its charging or discharging path, there is no diode. It is diode free, an attractive feature of the proposed topology. Power dissipation is further decreased because the load capacitance is gradually charged or discharged (Gurunadha 2017). Shari Jahan et al. reported RERL as a dual rail adiabatic logic circuit that satisfies zero-voltage switching and removes non-adiabatic energy loss through reversible logic (ZVS). Therefore, the area overhead is more in the reversible approach than in the static CMOS approach. In the circuit

Table 3.1 Comparative analysis of different types of Inverters

Sl. No	Inverter	Transistor count	PD (μW)	Delay (ps)	PDP (fJ)
1	PFAL (Jayanthi et al. 2016)	6	1.820	5	0.009
2	Proposed (Garg and Niranjan 2016)	5	0.053	–	–
3	ECRL (Chauhan and Krishan 2017)	4	6.493	–	–
4	DFAL (Gurunadha 2017)	3	510.16	–	–
5	SCRL (Ishwarya 2018)	4	279.16	–	–
6	Static CMOS (Pindoo et al. 2015)	2	143,300	–	–
7	PFAL(Pindoo et al. 2015)	6	42,900	–	–
8	2PASCL (Pindoo et al. 2015)	4	3690	–	–
9	RERL (Shari Jahan and Kayalvizhi 2012b)	16	0.005	260	1.30
10	DC-DB PFAL (Agrawal et al. 2017)	5	0.006	1249	7.49

design, transmission gates are employed to prevent non-adiabatic losses caused by signal degradation (Shari Jahan and Kayalvizhi 2012b). Sundar et al. have presented the inverter and linear feedback shift register circuits designed using a modified PFAL adiabatic approach. It implements basic inverter functionality. To lessen the energy consumption of the PFAL inverter design, it employs an additional drain gate connected NMOS transistor between the source and ground terminal of PFAL cross-coupled inverters (Sundar 2016). Agrawal et al. presented the inverter, basic gates, and multiplexer circuits designed using the DC-DB PFAL logic technique (Agrawal et al. 2017). A comparative analysis of different types of inverters is shown in Table 3.1.

Adiabatic Logic-Based Gates

Logic gates are the most fundamental digital electronic circuits with one or more inputs and a single output. Anitha et al. presented distinct power-efficient NOT, NOR, and NAND gates designed using ECRL, PFAL, and 2N-2N-2P adiabatic logic approaches and comparative analyses are done for power consumption, latency, and transistors count. Results show that the adiabatic logic consumes less energy than the conventional technique (Anitha et al. 2019). Sasipriya et al. have reported a two-phase adiabatic dynamic logic (2PADL)-based inverter design for low-power VLSI circuits. The proposed inverter circuit is like a static CMOS inverter with additional transistors for its energy recovery operation. It employs the PC and PC' sinusoidal clock signals, which are complementary. The two phases of the sinusoidal clock signals are evaluated and held. The proposed 2PADL quasi-adiabatic logic uses a two-phase sinusoidal clock signal, providing the benefit of gate overdrive and minimizing switching energy. The single rail two-phase logic operation removes the signal routing problem. It is appropriate for less energy and high-speed operation (Sasipriya and Bhaaskaran 2017). Priya et al. have presented a comparative analysis of various logic families like ECRL and PFAL and conventional techniques for the design of Inverter, NAND, and NOR circuits.

The adiabatic technique is the best option for low-power applications in particular frequency ranges. PFAL has likely to be used to realize reversible logic functions. By making PFAL fully reversible, the adiabatic switching approach achieves considerably reduced power consumption, and circuit energies are preserved rather than power dissipation. Depending on the system and application requirements, this technique reduces the power consumption of digital systems (Priya and Rai 2014). Sharma et al. presented the transistor count optimization in conventional adiabatic logic families. The proposed hybrid adiabatic approach optimizes the power and area by eliminating the need for dual polarity inputs for circuit operation. The presented work uses a trapezoidal power clock on 180 nm technology to optimize and build various circuits. The presented circuit optimizes energy-efficient realization for VLSI circuits (Sharma 2020). Blotti et al. presented a few circuit schemes for the semi-reversible adiabatic approach that simulated conventional and non-conventional solutions for minimizing the power consumption of CMOS digital circuits (Blotti et al. 2002a). Maurya et al. have reported the design of NAND and NOR gates using CMOS, PFAL, and 2PASCL logic techniques for VLSI applications. The proposed circuit simulations are performed using SPICE at a 0.18 μm technology node (Maurya and Kumar 2011). Sharma et al. have presented the design of XOR gates based on the CPL-adiabatic gated logic (CPLAG) technique. CPL circuits use only NMOS networks and reduce the capacitance. For the realization of logic, complementary and non-complementary inputs must be available.

Many researchers consider CPL to be a modified form of CVSL that addresses cross-coupled devices' sizing issues. The proposed circuit can be synchronized with the reference clock signal to reduce the power consumption of VLSI circuits. The proposed CPLAG XOR gate is examined for the capacitance involved in energy consumption for various voltage levels. The circuit's functional and operational robustness under other operating situations is also examined for different temperature ranges (Sharma and Noor 2013). Blotti et al. have presented a single-inductor 4-phase power-clock generator for PFAL gates. The existing circuits show an improvement in energy reduction two to four times (Blotti et al. 2002b). A comparative analysis of different types of basic gates is shown in Table 3.2.

Table 3.2 Comparative analysis of various types of basic Gates

Si. No	Basic gates	Transistor count	PD(μW)	Delay(ps)	PDP(zJ)
1	ECRL NOR (Chauhan and Krishan 2017)	10	1.89	–	–
2	ECRL Ex-OR (Chauhan and Krishan 2017)	14	4.81	–	–
3	CMOS NOT (Anitha et al. 2019)	2	60.8	85.37	51.90
4	ECRL NOT (Anitha et al. 2019)	4	627	91.17	57.4
5	PFAL NOT (Anitha et al. 2019)	6	623	0.162	0.101
6	2N2N2P NOT (Anitha et al. 2019)	6	0.008	112.6	89.8
7	ECRL NAND (Chauhan and Krishan 2017)	10	3.36		–
8	CMOS NAND (Anitha et al. 2019)	4	0.0662	19.2	12.71
9	ECRL NAND (Anitha et al. 2019)	6	0.0398	279.3	111.16
10	PFAL NAND (Anitha et al. 2019)	8	0.0650	469.2	304.9
11	2N2N2P NAND (Anitha et al. 2019)	8	0.0438	319.0	139.72
12	RERL NAND (Shari Jahan and Kayalvizhi 2012a)	24	0.320	0.066	212.12
13	Optimization AND/NAND (Sharma 2020)	8	0.052	–	–
14	CMOS NOR (Anitha et al. 2019)	4	0.106	48.05	0.50
15	ECRL NOR (Anitha et al. 2019)	6	0.04	44.09	17.81
16	PFAL NOR (Anitha et al. 2019)	8	0.095	0.011	0.112
17	2N2N2P NOR (Anitha et al. 2019)	8	0.082	31.1	25.50
18	Optimization OR/NOR (Sharma 2020)	8	0.0005	–	–
19	ECRL NOR (Chauhan and Krishan 2017)	10	1.89	–	–
20	ECRL Ex-OR (Chauhan and Krishan 2017)	14	4.81	–	–
21	CPLAG XOR (Sharma and Noor 2013)	7	0.00003	–	–
22	XOR (Sneha et al. 2019)	10	0.300	–	–

(continued)

Table 3.2 (continued)

Si. No	Basic gates	Transistor count	PD(μW)	Delay(ps)	PDP(zJ)
23	Optimization XOR/XNOR (Sharma 2020)	10	0.0005	–	–

Where HA = Half Adder, FA = Full Adder

Adiabatic Logic-Based Adder

In digital systems, adders are integral to arithmetic logic units. Hussain et al. (Venkatesh et al. 2018) presented a performance comparison of a one-bit hybrid full adder and a conventional full adder. Two or more logic styles are used in a hybrid approach, whereas only one is used in the traditional method. A conventional full adder is designed using CMOS logic, CPL full adder and hybrid adder are designed using transmission gate (TG) logic. Despite the delay improvements, CPL uses more power since the circuit has more switching activity. A lot of transistors are needed for CMOS and CPL adders.

On the contrary, the hybrid adder shows better performance matrix such as latency, power, and PDP, transistor counts (Hussain and Chaudhury 2018). Sajid et al. have shown the design of a carry look-ahead adder circuit. Proposed adder circuits perform the addition of two binary numbers. The easiest method of adder design is the use of gates to produce the required logic function. Adder is a prominent block in the arithmetic logic unit because of its high-speed operation (Sajid et al. 2013). Pujari et al. presented the realization of a low-power 32-bit carry look-ahead adder using the ECRL adiabatic technique. Comparative analysis of the adder design based on the proposed and conventional approaches is done with respect to power dissipation. It is found that the present method shows better performance (Pujari et al. 2019). Kumar et al. designed and implemented a full adder based on parallel computing adiabatic approach for ultra-low-power applications.

The proposed design performs better with sufficient output voltage levels. These full adders are superior candidates for ultra-low-power applications because of their improved performance at high speeds. Implemented new circuits that work fairly with varying temperature and voltage. The proposed circuit also achieves better with sufficient output voltage levels (Kumar and Kumar 2020). Kumar et al. have presented the design of adiabatic low-power full adder. The adiabatic logic full adder cell has lesser power dissipation than the existing full adder design (Fazal and Ahmer 2015). Saxena et al. designed full adders with adiabatic logic that consumes low power compared to full adders designed with static CMOS logic (Saxena 2011). Dhivya et al. have reported the power-efficient full adder design with analysis. The proposed 2PASCL adiabatic logic holds better power results than the existing adiabatic approach (Saxena 2011; Kumar and Kumar 2020; Pujari et al. 2019; Nithya and Dhivya 2018). Patpatia et al. introduced a full adder design using single-phase N-type and P-type CPAL techniques. The results show that the energy loss is reduced with the circuit design using a complimentary pass transistor adiabatic logic approach

(Patpatia et al. 2011). Kushawaha et al. designed the full adder using modified positive feedback adiabatic logic. Results exhibit that the proposed circuit's power dissipation is reduced compared to the positive feedback adiabatic logic (PFAL) (Kushawaha and Kushawaha 2016). Akshitha et al. have reported half adder and subtractor design using various partial adiabatic approaches for low-power applications. When proposed circuits are compared with the other partial adiabatic logic and conventional CMOS approach. It has been found that the half adders and half subtractors implemented using the PFAL technique typically save more power compared to the other approaches (Akshitha and Rajan 2019a). A comparative analysis of various types of full and half adders is shown in Table 3.3.

Adiabatic Logic-Based Subtractor

Subtractor circuits use two binary integers as input and subtract one binary number from the other. Similar to adders, it gives two outputs, difference and borrows. Akshitha et al. presented half adder and half subtractor designs using different partial adiabatic approaches for power reduction. It is observed that the average energy saving is more in proposed circuits using the PFAL approach compared to the other partial adiabatic methods, including the CMOS technique (Akshitha and Rajan 2019b). Deo et al. have reported 1-bit adiabatic full subtractor designed using different approaches. Comparative analysis of the proposed design shows the improved performance in terms of power dissipation of DCPAL than the 2N2N2P adiabatic technique (Deo and Mangang 2014). Katre et al. designed a power-efficient full subtractor based on CMOS, ECRL, and PFAL techniques. Power reduction is possible with the proper choice of adiabatic family and substrate bias voltage selection. PFAL adiabatic technique-based proposed circuit shows superior results compared to the ECRL and conventional approach (Katre et al. 2004). Mangla et al. presented combinational circuit design using an adiabatic approach for 180 nm CMOS technology. The proposed adiabatic logic utilizes less power supply and dissipates less power than traditional CMOS circuitry (Mangla and Mangla 2014). Comparative analysis of various types of half subtractors and full subtractors are illustrated in Table 3.4.

Adiabatic Logic-Based Comparator

A comparator is an electrical component that compares two voltages or currents and produces a digital signal that indicates which is more prominent. Parveen et al. presented the design of a low-power dynamic comparator based on an adiabatic inverter. Low-power techniques are preferred for high-speed applications since the need for portable battery-operated devices is increasing. The dynamic comparator is frequently used in constructing high-speed ADCs (analogue-to-digital converters).

Table 3.3 Comparative analysis of various types of Full Adder and Half Adder

Si. No	Adder	Transistor count	PD (μW)	Delay (ps)	PDP (aJ)
1	Conventional design HA (Shari Jahan and Kayalvizhi 2012b)	–	30.63	–	–
2	ECRL Design HA (Shari Jahan and Kayalvizhi 2012b)	–	2.973	–	–
3	2N-2N2P Design HA (Shari Jahan and Kayalvizhi 2012b)	–	3.81	–	–
4	PFAL Design HA (Akshitha and Rajan 2019a)	–	0.957	–	–
5	CAL Design HA (Akshitha and Rajan 2019a)	–	4.287	–	–
	HA (Katre et al. 2004)	16	2.26	–	–
6	Conventional Design FA (Akshitha and Rajan 2019a)	–	27.02	–	–
7	ECRL Design FA (Akshitha and Rajan 2019a)	–	4.059	–	–
8	2N-2N2P Design FA (Shari Jahan and Kayalvizhi 2012b)	–	2.548	–	–
9	PFAL Design FA (Akshitha and Rajan 2019a)	–	0.957	–	–
10	CAL Design FA (Akshitha and Rajan 2019a)	–	4.287	–	–
11	Static CMOS FA (Varma and Reddy 2013)	36	3.05	0.229	0.698
12	DCVSL FA (Varma and Reddy 2013)	30	8.38	0.136	1.139
13	XOR/XNOR and Multiplexer-Based FA (Varma and Reddy 2013)	12	2.96	1.98	5.86
14	1 Bit adder (Ranjith et al. 2017)	–	3399.1	0.078	265.12

Where HA = Half Adder, FA = Full Adder

Table 3.4 Comparative analysis of different types of Half Subtractors and Full Subtractor

Si. No	Subtractor	Transistor count	PD (Diff.) (μW)	PD (Borrow) (μW)	Delay (ns)	PDP
1	CMOS HS (Mangla and Mangla 2014)	–	0.00000423	–	–	–
2	HS (Mangla and Mangla 2014)	16	0.00000291	–	–	–
3	FS (Ranjith et al. 2017)	–	–	–	80.11	–
4	2N2N2P FS (Deo and Mangang 2014)	–	5.3155	45.168	–	–
5	DCPAL (Deo and Mangang 2014)	–	0.55348	42.045	–	–
6	CMOS (Katre et al. 2004)	–	8370	0.0055	–	–
7	ECRL (Katre et al. 2004)	–	0.025	142.5	–	–
8	PFAL(Katre et al. 2004)	–	122.5	106.25	–	–

Where HS = Half Subtractor, FS = Full Subtractor

It has high input impedance, full swing output, quick speed, and low energy dissipation (Parveen and Moyal 2015). Kumar et al. presented a less-power two-bit magnitude comparator design using an adiabatic approach. Results demonstrate that the suggested adiabatic logic-based technique enhances the performance with variable voltage and temperature situations (Kumar and Kumar 2016a).

Singh et al. presented the implementation of a 4-bit magnitude comparator. The proposed circuit design uses the NOR gate logic circuit. Proposed comparator is power efficient, high-speed and it can be used for larger N-bit magnitude comparators design (Singh and Jain 2018). Kumar et al. have designed a low-power two-bit magnitude comparator using an adiabatic approach. The NOR gate logic is used in this work for developing of the proposed circuit (Kumar and Kumar 2016b). Sivasathya et al. presented the implementation of a dual rail comparator by using a low-voltage successive approximation register. The energy dissipation by the double tail comparator is observed less than the dynamic comparator (Sivasathya et al. 2014). Shekhawat et al. have reported the low-power magnitude comparator circuit design. The proposed magnitude comparator simulation results have shown remarkable performance in terms of threshold loss, energy consumption, and area compared to the existing magnitude comparator (GDI technique) (Shekhawat et al. 2014). Alam et al. have shown the performance analysis of a 4-bit comparator circuit designed by ECRL and PFAL adiabatic approaches (Alam et al. 2017). Kaur et al. have presented the design and analysis of a comparator using adiabatic PFAL and ECRL approaches.

Table 3.5 Comparative analysis of different types of Comparators

Si. No	Comparator	Transistor Count	PD (μW)	Delay (ns)	PDP (fJ)
1	Bitwise competition logic for compact digital (Kim and Yoo 2007)	964	–	1.12	–
2	2-bit ECRL (Kaur et al. 2015)	110	0.000023	35.05	–
3	2-bit PFAL (Kaur et al. 2015)	92	0.0000016	46.139	–
4	64-Bit Digital Comparator Using Cmos Logic (Panda et al. 2014)	–	0.0000017	130.69	22.7
5	Double tail (Samuel et al. 2017)	–	31.48534	–	–
6	ECRL and 2PASCL (Samuel et al. 2017)	–	21.3287	–	–
7	2N-2N2P and 2PASCL (Samuel et al. 2017)	–	16.96743	–	–
8	4-bit ECRL (Alam et al. 2017)	100	0.0038	–	–
9	4-bit PFAL (Alam et al. 2017)	124	0.002	–	–

The output level of PFAL is better compared to ECRL-based 2-Bit comparator using 90 nm technology (Kaur et al. 2015). Samuel et al. have described the design of a novel modified comparator that combined two-phase adiabatic static clocked logic and 2N-2N2P adiabatic approach (2N-2N2P and 2PASCL). It uses two phases adiabatic static clocked logic and efficient charge recovery logic combination (ECRL and 2PASCL). The proposed comparator design using ECRL and 2PASCL-based comparator shows superior performance compared to other existing designs (Samuel et al. 2017). Comparative analysis of various types of comparators is shown in Table 3.5.

Adiabatic Logic-Based Multiplexer

Aron et al. demonstrated the power-efficient multiplexer design based on the PFAL decoder. The proposed design circuit performs superior in power consumption compared to the conventional CMOS-based decoder in energy consumption (Suguna and Rani 2020). Yadav et al. presented the energy-efficient logic circuits design of inverter and 2:1 multiplexer using PFAL, ECRL adiabatic approaches, and conventional CMOS approach. The adiabatic approach is a promising choice for low-power applications in a specific frequency band (Yadav et al. 2011). Sharma et al. presented a design of an adiabatic 2 × 1 multiplexer. It is found that the proposed circuit design using ECRL exhibit area efficiency, and the CAL design with energy efficiency (Sharma et al. 2016). Suguna et al. presented various logic approaches, including traditional CMOS, gate diffusion input (GDI), and adiabatic techniques. To design a combinational circuit, including the multiplexer, de-multiplexer, full adder, encoder, and decoder (Suguna and Rani 2019). Lolas et al. presented a design of low-power array architectures using a new adiabatic approach (Lolas et al. 1999). Aron et al. reported a PFAL-based decoder using power-efficient multiplexer. The PFAL-based decoder performs better in power dissipation than the traditional CMOS-based decoder. The presented Mux decoder has significantly decreased energy consumption by 41.867% compared to the CMOS-based decoder (Aron et al. 2015).

Bhati et al. presented a 2:1 PFAL and CMOS-based multiplexer design for low-power applications. Comparative analysis of PFAL and conventional techniques are carried out at different frequencies and voltages. It is observed that the PFAL circuits consumed less energy than traditional CMOS circuits. The adiabatic PFAL approach offers a significant power reduction, so better performance than the traditional conventional approach. However, PFAL suffers from a considerable switching time, so it is not applicable where the latency is critical (Bhati and Rizvi 2016). A comparative analysis of various types of multiplexers is shown in Table 3.6.

Table 3.6 Comparative analysis of different types of Multiplexers

Si. No	Multiplexer	Transistor count	PD (μW)	Delay (ns)	PDP (fJ)
1	PFAL-Based Power-Efficient Mux-Based Decoder (Aron et al. 2015)	12	41.482	–	–
2	CMOS-based (Aron et al. 2015)		71.358	–	–
3	8:1 MUX (Singh and Sinha 2016)	66	9.9	–	–
4	CMOS 2:1 MUX (Bhati and Rizvi 2016)	16	1.31	–	–
5	PFAL 2:1 MUX (Bhati and Rizvi 2016)	12	0.166	–	–
6	PFAL 2:1 MUX (Sharma et al. 2016)	18	29.243	–	–
7	ECRL 2:1 MUX (Sharma et al. 2016)	16	32.068	–	–
8	DPCAL 2:1 MUX (Sharma et al. 2016)	17	32.659	–	–
9	CAL 2:1 MUX (Sharma et al. 2016)	20	28.136	–	–
10	CEPAL 2:1 MUX (Turaga et al. 2014)	12	1.523	–	–
11	ECRL 2:1 MUX (Ram and Rajasekhar 2012)	10	268 m	–	–
12	PFAL 2:1 MUX(Ram and Rajasekhar 2012)	12	213 m	–	–
13	PFAL 2:1 MUX (Suguna and Rani 2019)	12	0.41	0.4	0.16

Adiabatic Logic-Based Multiplier

Kato et al. presented a 4 × 4-bit multiplier, half adder, full adder, XOR, and NAND circuits using a two-phase clocked sub-threshold adiabatic logic approach and conventional technique. The proposed circuit employs two-phase clock supply voltages with different amplitudes and frequencies. It is observed that the proposed circuit has an ultra-low-power characteristic to the conventional approach (Kato 2012). Dutta et al. reported a power-efficient vedic multiplier design using CPAL, ECRL, 2N-2N2P adiabatic and traditional techniques. It is found that the minimized PDP of the proposed CPAL Vedic multiplier design is compared to the abovementioned approach (Dutta and Chattopadhyay 2019). Sathe et al. proposed an energy-efficient 16-bit multiplier by GHz-class charge recovery logic. A boost logic implementation achieves five times higher energy efficiency than its minimum-energy pipelined, voltage-scaled, static CMOS equivalent in 16-bit multipliers with a 0.13-m CMOS process at 1 GHz, but at the cost of three times more delay (Sathe et al. 2007). Kumar et al. presented a low-power multiplier design with energy-efficient full adder using a double-pass transistor with asynchronous adiabatic logic (DPTAAL). Asynchronous adiabatic circuits are very low-power circuits that preserve energy for reuse, reducing the amount of energy drawn directly from the power supply (Kishore Kumar et al. 2013).

Yuejun et al. have demonstrated a multi-valued adiabatic logic (MVAL) ultra-low-power multiplier in a 65 nm CMOS technology. MVAL is a technique for energy efficiently using multiple threshold transistors and switch-level circuits. The presented MVAL hardware architecture can be used for energy-efficient and area reduction. Apart from the MVAL function, the proposed method supports multi-valued units with logic 0, 1, and 2. The energy-effective and the multi-valued adiabatic logic multiplier are implemented in the 65 nm CMOS process (Yuejun et al. 2018). Chanda et al. have showed an energy-efficient Vedic multiplier structure using energy-efficient adiabatic logic (EEAAL). The power consumption of the proposed multiplier is significantly low because the energy transferred to the load capacitance is mostly recovered (Chanda et al. 2013). Aradhya et al. have reported ECRL-based 8-bit multiplier designs and compared them with the CMOS designs (ultra low power adiabatic vedic multiplier", 2013). A comparative analysis of different types of multipliers is shown in Table 3.7.

Adiabatic Technique-Based Sequential Circuits

Various adiabatic logic-based sequential circuits are discussed in this section. A design whose output depends on the current set of inputs and previous output variables is called sequential design. Consequently, memory components capable of storing binary information are in sequential circuits.

Table 3.7 Comparative analysis of various types of Multipliers

Si. No	Multiplier	Transistor Count	PD (μW)	Delay (ns)	PDP (aJ)
1	4-bit CMOS (Kishore Kumar et al. 2013)	–	2.74	–	–
2	4-bit DPTAAL (Kishore Kumar et al. 2013)	–	1.75	–	–
3	MVAL multiplier (Yuejun et al. 2018)	–	110pW	–	–
4	2*2 Vedic (Chanda et al. 2013)	–	27	0.23	–
5	Vedic ECRL (ultra low power adiabatic vedic multiplier", 2013)	–	34.208	21.001	–
6	2-bit Vedic CPAL (Dutta and Chattopadhyay, 2019)	–	7.09	2.008	0.142

Flip-Flops

Flip-flop is a device which stores a single bit of data. It has 2 stable states and is used to store state information. Store data can be changed by applying varying inputs. Maheshwari et al. have reported five distinct adiabatic flip-flop circuit designs using novel resettable adiabatic buffers with various adiabatic techniques, like EACRL (efficient adiabatic charge recovery logic), Improved ECRL, PFAL, CPAL, and CAL. The proposed circuit design based on the PFAL gives superior results in terms of speed, energy, and area performance than the other adiabatic methods (Maheshwari et al. 2017). Gurunadha et al. proposed a positive edge-triggered D flip-flop design using a DFAL-based frequency divider- by-3 (Gurunadha 2017). Lin et al. presented low-voltage adiabatic flip-flops based on power-gating CPAL circuits with DTCMOS (dual-threshold CMOS) techniques.

Proposed circuit shows the superior performance in terms of speed and low power consumption (Aradhya et al. 2016). Xin et al. had proposed 2-phase CPAL adiabatic flip-flops operating on near-threshold and super-threshold regions. Medium-voltage adiabatic flip-flops employing circuits produced the low-power dissipation with less manufacturing cost (Lin et al. 2011). Chandra Shekar et al. had presented the design of D, SR, JK, and T flip-flops using conventional CMOS and ECRL approaches at 45 nm technology nodes using virtuoso tools. It is observed that the negative edge triggering gives extra performance merits of reducing clock skew and jitters than the positive edge trigger and pulsed flip-flop. This analysis shows a negative edge-triggered ECRL circuit of SR, JK, D, and T flip-flop shows significant improvement in power consumption as that of CMOS-based flip-flop. It is observed that the proposed circuit design based on the ECRL approach performs better in power dissipation than the CMOS-based approach (Xin et al. 2011). A comparative analysis of different types of the D flip-flops is illustrated in Table 3.8.

Table 3.8 Comparative analysis of different types of D flip-flop

Si. No	Flip-Flop	Transistor count	PD(μW)	Delay(ns)	PDP(aJ)
1	Two-phase clocking sub-threshold adiabatic logic (Chandra Shekar 2018)	–	580,000	–	–
2	FS-TSPC-DET flip-flop for IoT Applications (Dhoble and Kale 2014)	–	1,140,000	0.53	604.200
3	DFF (Garg and Niranjan 2016)	–	84,390,000	–	–
4	PFAL Single Edge Triggered Semi-Adiabatic D FF (Pavan Kumar et al. 2021)	–	35,000	–	–
5	ECRL-based SR FF (Ng and Lau 2000)	–	5.12	–	–
6	ECRL-based JK FF (Ng and Lau 2000)	–	9.36	–	–
7	ECRL-based D FF (Sharma et al. 2013)	–	1.063	161.1	0.171
8	ECRL-based SR FF (Xin et al. 2011)	–	22.60	22	0.497
9	ECRL-based JK FF (Xin et al. 2011)	–	56.43	0.5841	0.032
10	ECRL-based D FF (Xin et al. 2011)	–	53.83	6.042	0.325
11	ECRL-based T FF (Xin et al. 2011)	–	57.65	5.004	0.288

Shift Register

A digital memory circuit called a shift register is used in data processing systems, computers, and calculators. Shift registers have two ends, where bits enter and exit. Flip-flops are used for the realization of shift registers. Turaga et al. showed the realization of a 4-bit SISO (serial-in serial-out) shift register, 2-to-1 multiplexer, and basic gates—NOR, XOR, NOT, NAND using CEPAL (complementary energy path adiabatic logic). This static adiabatic logic has demonstrated its benefit by minimizing the energy dissipation in every cycle (Turaga et al. 2014). Priyadarshini et al. had presented the design of twin edge-triggered shift registers. It showed improved performance regarding low energy consumption, small area, and quick operations (Praveen et al. 2020). Ramachandran et al. had presented the proposed design of all-optical shift registers by D flip-flop. All-optical shift registers are designed with interconnected D flip-flop are operated by conventional clock pulses. PISO, designed as a 2-bit shift register using a D flip-flop, is developed using a Mach–Zehnder interferometer-semiconductor optical amplifier based on all-optical logic gates (Priyadarshini et al. 2019).

Sundar et al. proposed a linear feedback shift register using modified positive feedback adiabatic approach for ultra-low-power application. The proposed circuit power consumption is significantly less than the CMOS technology design (Sundar 2016). Vaddi et al. presented the implementation of a SIPO-based shift register design using static clocked logic based on the PFAL approach. The proposed design exhibits low power and high speed than existing designs (Manohari Ramachandran et al. 2019). Sarasvathi et al. created an 8-bit universal shifter using DFAL (Diode Free Adiabatic Logic) logic. The proposed circuit shows the superior performance in terms of transistor count, power dissipation, and delay compared to the existing design (Panada et al. 2021). Madan et al. reported a design of Sequential Circuits based on the 2N-2N2P, ECRL, and PFAL Adiabatic Logic Families. A comparative analysis of all design is done and it is observed that the PFAL adiabatic logic family consumes the minimum power consumption (Sarasvathi and Saraswathi 2019). Niranjan et al. showed low-power and high-performance shift registers using the pulsed latch technique. Pulsed-latch technique retains the advantages of both latches and flip-flops. Thus, high speed and lower power consumption are both possible. Present work, the pulsed latch technique is utilized to decrease the latency of different shift registers without increasing energy dissipation. Due to heavy pipelining, there is a requirement for low-power edge-triggered flip-flops in very high-speed VLSI circuits. However, for low-power usage the transition from the flip-flop to the pulsed latch technique has been quite successful in these very fast VLSI devices. The timing issue between the pulse latches has been resolved in the present work using a non-overlapped delayed pulse clock in the pulse latch approach (Madan 2017). Comparative analysis of different types of shift registers is illustrated in Table 3.9.

Counter

A counter is a device that counts the occurrences of a specific event or process, often with a clock Saxena et al. proposed an energy-efficient counter design on 28 nm FPGA. It is observed that the change in ambient temperature significantly alters the leakage power, but logic, signals, and IOs power remains unaffected (Niranjan 2018). Sharma et al. presented the implementation of a less-power Johnson counter based on the complimentary pass transistor adiabatic logic (CPAL) (Patel et al. 2017). Hafeez et al. proposed a digital CMOS parallel counter architecture based on state look-ahead logic (Himanshi Sharma 2015). Hwang et al. have showcased a low power and voltage divide-by-2/3 counter design using the pass transistor logic circuit. Only one transistor is required to realize the counting logic and the mode selection control when employing a wired-OR method. (Abdel-Hafeez and Gordon-Ross 2011). Current et al. had presented the proposed parallel counter design using four-valued threshold logic (Hwang and Lin 2012).

Table 3.9 Comparative analysis of different types of shift registers

Si. No	Shift register	Transistor count	PD (μW)	Delay (ns)	PDP (fJ)
1	Linear feed back (Sundar 2016)	–	1200	–	–
2	ECRL PIPO (Sarasvathi and Saraswathi 2019)	–	–	1.80	–
3	2N2N-2P PIPO (Sarasvathi and Saraswathi 2019)	–	–	2.02	–
4	PFAL PIPO (Sarasvathi and Saraswathi 2019)	–	–	2.6	–
5	SISO SR with pulsed latch technique (Madan 2017)	–	246.3	24.34	5.99
6	PISO SR with pulsed latch technique (Madan 2017)	–	489.7	27.67	13.55
7	SIPO SR with pulsed latch technique (Madan 2017)	–	246.3	34.31	8.45
8	PIPO SR with pulsed latch technique (Madan 2017)	–	406.3	37.62	15.28

Akhila et al. had presented the design of a sub-threshold adiabatic logic-based Johnson's ring counter. Compared to static CMOS, the sub-threshold adiabatic approach is a unique technique for low-energy and low-frequency digital circuits (Current 1978). Mohd et al. presented a carry-based reduction parallel counter design using a reduction stage and a single (2n-1 -1, n-1) parallel counter (Akhila and Kumar 2018). Kumar et al. proposed the method of PUF for IoT devices. The proposed adiabatic PUF employs a reliable energy recovery approach to get excellent energy efficiency and a temporal ramp voltage to ensure responsible startup behaviors (Mohd et al. 2013). Bhargave et al. proposed a low-power 4-bit Johnson counter based on a power-gating CPAL adiabatic approach. According to simulation results, conventional technique in the frequency range of 5–100 MHz, the proposed architecture dissipates just 10 to 15% of the power (Kumar and Thapliyal 2020). Krishnaveni et al. showed a high-speed parallel counter based on state look-ahead logic. It is found that the presented parallel counter power dissipation is reduced drastically compared to the existing parallel counter. The counter frequency is greatly improved by decreasing the transistor count, which is helpful in advanced circuit design techniques (Bhargave et al. 2016).

Kumar et al. showed the realization of an efficient Johnson counter using various approaches like DFAL, TG, GDI, 2PASCL, CPL, and CMOS. DFAL approach-based proposed counter design shows a 60% improvement in power dissipation among other existing approaches (krishnaven and saidulu 2023). Kumar et al. presented the design of a low-power 4-bit synchronous counter using adiabatic logic. In designing VLSI circuits, power dissipation has become a significant concern. Different techniques are available to reduce this power dissipation.

Table 3.10 Comparative analysis of different types of counters

Sl. No	Counter	Transistor count	PD (mW)	Delay (ns)	PDP (fJ)
1	DFAL (krishnaven and saidulu)	–	20.33	35.82	0.728
2	Parallel CDMFF (Aradhya et al. 2016)	–	0.136	–	–
3	CMOS (Bharatkumar et al. 2017)	180	75.7	–	–
4	ECRL (Bharatkumar et al. 2017)	84	14.6	–	–
5	PFAL (Bharatkumar et al. 2017)	132	17.3	–	–
6	2 Pa (Bharatkumar et al. 2017)	132	23.3	–	–
7	Proposed up-down (Kumar et al. 2017)	–	0.012	–	–
8	4-bit parallel-based CDCAL T- FF (Sharma et al. 2013)	–	–	–	46

In an adiabatic logic, the charge stored in the load capacitor is recovered, while in conventional CMOS, it is transferred to the ground, which wastes energy. Proposed circuit design using adiabatic logic in adiabatic logic, the power dissipation can be minimized compared to conventional CMOS (Bharatkumar et al. 2017). Katreepalli et al. presented an energy-efficient synchronous counter design. The proposed circuit uses power-efficient synchronous counters that reduce energy dissipation due to the clock distribution for various flip-flops and it offers high reliability (Kumar et al. 2017). A comparative analysis of various types of counters is shown in Table 3.10.

Result Analysis and Discussion

In the literature review, combinational circuits like basic gates (NOT, NAND, AND, OR, NOR, Ex-OR, and Ex-NOR), inverters, half adders, full adders, half subtractors, full subtractors, comparators, multiplexers, and multipliers are analyzed. It is observed that the performance matrices such as energy consumption, latency, power delay product, and transistor count are better in adiabatic techniques. Various types of an inverter are analyzed from the existing literature and illustrated in Table 3.1. Table 3.1 shows that RERL (Reversible Energy Recovery Logic)-based inverter (Shari Jahan and Kayalvizhi 2012b) shows better power dissipation performance than existing inverters, but it requires more area.

It is observed that the power dissipation in 2N-2N2P-based NOT gate (Anitha et al. 2019) has significantly lower energy consumption than the other similar techniques presented literature, in Table 3.2. Similarly, ECRL NAND gate (Anitha et al. 2019), optimized OR/NOR gate (Sharma 2020), and CPLAG XOR (Sharma and Noor 2013) lead the superb results in energy consumption. A comparative analysis of half and full adder is shown in Table 3.3. It is found that the PFAL-based half adders and full adders (Akshitha and Rajan 2019a) and DCPAL-based full subtractors outperform in terms of power dissipation (Deo and Mangang 2014). Comparator analysis is carried out in Table 3.5. It is found that the 2-bit PFAL- (Kaur et al. 2015) based comparator shows superior results in power dissipation.

Similarly, sequential circuit designs such as a flip-flop, shift register, and counter are analyzed. A relative analysis of flip-flop is shown in Table 3.8. Analysis of the flip-flop is carried out, and it is found that ECRL-based D flip-flop offers superior performance in terms of power dissipation (Sharma et al. 2013). Likewise, comparative analysis of shift registers and counters is shown in Tables 3.9 and 3.10. It is observed that SIPO and SISO shift register with pulsed latch technique (Madan 2017) and proposed 4-bit binary counter (Katreepalli and Haniotakis 2019) show better results in PD.

Conclusion

The increasing demand for portable electronic devices with long-life batteries and reliable functionality has increased interest in low-power design. The main idea of this paper is to give detail description of the designs of high-performance and power-efficient combinational and sequential circuits based on different adiabatic approaches. The methods are mainly implemented using ECRL, 2N-2N2P, CPAL, PFAL, MPFAL, DC-DB PFAL logic, etc. So, it is observed that adiabatic logic has to be devised to optimize the circuit area, speed, and power performance than the existing techniques. It has been observed that the DC-DB PFAL is the best approach which outperforms the other adiabatic techniques. The analysis shows that the power dissipation is at its minimum when the circuits are designed using DC-DB PFAL. However, selecting the proper design approach can optimize the area and delay. Hence, it is one of the superior techniques for low-power devices. Low-power approaches are used in applications of implantable biomedical devices, cryptographic hardware such as smart cards, sensors, digital signal processing systems, and embedded systems at particular frequency choices. Adiabatic logic is suitable for implementing energy-aware and performance-efficient VLSI (very-large-scale integration) circuitry.

References

Abdel-Hafeez S, Gordon-Ross A (2011) A digital CMOS parallel counter architecture based on state look-ahead logic. VIEEE Trans Very Large Scale Integr Syst 19(6):1023–1033. https://doi.org/10.1109/TVLSI.2010.2044818

Agrawal A, Gupta TK, Dadoria AK (2017) Ultra low power adiabatic logic using diode connected DC biased PFAL logic. Adv Electr Electron Eng 15(1):46–54. https://doi.org/10.15598/aeee.v15i1.1974

Akhila C, Kumar GR (2018) Design of sub-threshold adiabatic logic based Johnson's ring counter. J Emerg Technol Innov Res 5(9):284–293

Akshitha, Rajan N (2019a) Power reduction of half adder and half subtractor using different partial adiabatic logic styles. In: Proceedings of the international conference on intelligent sustainable systems, no. Iciss, pp 87–92. https://doi.org/10.1109/ISS1.2019.8908104

Akshitha, Rajan N (2019b) Power reduction of half adder and half subtractor using different partial adiabatic logic styles. In: Proceedings of the international conference on intelligent sustainable systems, pp 87–92. https://doi.org/10.1109/ISS1.2019.8908104

Alam S, Ghimiray SR, Kumar M (2017) Performance analysis of a 4-bit comparator circuit using different adiabatic logics. Innov Power Adv Comput Technol 1–5. https://doi.org/10.1109/IPACT.2017.8245210

Anitha A, Rooban S, Sujatha M (2019) Implementation of energy efficient gates using adiabatic logic for low power applications. Int J Recent Technol Eng 8(3):3327–3332. https://doi.org/10.35940/ijrte.C4982.098319

Anuar N, Takahashi Y, Sekine T (2010) Two phase clocked adiabatic static CMOS logic and its logic family. J Semicond Technol Sci 10(1):1–10. https://doi.org/10.5573/JSTS.2010.10.1.001

Aradhya HVR, Madan HR, Suraj MS, Mahadikar MT, Muniraj R, Moiz M (2016) Design and performance comparison of adiabatic 8-bit multipliers. In: 2016 IEEE international conferences distributed computing, VLSI, electrical circuits and robotics discover 2016 – proceedings, pp 141–147. https://doi.org/10.1109/DISCOVER.2016.7806237

Aron S, Garg S, Niranjan V (2015) PFAL based power efficient mux based decoder. In: Proceedings of international conference on computing, communication & automation, pp 1010–1013. https://doi.org/10.1109/CCAA.2015.7148523

Athas WC, Svensson LJ (1994) Reversible logic issues in adiabatic CMOS. Proc Work Phys Comput PhysComp 1994:111–118. https://doi.org/10.1109/PHYCMP.1994.363692

Bharatkumar KR, Babu MR, Lakshmi VA, Niharika NS (2017) Implementation of efficient Johnson counter using diode free adiabatic logic (DFAL). IOSR J Electron Commun Eng 12(02):01–05. https://doi.org/10.9790/2834-1202030105

Bhargave G, Uniyal S, Sheokand P (2017) Low power adiabatic 4-Bit Johnson counter based on power-gating CPAL logic. In: 2nd IEEE international conference on innovative applications of computational intelligence on power, energy and control with their impact humanit. CIPECH 2016, pp 297–301. https://doi.org/10.1109/CIPECH.2016.7918786

Bhati P, Rizvi NZ (2016) Adiabatic logic: an alternative approach to low power application circuits. In: Proceedings of international conference on electrical, electronics, and optimization techniques, pp 4255–4260. https://doi.org/10.1109/ICEEOT.2016.7755521

Bindal V (2016) Adiabatic logic circuit design. Int J Innov Sci Eng Technol 3(3):688–694

Blotti A, Di Pascoli S, Saletti R (2002a) A comparison of some circuit schemes for semi-reversible adiabatic logic. Int J Electron 89(2):147–158. https://doi.org/10.1080/00207210010110116657

Blotti A, Borghese S, Saletti R, Elettronica I (2002b) Single-inductor four-phase power-clock generator for positive-feedback adiabatic logic gates. Informatica I:533–536

Chandra Shekar P (2018) Design of sequential circuits using adiabatic logic. Int J Res Electron Electron 5(2):14–17

Chanda M, Banerjee S, Saha D, Jain S (2013) Novel transistor level realization of ultra low power adiabatic vedic multiplier. In: Proceedings of IEEE, pp 801–806 (2013)

Chaudhary P, Girdhar D (2013) Power analysis of CMOS combinational logic circuits using adiabatic reduction technique at 180nm technology. Int J Eng Res Appl 3(6):1604–1607

Chauhan P, Krishan B (2017) Design and analysis of various gates using efficient charge recovery logic (ECRL). Int J Signal Process Image Process Pattern Recognit 10(11):1–12. https://doi.org/10.14257/ijsip.2017.10.11.01

Current K, Mow D (1978) Parallel counter design using four-valued threshold logic. In: Proceedings of IEEE, pp 800–803. https://doi.org/10.1109/icassp.1978.1170553

Cutitaru M, Belfore LA (2013) A partially-adiabatic energy-efficient logic family as a power analysis attack countermeasure. In: Proceeding of conference record - Asilomar conference on signals, systems and computers, pp 1125–1129. https://doi.org/10.1109/ACSSC.2013.6810469

Deo N, Mangang RK (2014) Comparative analysis of 1-bit adiabatic full subtractor designed in 45nm technology. Int J Eng Trends Technol 10(11):541–544

Dhoble PG, Kale AD (2014) A review paper on design of positive edge triggered D flip-flop using VLSI technology. Int J Eng Res Technol 3(2):1512–1515

Dutta K, Chattopadhyay S (2019) Design of power efficient vedic multiplier using adiabatic logic. In: Proceeding of IEEE.https://doi.org/10.1109/UPCON47278.2019.8980057

Fazal S, Ahmer M (2015) Design & analysis of low power full adder. Mukt Shabd J 4(11):1174–1178

Maurya AK, Kumar G (2011) Adiabatic logic : energy efficient technique for VLSI applications. In: International conference on computer & communication technology (ICCCT)-2011 40, pp 234–238

Garg S, Niranjan V (2016) A new cascadable adiabatic logic technique. Electr Electron Eng Int J 5(1):21–36. https://doi.org/10.14810/elelij.2016.5102

Gurunadha R (2017) Implementation of low power digital circuits using DFAL technique. Int J Electron Eng Res 9(8):1135–1145

Hänninen I, Snider GL, Lent CS (2014) Adiabatic CMOS: limits of reversible energy recovery and first steps for design automation. Lecture notes in computer science (including Subseries Lecture notes in artificial intelligence. Lecture notes bioinformatics), vol 8911, pp 1–20. https://doi.org/10.1007/978-3-662-45711-5_1

Himanshi Sharma RS (2015) Design of a low power adiabatic logic based Johnson counter. In: IEEE 2015 international conference on green computing and internet of things, 2015, pp 270–274

Hussain I, Chaudhury S (2018) Performance comparison of 1-bit conventional and hybrid full adder circuits. Lect Notes Electr Eng 462:43–50. https://doi.org/10.1007/978-981-10-7901-6_6

Hwang YT, Lin JF (2012) Low voltage and low power divide-By-2/3 counter design using pass transistor logic circuit technique. IEEE Trans Very Large Scale Integr Syst 20(9):1738–1742. https://doi.org/10.1109/TVLSI.2011.2161598

Ishwarya DRSS (2018) Comparative analysis of various adiabatic logic techniques. Int J Eng Res Technol 6(14):1–6

Ito T (2003) Research and development of advanced CMOS technologies. Fujitsu Sci Tech J 39(1):3–8

Jayanthi D, Shankar AB, Raghavan S, Rajasekar G (2016) High speed multioutput circuits using adiabatic logic. https://doi.org/10.1109/ICETETS.2016.7603058

Turaga SD, Jyothi EA, Sai KJ (2014) Power reduction technique using adiabatic logic. In: Proceedings of international conference on circuit, power and computing technologies [ICCPCT] dissipation, pp 1284–1290

Kato K, Takahashi Y, Sekine T (2012) Two phase clocked subthreshold adiabatic logic circuit. Lett IEICE Electron Express 2(12):7–8. https://doi.org/10.1049/el.2020.0423

Katre SS, Chiwande SS, Keote ML, Wakode SM (2004) Efficient power conservation using adiabatic subtracter. Int J Innov Res Electr Electron Instrum Control Eng 3(3):126–128. https://doi.org/10.17148/IJIREEICE.2015.3329

Katreepalli R, Haniotakis T (2018) Energy-efficient synchronous counter design with minimum hardware overhead. In: Proceedings of 2017 IEEE international conference on communication and signal processing, pp 1423–1427. https://doi.org/10.1109/ICCSP.2017.8286619

Katreepalli R, Haniotakis T (2019) Power efficient synchronous counter design. Comput Electr Eng 75:288–300. https://doi.org/10.1016/j.compeleceng.2018.01.001

Kaur R, Ashwani E, Singla K (2015) Design and analysis of comparator using adiabatic ECRL and PFAL techniques. Int J Adv Comput Technol 4(6):29–33

Kim S, Papaefthymiou MC (1999) Single-phase source-coupled adiabatic logic. In: Proceedings of the international symposium on low power electronics and design, digest of technical papers, pp 97–99. https://doi.org/10.1145/313817.313876

Kim JY, Yoo HJ (2007) Bitwise competition logic for compact digital comparator. In: 2007 IEEE Asian Solid-State Circuits Conferences A-SSCC, pp 59–62. https://doi.org/10.1109/ASSCC. 2007.4425682.

Kim C, Yoo SM, Kang SM (1999) NMOS energy recovery logic. In: Proceedings of IEEE Gt. Lakes symposium VLSI, pp 310–313. https://doi.org/10.1109/glsv.1999.757440

Kim S, Papaefthymiou MC (2001) True single-phase adiabatic circuitry. IEEE Trans Very Large Scale Integr Syst 9(1):52–63. https://doi.org/10.1109/92.920819

Kishore Kumar A, Somasundareswari D, Duraisamy V, Shunbaga Pradeepa T (2013) Design of low power multiplier with energy efficient full adder using DPTAAL. VLSI Des. https://doi.org/ 10.1155/2013/157872

krishnaven M, saidulu BKS (2023) High speed parallel counter based on state look ahead flip flop data. Indian J Sci Res

Kramer A, Denker JS, Flower B, Moroney J (1999) 2Nd order adiabatic computation with 2N-2P and 2N-2N2P logic circuits. In: High-performance system design: circuits and logic, pp 241–246. https://doi.org/10.1109/9780470544846.ch3

Kumar D, Kumar M (2016b) Design of low power two bit magnitude comparator using adiabatic logic. In: International symposium on intelligent signal processing and communication systems, vol 1, pp 3–8. https://doi.org/10.1109/ISPACS.2016.7824703

Kumar D, Kumar M (2020) Implementation of parallel computing and adiabatic logic in full adder design for ultra - low - power applications. SN Appl Sci. https://doi.org/10.1007/s42452-020-3188-z

Kumar SD, Thapliyal H (2020) Design of adiabatic logic-based energy-efficient and reliable PUF for IoT devices. ACM J Emerg Technol Comput Syst 16(3). https://doi.org/10.1145/3390771

Kumar YP, Ramarao K, Rao SM, Nagasripooja S, Sateela B (2017) Design of low power 4bit synchronous counter using adiabatic logic. SSRG Int J Comput Trends Technol 72–74

Kumar D, Kumar M (2017) Design of low power two bit magnitude comparator using adiabatic logic. In: 2016a international symposium on intelligent signal processing and communication systems, ISPACS 2016a, 2017, vol 1, pp 3–8. https://doi.org/10.1109/ISPACS.2016.7824703

Kushawaha SPS, Sasamal TN (2016) Modified positive feedback adiabatic logic for ultra low power adder. In: 2nd international conference on computational intelligence and communication technology, pp 378–381. https://doi.org/10.1109/CICT.2016.80

Kushawaha SPS, Kushawaha TN (2016) Modified positive feedback adiabatic logic for ultra low power adder. In: Proceedings of international conference on computational intelligence & communication technology, pp 378–381. 0.1109/CICT.2016.80

Lin J, Hu J, Chen Q (2011) Low voltage adiabatic flip-flops based on power-gating CPAL circuits. Adv Control Eng Inf Sci Low 15:3144–3148. https://doi.org/10.1016/j.proeng.2011.08.590

Lolas CZ, Soudris D, Karafyllidis I, Thanailakis A (1999) A new adiabatic technique for designing low power array architectures. Proc IEEE Int Conf Electron Circuits Syst 2:795–798. https://doi. org/10.1109/ICECS.1999.813228

Madan G (2017) A comparative study of power dissipation of sequential circuits for 2N-2N2P, ECRL and PFAL adiabatic logic families. Int J Res Sci Innov IV(Xii):59–63

Maheshwari S, Bartlett VA, Kale I (2017) Adiabatic flip-flops and sequential circuit design using novel resettable adiabatic buffers. In: Proceedings of European conference on circuit theory and design, vol 2, pp 7–10. https://doi.org/10.1109/ECCTD.2017.8093257

Mangla K, Mangla N (2014) Power dissipation of combinational circuits by adiabatic technique for 180nm CMOS technology. IJLTEMAS III(Vi):179–186

Manikandan A, Ajayan J, Arasan CK, Karthick S, Vivek K (2015) High speed low power 64-bit comparator designed using current comparison based domino logic. In: 2nd international conference on electronics and communication systems, ICECS 2015, 2015, no. June 2015, pp 155–161. https://doi.org/10.1109/ECS.2015.7124848

Manjurathi B (2009) Low power application for true single phase energy recovery logic. Int J Recent Trends Eng 2(8):2009

Manohari Ramachandran NM, Prince S, Kambham A (2019) Design and simulation of all optical shift registers using D. Microw Opt Technol Lett 1–12. https://doi.org/10.1002/mop.32350

Mohd BJ, Abed S, Alouneh S (2013) Carry-based reduction parallel counter design. Int J Electron 100(11):1510–1528. https://doi.org/10.1080/00207217.2012.751320

Nandal A, Kumar D (2017) A study on adiabatic logic circuits for low power applications. Int J Eng Res Technol 5(3):1–7

Ng KW, Lau KT (2000) ECRL-based low power flip-flop design. Microelectronics J 31:365–370

Niranjan V (2018) Low power and high performance shift registers using pulsed low power and high performance shift registers using pulsed. ICTACT J Microelectron 03(04):494–502. https://doi.org/10.21917/ijme.2018.0088

Nithya A, Dhivya S (2018) Design and analysis of power efficient full adder in 30nm technology. Int J Pure Appl Math 118(20):763–771

Oklobdzija VG, Maksimovic D, Lin F (1997) Pass-transistor adiabatic logic using single power-clock supply. IEEE Trans Circuits Syst II Analog Digit Signal Process 44(10):842–846. https://doi.org/10.1109/82.633443

Panada JVS, Vadd K, Bigneswar, Nayana JH (2021) Implementation of SIPO based shift register using adiabatic logic. Sci Technol Dev 10(3):195–204

Panda S, Behera A, Jena MR, Nath S (2014) A novel dedicated low power 64 bit digital comparator using CMOS logic. J Embed Syst 2(2):28–31. https://doi.org/10.12691/jes-2-2-2

Parveen H, Moyal V (2015) Implementation of low power adiabatic based inverter for dynamic comparator. Int J Sci Res 6(1):2320–2323. https://doi.org/10.21275/ART20164642

Patel C, Vishwavidyalaya DS, Agarwal P, Vishwavidyalaya DS (2017) Environment friendly energy efficient counter design on 28nm FPGA. Int J Emerg Technol 8(1):431–434

Patpatia B, Arora N, Mehta K, Swami N (2011) An adiabatic single phase N-type and P-type CPAL technique for full adder design. In: Proceedings of IEEE, pp 244–247

Pindoo IA, Singhy T, Singh A, Chaudhary A, Kumar PM (2015) Power dissipation reduction using adiabatic logic techniques for CMOS inverter circuit. In: Proceeding of ICCCNT. https://doi.org/10.1109/ICCCNT.2015.7395216

Praveen J, Bhuvanesh M, BS N, Bhanupriya HK, Ananda Kumar K (2020) A design and implementation of adiabatic logic on low power application circuits. IJAST 29(7):10130–10140

Priya A, Rai A (2014) Adiabatic technique for power efficient logic circuit design. Int J Electron Commun Technol 5(1):70–78

Priyadarshini KM, Ernest Ravindran RS, Kumar RV, Harish R, Sai Bhattar SS, Pavan Sri Kalian T (2019) Design and implementation of dual edge triggered shift registers for IoT applications. Int J Sci Technol Res 8(10):3585–3594

Pujari M, Desai A, Basavaraj C (2019) Implementation of low power 32-bit carry-look ahead adder using adiabatic logic. Int Res J Eng Technol 6(10):1387–1393

Ranjith KG, Chavan AP, Aradhya HR (2017) Design and implementation of 8-bit ALU based on sub-threshold adiabatic logic (SAL). Commun Appl Electron 7(4):39–43. https://doi.org/10.5120/cae2017652648

Pavan Kumar RSHKVKVL, Prabhakar VSV, Naresh K, Gopi Krishna N (2021). Design and analysis of wideband rectenna for IoT applications. SSRN Electron J 12(3):3055–3063. https://doi.org/10.2139/ssrn.3769225

Ram NLSPS, Rajasekhar K (2012) Power optimized energy efficient hybrid circuits design by using a novel adiabatic techniques. Int J Eng Res Technol 1(7):1–5

Rani A, Kadam P (2013) Adiabatic split level charge recovery logic circuit. Int J Comput Appl 65(25):18–22

Rao GS (2017) Design of power efficient digital systems using adiabatic techniques. Int J Adv Res Electron Commun Eng 5(1):132–143

Swathi SM, Kendri S, Khanai R (2018) Partial adiabatic logic. Int J Comput Appl 182(14):10–15. https://doi.org/10.5120/ijca2018917653

Sajid A, Nafees A, Rahman S (2013) Design and implementation of low power 8-bit carry-look ahead adder using static CMOS logic and adiabatic logic. Int J Inf Technol Comput Sci 5(11):78–92. https://doi.org/10.5815/ijitcs.2013.11.09

Samanta S, Mahapatra R, Mal AK (2019) Adiabatic adder: modeling, design and simulation. Adv Appl Math Sci 18(9):977–985

Samuel TSA, Darwin S, Arumugam N (2017) "Design of adiabatic logic based comparator for low power and high speed applications", ONLINE) ICTACT. J Microelectron 03(01):365–369. https://doi.org/10.21917/ijme.2017.064

Sanadhya M, Kumar MV (2015) Recent development in efficient adiabatic logic circuits and power analysis with CMOS logic. Procedia Comput Sci 57:1299–1307. https://doi.org/10.1016/j.procs.2015.07.439

Sarasvathi GKS, Saraswathi S (2019) 8-bit universal shifter using verilog. IJSRD Int J Sci Res Dev 6(12):615–618

Sasipriya P, Bhaaskaran VSK (2017). Design of low power VLSI circuits using two phase adiabatic dynamic logic (2PADL). J Circuits Syst Comput 27(4):1850052. https://doi.org/10.1142/s02181 26618500524.

Sathe VS, Chueh JY, Papaefthymiou MC (2007) Energy-efficient GHz-class charge-recovery logic. Proc IEEE J Solid-State Circuits 42(1):38–46. https://doi.org/10.1109/JSSC.2006.885053

Saxena P (2011) An adiabatic approach for low. Int J Comput Sci Eng 3(9):3207–3221

Shari Jahan CS, Kayalvizhi N (2012a) Adiabatic technique for designing energy efficient logic circuits. Commun Comput Inf Sci CCIS 305:100–107. https://doi.org/10.1007/978-3-642-32112-2_13

Shari Jahan CS, Kayalvizhi N (2012b) Adiabatic technique for designing energy efficient logic circuits. In: Communications in computer and information science CCIS, vol 305, pp 100–107. https://doi.org/10.1007/978-3-642-32112-2_13

Sharma M (2020) Adiabatic logic based circuit optimization for ultra low power applications. J Inf Optim Sci 41(1):85–98. https://doi.org/10.1080/02522667.2020.1715560

Sharma M, Noor A, Vihar P, Delhi N (2013) Positive feed back adiabatic logic: PFAL single edge triggered semi-adiabatic D flip flop. African J Basic Appl Sci 5(1):42–46. https://doi.org/10.5829/idosi.ajbas.2013.5.1.1118

Sharma M, Noor A (2013) CPL-adiabatic gated logic (CPLAG) XOR gate. In: Proceedings of the 2013 international conference on advances in computing, communications and informatics, pp 575–579. https://doi.org/10.1109/ICACCI.2013.6637236

Sharma M, Noor A (2015) Reconfigurable CPLAG and modified PFAL adiabatic logic circuits. Adv Electron 1–10. https://doi.org/10.1155/2015/202131

Sharma A, Sohal H, Sharma K (2016) Area and power analysis of adiabatic 2x1multiplexer designon 65nm cmos technology. In: Proceedings of IEEE

Shekhawat V, Sharma T, Sharma KG (2014) Low power magnitude comparator circuit design. Int J Comput Appl 94(1):22–24. https://doi.org/10.5120/16308-5535

Singh P, Jain PK (2018) Design and analysis of low power, high speed 4 - bit magnitude comparator. In: 2018 international conference on recent innovations in electrical, electronics and communication engineering, vol 3, no. 2, pp 1680–1683. https://doi.org/10.1109/ICRIEECE44171.2018.9008504

Singh VP, Sinha SRP (2016) Design and implementation of power efficient 8:1 multiplexer based on adiabatic logic. Int J Sci Res 5(2):185–188. https://doi.org/10.21275/v5i2.nov161045

Sivasathya S, Manikandan T, Venkatesan Gkd P (2014) Implementation of double tail comparator for low voltage successive approximation register. Unique J Eng Adv Sci 52–56

Sneha HKM, Dwijesh B, Magadum S, Sagar K (2019) Design and implementation of low power 8-bit carry-look ahead adder using static cmos logic and adiabatic logic. Int J Res Appl Sci Eng Technol 7(5):2857–2862. https://doi.org/10.22214/ijraset.2019.5471

Suguna T, Rani MJ (2019) Analysis of combinational circuits using positive feed back adiabatic logic. Int J Innov Technol Explor Eng 8(8):3390–3399

Suguna T, Rani MJ (2020) Analysis of adiabatic hybrid full adder and 32-bit adders for portable mobile applications. Int J Interact Mob Technol 14(5):73–94. https://doi.org/10.3991/IJIM.V14 I05.13343

Sundar MS (2016) Ultra low power design of combinational logic circuits. Int J VLSI Syst Des Commun Syst 5(9):0235–0238. https://www.ijsr.net/archive/v5i9/17091603.pdf

Swaroop BM (2013) Optimization of power in hybrid circuits using adiabatic techniques. Int J Eng Res Technol 2(8):1630–1636

Upadhyay S, Nagaria RK, Mishra RA (2013a) Low-power adiabatic computing with improved quasistatic energy recovery logic. VLSI Des 2013:1–9. https://doi.org/10.1155/2013/726324

Upadhyay S, Mishra RA, Nagaria RK, Singh SP (2013b) DFAL : diode-free adiabatic logic circuits. ISRN Electron 1–12. https://doi.org/10.1155/2013/673601.

Varma PD, Reddy RR (2013) A novel 1-bit full adder design using DCVSL XOR/XNOR gate and pass transistor multiplexers. Int J Innov Technol Explor Eng 2(4):142–146. https://doi.org/10.1007/978-981-10-4280-5

Venkatesh C, Mohanapriya A, Anandhi RS (2018) Performance analysis of adiabatic techniques using full adder for efficient power dissipation. ICTACT J Microelectron (ISSU). 4(1):510–514. https://doi.org/10.21917/ijme.2018.0090

Wang WY, Lau KT (1998) Low power switched output adiabatic logic. Int J Electron 84(6):589–594. https://doi.org/10.1080/002072198134436

Xin Z, Hu J, Chen Q (2011) Adiabatic two-phase CPAL flip-flops operating on near-threshold and super-threshold regions. In: Procedia environmental sciences PART A, vol 11, pp 339–345. https://doi.org/10.1016/j.proenv.2011.12.054

Yadav RK, Rana AK, Chauhan S, Ranka D, Yadav K (2011) Adiabatic technique for energy efficient logic circuits design. In: Proceedings of ICETECT, pp 776–780

Ye Y, Roy K (2001) QSERL: quasi-static energy recovery logic. IEEE J Solid-State Circuits 36(2):239–248. https://doi.org/10.1109/4.902764

Yuejun Z, Dailu D, Zhao P, Pengjun W, Qiaoyan Y (2018) An ultra-low power multiplier using multi-valued adiabatic logic in 65 nm CMOS process. Microelectronics J 78(818):26–34. https://doi.org/10.1016/j.mejo.2018.05.016

Zhang W, Hu J, Yu L (2011) Adiabatic computing for CMOS integrated circuit with dual-threshold CMOS and gate- length biasing techniques. Inf Technol J 10(12):2392–2398

Zhou Z (2001) CMOS as a research platform. In: Biennial university microelectronics symposium - proceedings, pp 70–73. https://doi.org/10.1109/ugim.2001.960296

Chapter 4
Low Power Methodologies
for FPGA—An Overview

K. Umapathy, D. Muthukumaran, S. Chandramohan, M. Sivakumar, and Oliver James

Introduction

Because of their reconfiguring characteristic, FPGA's are more appropriate for adaptive systems in general. The relevant applications include recognition of images or patterns, recovery of failures online, etc. (Hassan et al. 2005; Paulsson et al. 2006). Less efficiency is the only constraint of FGGA in comparison with ASIC's as far as the requirement of extra circuit for reconfiguration. Nowadays, more attention is focused on enhancement of efficiency in energy in FPGA's (Betz et al. 1999). This is because of increased requirement for applications connected with low power. There is an increased requirement for low power especially for portable devices and devices operated with battery. In case of non-portable applications, the reduction in consumption of power will have economical benefits with respect to functioning, cooling, etc. To put FPGA's into the track of energy efficiency; four methodologies can be implemented with respect to—system, device, circuit and architecture (Lamoureux et al. 2008).

K. Umapathy (✉) · D. Muthukumaran · S. Chandramohan
Department of ECE, SCSVMV Deemed University, Kanchipuram, Chennai, India
e-mail: umapathykannan@gmail.com

S. Chandramohan
e-mail: chandramohan@kanchiuniv.ac.in

M. Sivakumar
Department of ECE, Mohamed Sathak AJ College of Engineering, Chennai, India
e-mail: ece.sivakumar@msajce-edu.in

O. James
Institute of Basic Sciences, Centre for Cognition & Sociality, Seoul, South Korea

© The Author(s), under exclusive license to Springer Nature Singapore Pte Ltd. 2023
D. K. Sharma et al. (eds.), *Low Power Architectures for IoT Applications*, Springer Tracts in Electrical and Electronics Engineering, https://doi.org/10.1007/978-981-99-0639-0_4

Architecture of FPGA

Field programmable gate array is an electronic circuit of integrated type which comprises a number of blocks of hardware with internal programmable connections designed for a particular application. The internal connections can be integrated by means of programming for a specific design activity or application. The origin of FPGA has come from various memory devices of one time readable type and logic devices of programming type. The difference between above devices and FPGA is that devices of programmable type are actually manufactured and programmed at the site of factory but whereas FPGA is done in a style of repeated programming style.

The general composition of FPGA is shown in Fig. 4.1. The FPGA is composed of many numbers of logical blocks which are reconfigurable for implementing the digital circuits planned for. Nowadays, various logical components such as ALU's and memories can be embedded into FPGA in terms of rows and columns. In the above composition, the logical components are programmable and the embedded components are immovable by design. The dissipation of both static and dynamic power is significant in FPGA when compared to ASIC against the following reasons (Tuan et al. 2007).

(1) FPGA employs more percentage of configurations in the name of transistors both for programming and logical operations.
(2) It includes more number of switches meant for programming.

Fig. 4.1 Composition of FPGA

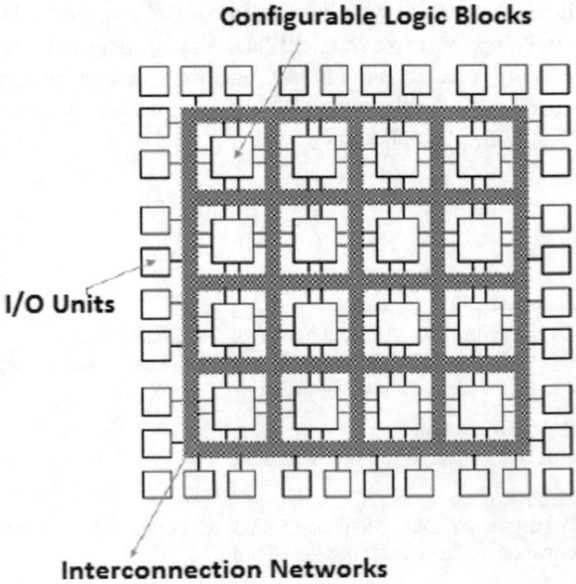

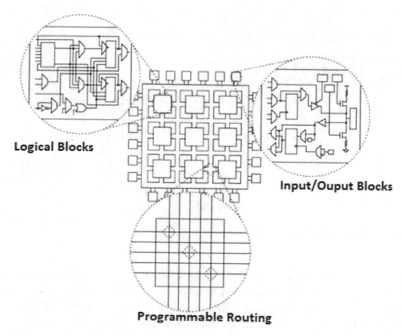

Logical Blocks

Input/Ouput Blocks

Programmable Routing

Fig. 4.2 Basic architecture of FPGA

As per latest surveys, in FPGA's 68% and 32% are suited for dissipation of dynamic power and static power, respectively (Tessier et al. 2007).

The architecture of FPGA at basic level comprises a lot number of basic components named as configurable logic blocks blended with a group of internal connections of programming type. There are different names for CLB as—logical block, logical component, etc. The architecture of FPGA in the basic form is given in Fig. 4.2.

Figure 4.3 illustrates the schematic diagram of CLB in a simplified form. A number of logical components put together form a CLB. The important trait of FPGA is a look-up table (LUT). A 4 X 5 input combination of data bits form an LUT in general. The typical examples are half adders, subtractors, encoders, multiplexers, etc. As shown in Figs. 4.2, 4.3-input LUT along with a full adder and D-type flip flop are shown forming a logic cell.

The component arrangement and their number in CLB vary from device to device. The CLB can be operated in two modes—normal mode and arithmetic mode of operation. The normal mode corresponds to four inputs LUT and the arithmetic mode corresponds to a full adder circuit with carry operation.

Modern versions of FPGA's include more number of CLB each one capable of handling more than one operation at a time. They can contribute to logical operations such as signal processing, courting, multiplexing, etc. The low level configurations of FPGA's have characteristics like consumption of low power, low density of logic and less amount of complexity per chip. The typical applications include management of clock, phase locked loops, transceivers of high speed, etc. On the other hand, in

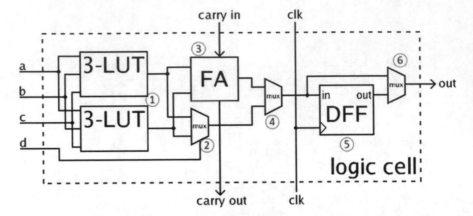

Fig. 4.3 CLB in simplified style

high end configuration, the system on chip (SOC) plays a vital role in combining the architecture of FPGA, intellectual property and a CPU into a single entity. These types of FPGA's contribute to consumption of low power, good level of integration, miniature size and wider band of frequencies. Cyclone V is a good example for high end configured FPGA as shown in Fig. 4.4.

The cyclone V system includes two portions—FPGA and a system of hard processor. The method of design of FPGA starts with sorting out computations to be done using the tool of development and a file of configuration connecting the CLB's and internal other components. This methodology is very much similar to that of cycle of development of coding but sticks to tuning hardware part of the application. To design the configuration of FPGA, two languages—VHDL and Verilog are

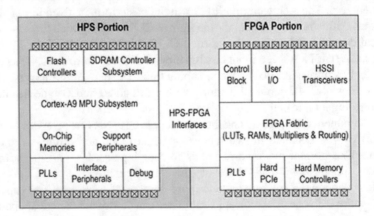

Fig. 4.4 Block diagram of cyclone V

```
module half_adder
    (
    i_bit1,
    i_bit2,
    o_sum,
    o_carry
    );

    input  i_bit1;
    input  i_bit2;
    output o_sum;
    output o_carry;

    assign o_sum   = i_bit1 ^ i_bit2;  // bitwise xor
    assign o_carry = i_bit1 & i_bit2;  // bitwise and

endmodule // half_adder
```

Fig. 4.5 Implementation of half adder using verilog

employed. Figure 4.5 illustrates the sample coding for implementation of half adders in Verilog language.

The implementation of full adder is shown in Fig. 4.6 along with its corresponding sample coding shown in Fig. 4.7. The coding is written in Verilog.

When the design process is completed, the above contents present in a text file will be converted to a file of configuration, which in turn wire the internal component as per the data given. The important thing to be remembered is programming with FPGA's requires two things—knowledge about both hardware and the corresponding language. Due to this constraint, devilment kits are available in the market to provide optimum solutions on FPGA using popular languages such as python, C++ , etc. The capacity of configuration, reconfiguration and optimization of various functions put FPGA for different types of applications such as image processing, machine learning, application specific circuits, etc.

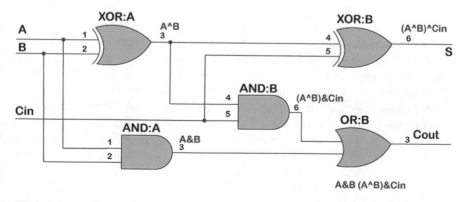

Fig. 4.6 A full adder circuit

Fig. 4.7 Coding for full
adder using verilog

```
module fulladder ( input [3:0] a,
input [3:0] b,
input c_in,
output reg c_out,
output reg [3:0] sum);
always @ (a or b or c_in) begin.
{c_out, sum} = a + b + c_in;
end.
```

Generally the devices used in medical electronics are employed for screening, tracking and curing of different conditions of diseases. The most important trait is their portability. The other relevant characteristics are consumption of low energy and powered by battery. Specifically, microcontrollers having low power are used for the above design of equipments. But recently FPGA's are gaining importance due to their reconfiguration property, parallelism, economics, etc. The chips made up of FPGA find wide applications in areas such as medical signal and image processing, identification of radio frequency, etc. Hence there is a need for low consumption of power in the topic (Kovacevic et al. 2014). In recent days, dissipation of power and heat factors are gaining more importance as far as scaling of CMOS devices is concerned. The internet and computing techniques have increased the above trend to a larger extent. The requirement is relevant embedded applications have to be operated by battery only for the purpose of portability. Hence the energy budget is concerned with requirements of power design and performance design at all levels. So reduction of power is a vital parameter for designing portable devices connected with communication and processing of signals. Another bothering factor required for FPGA programming is flexibility. But appropriate compromise has to be done between flexibility and performance. Due to the above reason, the chips connected with signal processing are subjected to design of dissipation of low power (Mangal et al. 2007).

The devices of embedded systems find usage ranging from portable applications to control applications in the industry. But the necessity for applications of multimedia and communication systems with good quality keeps on increasing every day. The parameters of constraints include consumption of low power, portability, techno-driven devices, etc. Hence the approaches used for design and the techniques related to configuration, development and consumption of power have to be properly handled as far as multimedia applications are concerned (Valderrama et al. 2011). FPGA's are extensively used in various applications like computer engineering, communication engineering, avionics, etc., due to their merits such as optimum performance, low cycle of design, economical nature, etc. But the constraint is the above merits increase the consumption of energy especially in controllers or processors (Li et al. 2011).

The dissipation of power is becoming an issue in the field of CMOS circuits and applications nowadays. The above device-oriented applications are dependent on embedded systems working on battery power. The reduction in power or energy is very much required at all layers of the design process. This concept of low power is employed for both computing devices and processing of signal techniques also. Additionally flexibility is the parameter needed for the devices based on FPGA. The arithmetic operation of multiplying is another operation needed for complex applications of DSP like FFT and process of filtering. In order to obtain optimum speed in execution, multipliers of parallel arrays are employed. The design of an energy efficient multiplier had been discussed in this paper with the concept of optimization of power (Tushar and Kshirsagar 2011). Due to growing capacity and economical factor of FPGS's, they can be employed for design of ASIC's. The dissipation of power is a bothering matter in case of ASIC's. Even though FPGA's are popular for many applications, they are not that famous for consumption of low power. They try to find place in the market of portability. If the power in FPGA is minimized, then a lot of benefits can be obtained like packages becoming economical, less heat, optimized power budgets, more reliability, etc. The tables of characterization in components of RTL and IP will give appropriate guidance for consumption of low power. A technique of employing an FTR filter is applied here (Wolff 2000).

Design at Level of System

The methodologies relevant to low power design under this section shall be decomposed into two categories—basic techniques and Run-time techniques based on their usage by the developers against the application. The following steps are correlated to basic low power methods.

(1) To reduce consumption of power, logical blocks which are coarse grained in nature are mostly employed for the applications rather than logical blocks which are fine grained (Kuon and Rose Feb. 2007).
(2) The concept of pipelining is applied to reduce impact of glitching and thereby decrease consumption of power. This can significantly lower the power in certain applications like multiplication of integers, DES standard, IIR filters, etc. (Wilton et al. 2004; Chandramohan and Senthilkumaran 2020).
(3) The optimization of word length is another technique applied for reducing consumption of power, accuracy and adaptability. This can significantly lower the power in certain applications like evaluation of polynomials, FIR filters, etc. (Constantinides 2006; Chandramohan and Senthilkumaran 2022).
(4) The idea of gating the clock shall be employed in the inactive areas to avoid the transition of signals thereby reducing the power. This step can be integrated with step 3 for better efficiency (Osborne et al. 2008a).

The following are the various step correlated with run time techniques.

(1) The concept of optimization of word length and configuration of run time can be integrated to provide adaptive smaller designs at a specified time interval (Osborne et al. 2008b; Gunasekaran et al. 2022).

(2) The configuration of run time concept can be employed to modify an existing
     design with respect to run time conditions. For example if a channel is affected
     by noise, a turbo coder which is powerful and has less efficiency can be employed
     to stabilize the bit rate of error (Liang et al. 2004; Umapathy et al. 2021).

Design at Level of Device

The following are the various techniques incorporated at the level of devices in
modern FPGA's from low power point of view.

(1) Modern FPGA's at the level of device, employ a three gate oxide technique
     to compromise between the parameters—static power and performance (Altera
     2007a; Yuvaraj et al. 2021; Chandramohan and Senthilkumaran 2021).
(2) The most thickness oxide is meant for use in the transistors larger in size and
     voltage. The moderate one is applied for the memory configuration and switches
     connected with memory. The least one is employed for common purposes.
(3) Modern FPGA's employ dielectric material of low value within the layers of
     metal by which the parasitic capacitance can be reduced. This in turn reduces
     the consumption of dynamic power.
(4) Because of correlation between the dynamic power and supply voltage, dynamic
     power can be reduced further by decreasing voltage supply. Xilinx and Altera
     reduce consumption of power by decreasing their supply from 1.2 V to 1 V and
     from 1.1 V to 0.9 V, respectively.
(5) Size of the look-up tables is increased with respect to logic blocks within FPGA
     in order to reduce both dynamic and static levels of power. The look-up tables
     employed will use only small transistors for the application (Altera 2007b;
     Umapathy et al. 2019).

Design at Level of Circuit and Architecture

Since there is a correlation between efficiency and resources of FPGA, the implementation of design at the level of circuit and architecture seems to be more significant.
Many studies in the past have done investigations on the design at the level of architecture for achievement of low power. The embedded components are incorporated
in the form of modules having more energy efficiency so that various connections
between the modules and resources are optimized (Kusse and Rabaey 1999). In order
to decrease the static power, the concept of power gating is employed to switches
in resources. One of the recent methodologies is to decrease the power of glitching
in FPGA. Generally glitching comes to picture when the input values at the gate or
LUT change at various times because of difference in propagation delays in those
signals. Latest report says that 31% of the dynamic power dissipated is accountable
with the impact of glitching. Figure 4.8 shows the impact of glitching in FPGA's. A
circle in the output signal shows the effect of glitching.

Fig. 4.8 Glitching effect in logic gates

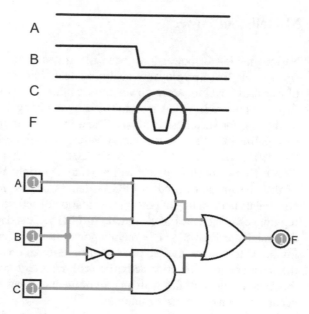

The effect of glitching can be minimized by including the delay elements in configured form against inputs of each logic component present in FPGA as shown in Fig. 4.9.

Fig. 4.9 Logic Components configured with delay elements

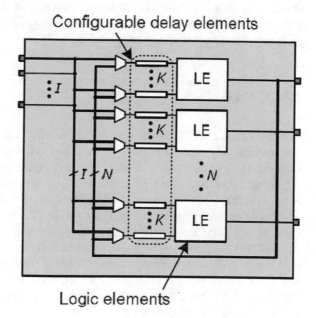

Modeling of Power

Various models of power have been illustrated in the past. The model of power (Betz et al. 1999) employs an analytical technique of first order and capacitance of transistor level for static power and dynamic power respectively. The static and dynamic powers in FPGA are evaluated by applying switching activity data rather than going for vectorless methods. The above model of power has been improved to stabilize FPGA's with the supply voltages and threshold voltages programmed (2004; Umapathy and Chandramohan 2019; Chandramohan and Senthilkumaran 2249). These models of power will provide an insight about consumption of power of different modules used in FPGA such as adders, multipliers, etc. One of the constraints in modeling of power is estimation of activity connected with finding the toggling characteristics of each node in FPGA. This data is very much required to determine the dissipation of dynamic power for a particular application. One of the important techniques available is vectorless estimation of activity which determines the input and logic function activities with respect to particular node. The merit of this technique is very fast with no requirement of input vectors. The demerit is poor accuracy when compared to simulation.

Many systems in the past incorporated vectorless methodologies in order to model the interactions which are complex in nature. Some of the above methods are very slow when compared to methods of simulation. A survey on comparison of vectorless methods was done (Lamoureux and Wilton 2006) to identify the fastest vectorless method to be employed for FPGA CAD. The main objective of the survey is to determine a technique which is most accurate and faster so that it can be compatible with the design flow of FPGA. The ultimate result of integration of above methods gives rise to a new tool of estimation called ACE 2.0.

FPGA CAD

The CAD tools of FGPA do have an inevitable effect on the consumption of power. The mapping of programming of FPGA linked to the application comes in various stagesmapping of technology, level of synthesis, routing, etc. Various types of algorithms are enunciated with appropriate levels of synthesizing FPGA. In this system (Chen et al. 2003), the reduction of power is achieved by decreasing power connected with total operations and the compactness of the circuit. The technique discussed in Chen et al. (2005) indicates that allocating low value of supply for FPGA's with the available facilities will be the optimum solution. The algorithms employed for mapping of low power techniques are detailed in these works (Li et al. 2004; Wang and Kwan 1997; Wang et al. 2001). The reduction of power is achieved by above algorithms by applying the absorption methodology with respect to possible nodes in the network. The cluster methods of low power are also enunciated in Sanadhya and Sharma (2023), Sharma et al. (2021). These methods reduce the power by the same absorption technique by integrating the look-up tables into clusters. The placement and routing techniques of low power are illustrated in (Pannu and Sharma 2021; Pannu and Sharma 2020; Pannu et al. 2020). Here the reduction of power is obtained by direct placement and routing of wires of better activity. In the system of [44], power is minimized by selecting appropriate configurations of LUT with less amount of leakage power. This work (Tessier et al. 2007) describes the connecting of logical memories to memories physically available in FPGA's. The selection of correct mapping technique and configuration help to achieve the reduction in power.

Conclusion

In this review paper, inevitable improvements are discussed in order to enhance the efficiency of power/energy in FPGA's. These improvements are illustrated from the level of low process to level of high process. The design methodologies at the level of system, device, circuit and architecture were enunciated in detail. Moreover, the recent survey on power modeling was also explained. It is obvious that power can be saved to a significant level at the level of system. The optimization of system scheduling is the main reason for the reduction of power at the level of system. If "deep-sleep" state is exploited effectively, then the reduction in dissipation of power can be achieved easily. The embedding concept of FPGA can be employed for compromising the system level parameters by which reduction of power can be achieved. As an extension, appropriate benchmarks incorporated with adaptive systems have to be developed. These benchmarks will provide a promising situation to cover the reduction of power as far as functional adaption is concerned.

References

Altera (2007a) Quartus II handbook, vol 3
Altera (2007b) Quartus II handbook, vol 2
Betz V, Rose J, Marquardt A (1999) Architecture and CAD for deep-submicron FPGAs. Kluwer Academic Publishers
Chandramohan S, Senthilkumaran M (2020) SD-NFV based network optimization: an architectural framework for industrial IoT. Int J Futur Gener Commun Netw. ISSN: 2233-7857
Chandramohan S, Senthilkumaran M (2019) A self-configurable edge computing for industrial IoT. Int J Eng Adv Technol (IJEAT) 9(2). ISSN: 2249-8958
Chandramohan S, Senthilkumaran M (2021) SDN-based dynamic resource management and scheduling for cognitive industrial IoT. Int J Intell Comput Cybern 15(3):425–437. https://doi.org/10.1108/IJICC-08-2021-0184,August
Chandramohan S, Senthilkumaran M (2022) Adaptive computing optimization for industrial IoT using SDN with edge computing. IEEE Xplore. https://doi.org/10.1109/ICCMC53470.2022.9754048
Chen D, Cong J, Fan Y (2003) Low-power high-level synthesis for FPGA architecture. Low Power Electron Des 134–139

Chen D, Cong J, Xu J (2005) Optimal module and voltage assignment for low-power. In: Proceedings of Asia South Pacific Design Automation Conferences, pp 850–855

Constantinides G (2006) Word-length optimization for differentiable nonlinear systems. ACM Trans Design Autom Electron Syst 11(1):26–43

Gunasekaran K, Muthukumaran D, Umapathy K, Yuvaraj SA (2022) FPGA based implementation of brent kung parallel prefix adder. Intell Syst Ref Libr 215: 191–198. ISSN: 1868-4408. Springer

Hassan H, Anis M, El Daher A, Elmasry M (2005) Activity packing in FPGAs for leakage power reduction. In: Proceedings of design automation and test in Europe, pp 212–217

Kovacevic J et al (2014) FPGA low-power implementation of QRS detectors. In: 2014 3rd Mediterranean IEEE conference on embedded computing (MECO),15–19 June 2014, Print ISSN: 2377-5475: https://doi.org/10.1109/MECO.2014.6862667

Kuon I, Rose J (2007) Measuring the gap between FPGAs and ASICs. IEEE Trans Comput-Aided Design 26(2):203–215

Kusse E, Rabaey J (1999) Low-energy embedded FPGA structures. In: Proceedings of international symposium low power electronics and design, pp 155–160

Lamoureux J, Wilton SJE (2006) Activity estimation for field-programmable gate arrays. In: Proceedings of international conferences on field- programmable. Logic and applications, pp 87–94

Lamoureux J et al (2008) An overview of low power techniques for field programmable arrays. In: NASA/ESA conference on adaptive hardware and systems, IEEE, pp 338–345. https://doi.org/10.1109/AHS.2008.71

Li H, Katkoori S, Mak W-K (2004a) Power minimization algorithms for LUT-based FPGA technology mapping. ACM Trans Design Autom Electron Syst 9(1):33–51

Li F, Lin Y, He L, Cong J (2004b) Low-power FPGA using pre-defined dual-Vdd/dual-Vt fabrics. In: Proceedings of ACM international symposium on field- programmable. gate arrays, pp 42–50

Li L-W et al Research on low power design methodology of register files based on FPGA. In: IEEE 2011 international conference on electric information and control engineering (ICEICE) - Wuhan, China, pp 673–676. https://doi.org/10.1109/iceice.2011.5777539

Liang J, Tessier R, Goeckel D (2004) A dynamically reconfigurable power efficient turbo coder. In Proceedings of IEEE symposium on field-programmable custom computing machines. IEEE Computer Society Press, pp 91–100

Mangal SK et al (2007) FPGA implementation of low power parallel multiplier. In: IEEE international conference on VLSI design held jointly with 6th international conference on embedded systems (VLSID'07), 06–10 January 2007. https://doi.org/10.1109/VLSID.2007.85

Osborne WG, Luk W, Coutinho JGF, Mencer O (2008a) Power and branch aware word-length optimisation. Custom Computing Machines, IEEE Computer Society Press, Proceedings of IEEE Symposium on Field-Programmable

Osborne WG, Luk W, Coutinho JGF, Mencer O (2008b) Reconfigurable design with clock gating. In: Proceedings of international symposium on systems, architectures, modelling and simulation

Pannu P, Sharma DK (2020) A Low profile quad-port Ultra Wide Band- Multiple Input Multiple Output antenna using a defected ground structure with dual notch behaviour. Int J RF Microw Comput-Aided Eng Wiley Publ 30(9)

Paulsson K, Hubner M, Becker J (2006) Strategies to on-line failure recovery in self-adaptive systems based on dynamic and partial reconfiguration. Proceedings of NASA/ESA conferences on adaptive hardware and system, IEEE, pp 288–291

Pannu P, Sharma DK (2020) Miniaturize four-port UWB-MIMO antenna with tri-notchedband characteristics. Microw Opt Technol Lett Wiley Publ 63(5):1489–1498

Pannu P, Sharma DK (2021) Cordate-shaped UWB-MIMO antenna with notch band characteristic and high isolation. World J Eng Emerald Publication U.K 18(3):480–489

Sanadhya M, Sharma DK (2023) Low power architecture of logic gates using adiabatic techniques. Indones J Electr Eng Comput Sci 25(2):805–813

Sharma R, Kumar R, Sharma DK et al (2021) Water pollution examination through quality analysis of different rivers: a case study in India. Environ Dev Sustain (2021). https://doi.org/10.1007/s10 668-021-01777-3

Tessier R, Betz V, Neto D, Egier A, Gopalsamy T (2007) Power-efficient RAM mapping algorithms for FPGA embedded memory blocks. IEEE Trans Comput Aided Design 26(2):278–289

Tuan T, Rahman A, Das S, Trimberger S, Kao S (2007) A 90-nm low-power FPGA for battery-powered applications. IEEE Trans Comput Aided Design 26(2):296–300

Tushar V, Kshirsagar RV (2011) Design of low power column bypass multiplier using FPGA. In: IEEE 2011 3rd international conference on electronics computer technology (ICECT)-Kanyakumari, India, pp 431–435. https://doi.org/10.1109/ICECTECH.2011.5941786

Umapathy K, Chandramohan S (2019) IOT enabled smart classroom with real time data monitoring. Int J Innov Technol Explor Eng (IJITEE) 9(2):4933–4937. ISSN: 2278-3075

Umapathy K, Muthukumaran D, Chandramohan S (2019) RF energy harvesting using wireless sensor network for low power applications. Int J Eng Adv Technol (IJEAT) 9(2):3469–3471. ISSN: 2249-8958

Umapathy K, Yuvaraj SA, Gunasekaran K, Muthukumaran D (2021) FPGA based implementation of hamming encoder and decoder. In: Lecture notes in networks and systems. Springer Nature, pp 245–251. ISSN: 2367-3370

Valderrama C et al (2011) Programmable logic (SPL). In: IEEE 2011 VII Southern conference on programmable logic (SPL) - Cordoba, Argentina (2011.04.13–2011.04.15)] 2011 VII Southern conference on programmable logic (SPL) - FPGA and ASIC convergence, pp 269–274. https://doi.org/10.1109/spl.2011.5782660

Wang C-C, Kwan C-P (1997) Low power technology mapping by hiding high-transition paths in invisible edges for LUT based FPGAs. In: Proceedings of IEEE international symposium on circuits and system, pp 1536–1539

Wang Z-H, Liu E-C, Lai J, Wang T-C (2001) Power minimization in LUT-based FPGA technology mapping. In: Proceedings of ACM Asia South pacific design automation conferences, pp 635–640

Wilton SJE, Ang S-S, Luk W (2004) The impact of pipelining on energy per operation in field programmable gate arrays. In: Proceedings of field programmable logic and applications, LNCS, vol 3203, pp 719–728

Wolff FG et al (2000) High-level low power FPGA design methodology. In: IEEE 2000 national aerospace and electronics conference. NAECON 2000. Engineering Tomorrow - Dayton, OH, USA, pp 554–559. https://doi.org/10.1109/NAECON.2000.894960

Yuvaraj SA, Gunasekaran K, Muthukumaran D, Umapathy K (2021) FPGA implementation of parallel adders using reversible logic gates. In: Lecture notes in networks and systems. Springer Nature, pp 429–435. ISSN: 2367-3370

Chapter 5
IoT Devices Based Low Power Dependability

K. Umapathy, S. Omkumar, S. Chandramohan, M. Sivakumar,
and Wasana Boonsong

Introduction

With the proliferation of IoT technology, the design of low power IoT devices becomes easier, which can be implemented in the current smart environments, such as smart homes, smart cities, and smart industries. It is the wireless network of standard physical devices that can be monitored and controlled through the Internet. To analyse the collected data, the IoT network provides the necessary information to take decisions. The IoT structure is shown in Fig. 5.1.

IoT is a broad term in which various different objects are linked to the internet for catering to innovative and best services in the digital world (Samie et al. 2016; Umapathy et al. 2020a). Technical enhancements in communication engineering, embedded systems, transducers, etc. play an inevitable role in the design of low power portable economical devices (Muthukumaran et al. 2022).

The above are the vital parameters employed for various applications such as patient monitoring systems, home and office automation, smart glasses for the blind, etc. (Miorandi et al. 2012; Umapathy et al. 2020b). They provide essential support and aid for IoT to achieve the required application. The System of IoT is shown in Fig. 5.2 with different layers. Basically, IoT is a blend of various objects, machines,

K. Umapathy (✉) · S. Omkumar · S. Chandramohan
Department of ECE, SCSVMV Deemed University, Kanchipuram, India
e-mail: umapathykannan@gmail.com

S. Chandramohan
e-mail: chandramohan@kanchiuniv.ac.in

M. Sivakumar
Department of ECE, Mohamed Sathak AJ College of Engineering, Chennai, India
e-mail: ece.sivakumar@msajce-edu.in

W. Boonsong
Department of EE, Rajamangala University of Technology, Songkhla, Thailand
e-mail: wasana.b@rmutsv.ac.th

© The Author(s), under exclusive license to Springer Nature Singapore Pte Ltd. 2023   99
D. K. Sharma et al. (eds.), *Low Power Architectures for IoT Applications*, Springer Tracts in Electrical and Electronics Engineering, https://doi.org/10.1007/978-981-99-0639-0_5

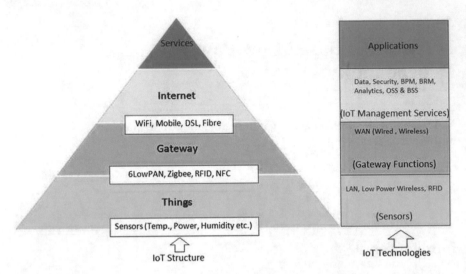

Fig. 5.1 Structure of IoT

Fig. 5.2 Architecture of IOT

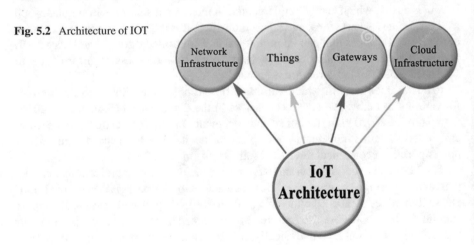

devices; human beings, etc. interlinked to each other with the aid of the internet either in the wired or wireless form (Xu et al. 2014; Mangayarkarasi et al. 1964).

Related Works

Internet of things is a new transformation of the Internet. It is guided by improved sensor networks, advanced Wireless networks and cloud technologies. With the recent advent of IoT, we can build smart homes, smart agriculture, and intelligent lightning, also that the important strength of IoT technology is a high impact on every day as manufacturing industries become "Smarter" (Chandramohan and Senthilkumaran 2020a). In Sanadhya and Sharma (2022), the author introduces edge computing architecture for the IIoT model in which the data computing is perform better at the "edge" of the sensor node. Moreover, in this work cluster-based dynamic scheduling nodes deployed at the edge can allow the offloading of traffic for better execution.

Edge Computing is emerging as a significant element in the smart industry to bring legacy in the context of Industrial IoT (IIoT). With the advancements in the current manufacturing industry such as smart manufacturing, augmented reality, SDN, Virtualization and a multitude of IoT applications, there is a great demand for infrastructure with edge computing capabilities. In the conventional cloud computing method, processing these huge data via centralized servers will demand pressure on the data transmission cost, bandwidth allocation, and other resources. To overcome the aforementioned issues, we proposed an edge computing method for the Industrial IoT (Sanadhya and Sharma 2022).

In Atzori et al. (2010), the author presented the Internet of Things. The principal empowering element of this promising worldview is the mix of a few innovations and correspondence arrangements. Distinguishing proof and following innovations, wired and remote sensor and actuator organizations, upgraded correspondence conventions (imparted to the Cutting edge Web), and dispersed insight for savvy objects are only the most pertinent.

In such a complicated situation, this overview is coordinated with the people who need to move towards this mind-boggling discipline and add to its turn of events. Various dreams of this Web of Things worldview are accounted for, and empowering advances are looked into. The fundamental thought of this idea is the inescapable presence around us of different things or items—like Radio-Recurrence ID (RFID) labels, sensors, actuators, cell phones, and so on. IoT is an original worldview that is quickly making strides in the situation of present-day remote broadcast communications. Lee et al. introduced that the Web of Things (IoT), likewise called the Web of Everything or the Modern Web, is another innovation worldview imagined as a worldwide organization of machines and gadgets fit for communicating with one another. The IoT is perceived as one of the main areas of future innovation and is acquiring huge consideration from a great many enterprises.

In this paper, the authors discussed few IoT advancements that are fundamental in the organization of effective IoT-based items and administrations. What's more, it looks at the technique and the genuine choice methodology generally utilized in the defence of innovation projects and outlines how the genuine choice methodology can be applied to IoT speculation. Zhang et al. presented that, in recent years, distributed computing has moulded the product business and made the turn of events and arrangement of web administrations more straightforward than at any time in recent memory. Public cloud suppliers, for example, Amazon and Microsoft offer pay more only as costs arise administrations for the overall population (Lee and Lee. 2015).

In Zhang et al. (2015b), Want et al. (2015) and Salman et al. (2015), the authors discussed that different endeavours exist to address the difficulties of IoT. Cisco's

Haze Processing gives registering assets nearer to the edge. Our contentions reinforce the requirement for mist like registering stages. Also, this paper discussed Gross domestic product design can use such assets. Likewise significant are frameworks, for example, Edge Processing from Akamai, and Intel's Insightful Edge. In this proposed model appears to underline on being clever doors or intermediaries for information streaming into and from the cloud. A couple of plan choices are single-essayist time-series information, piecing for execution and effective information sharing. In Sanadhya and Sharma (2022), the authors discussed a versatile distributed computing can be contended by thinking about the extraordinary benefits of engaged portable processing. Then the extensive variety of potential versatile, cloud applications has been perceived in recent surveys. The advantage of mobile computing is discussed, for example, picture handling, regular language handling, sensor data, and media search. Cao et al. consider that information is being produced at the organization's edge all the more habitually; so handling information there would be more viable. Because of the way distributed computing isn't generally compelling for handling information when the information is created at the organization's edge, past work on miniature data centres, cloudlets and haze figuring has been acquainted with the local area. The justifications for why edge processing is more compelling than distributed computing for explicit registering administrations are presented in this work (Sharma et al. 2021).

The growth of IoT and the advancement of cloud administrations push the skyline of another registering worldview. EC has addressed concerns about reaction time requirements, battery duration limitations, transmission capacity cost savings, and information security.

The edge follows the analysis starting from cloud computing from scratch to smart city with respect to edge processing idea (Preeti Pannu and Sharma 2021). Moreover, since the registering power on the cloud exceeds the limit of the things at the edge, moving all calculating tasks to the cloud has proven to be a viable method for handling information. In any case, rather than rapidly increasing, the organization's capability has come to a halt. Therefore, the increase in the amount of information produced at the edge and the speed of information travel is becoming a bottleneck for the cloud and edge computing paradigm (Pannu and Sharma 2020; Pannu et al. 2020; Yetgin et al. 2015, 2018; Abdul-Qawy and Srinivasulu 2018).

Energy Efficiency

The consumption of power assumed by various devices connected to the IoT network may vary from time to time. It may not be fixed all the time. This consumption of power relies on various factors such as technical methodology, type of architecture, mode of power of connected elements, etc. Ultimately, the power is correlated to the window of time which means the spacing between the regular sensor data.

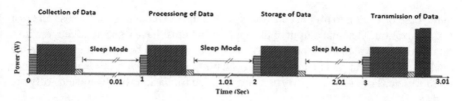

Fig. 5.3 Device operations with time

To satisfy the constraints of quality of service, the expected objectives of design to be achieved are consumption of low power and management of energy efficiency. The device functions of IoT can be categorized into the following-

- Collection of Data
- Processing of Data
- Storage of Data
- Transmission of Data

The consumption of low power and management of energy efficiency can be achieved in all the stages of sensors, controllers, memories, etc. are of radiating low power (Samie et al. 2016; Umapathy et al. 2020c). Figure 5.3 shows various operations of an IoT device as far as the time factor is concerned. There are four stages with different possible values of consumption of power. Generally, the transmission of data can be done at the earliest after processing. But as shown in Fig. 5.3, data before the transmission has been stored in memory for a while once processing is completed. Selecting any of the above two approaches depends upon the size of memory, consumption of power for data buffering, etc. In parallel, the software has to be optimized appropriately in order to achieve a significant reduction in the consumption of power (Tiwari et al. 1996; Chatzigeorgiou and Stephanides 2002; Chandramohan and Senthilkumaran 2020b).

In the case of the design of hardware, the reduction in consumption of power can be obtained drastically if the sleep mode of operation of the device is handled appropriately. If certain types of processors have less power leakage such as RAM with ferroelectric characteristics, SOI in fully depleted mode, etc. can be employed for the design. In the case of software design, the concept of optimization has to be applied for various control and communication tasks in order to decrease the time correlated with the active mode of operation (Umapathy and Chandramohan 2019). In short, the software has to be executed at the frequency of highest.

Approximation on IoT

The concept of approximation plays a vital role in applications of IoT since they are connected with the real-time world with noisy data of input (Samie et al. 2016; Chandramohan and Senthilkumaran 2022). The initial level of approximation occurs in the case of analog to digital converters where the device will come across an error in quantization. The final output of the application must have a specified range with a set of tolerance values. The property of error tolerance can be utilized to balance the quality of output in parameters such as consumption of power, efficiency, usage of memory, etc. The above property can be exploited for various hardware and software parts as follows-

(1) **Collection of Data**: The quality of data collected depends upon the rate of sampling and percentage of resolution. As an example, an MRI provides the electrical signal of the brain at the rate of 200 samples per second with a resolution of 10 bits (Gia, et al. 2015; Chandramohan and Senthilkumaran 2021). The property of sparseness in input data can be exploited to reduce the volume of data without compromising the information loss (Zhang et al. 2015a). This methodology is said to be compressed sensing. The typical examples are patient monitoring systems in wireless mode (Li et al. 2013; Bortolotti et al. 2016).

(2) **Processing and Control of Data**: The level of approximation can be employed in both hardware and software by selecting those components or parts very specific to various arithmetic operations. The typical operations showing an inclination towards approximation are division, Fourier transformation, multiplication, etc. (Han and Orshansky 2013).

(3) **Storage of Data**: In this mode of operation, the error in tolerance can be exploited to reduce energy consumption by decreasing memory capacity and instants of memory operations. A good illustration of the above is enunciated in Bortolotti et al. (2014) for a signal processor with low power.

(4) **Transmission of Data**: The reduction of data in transmission will become a key concern for the applications of IoT needing wireless communication. Hence the concept of compression of data can be applied.

This compression of data can exploit the specific properties of IoT in reducing the consumption of power thereby. A patient monitoring system with a compression technique is illustrated in Samie et al. (2015). By including a small percentage of an error on the input side, it is possible to encode the data easily with code words of small length aiming for a good ratio of compression.

IoT devices have the shortest communication range and the WiFi router is a choice for the 802.11 specific with power-saving features, ensuring that data flow between IoT devices doesn't require any additional points of interaction for network relationships. LoRa operates in astronomical regions, so that low power devices may convey information more easily without having to interpret the rules for interacting with low power IoT devices. The Transmission Control Protocol is widely used by these devices because the low power means that a low power device's WiFi receiving wire spans more limited areas.

Reliability on IoT

Generally, a reduction in supply voltage will reduce the consumption of energy and power. But this will lead to an increased probability of coming across failures. The failures which are independent of time involve the errors in the software caused due to noise in supply voltage and radiations from particles of energy. The failures which are time-dependent are mainly due to instability in temperature and induced effect I degradation (Amrouch et al. 2014). A six-transistor static RAM model is discussed below with a range of voltage from 0.5 V to 1.2 V with the application of predictive technique (Santen et al. 2016).

(1) **Noise Resiliency**: This parameter is mainly dependent on the range of supply voltage. To represent this noise, a term called static noise margin (SNM) is employed to identify the impact of parasitic coupling and thermal noise.
(2) **Radiation Resiliency**: This parameter is also dependent upon the voltage. The radiation of particles extrinsic to static RAM will create a charge which in turn destroys values stored already if it is stronger than the critical charge (Qin) of SRAM.
(3) **Ageing Resiliency**: This parameter is used to represent the defects or faults generated when the electric fields are in contact with the transistors during their operation. These defects in course of time concatenate with each other and increase transistor delay thereby decreasing the speed of operation.

The proposed IoT low power method generates viable communication in terms of a good signal-to-noise ratio (SNR) with a minimum bit error rate (BER). For that purpose, we mentioned Δ to model the maximum limit of coverage areas. For example, the proposed value is ρ to 12.5 dB, therefore SNR between the low power IoT devices is formulated as follows:

$$SNR_{dB} = 10\log_{10}\left(\frac{|S_c(m,k)|^2}{\Delta(m,k)^2}\right) \tag{5.1}$$

To fully utilize the capabilities of IoT systems, it is vital that the special security concerns that IoT presents be addressed. Security also offers a major critical concern for IoT's practical deployment. For immediate adaptation in IoT contexts, conventional methods could be unworkable and noise-intolerant. In this paper, we propose noise-resilient and low power reliability for securing communication in IoT networks to address these concerns. Practically a higher value of SNM amounts to a larger amount of noise resiliency. As shown in Fig. 5.4, the reduction in supply voltage amounts to a low value of SNM which in turn amount to failures due to noise.

As shown in Fig. 5.5, the reduction in the supply voltage will reduce the critical charge with respect to radiations. The number of defects depends on the amplitude of electric fields which in turn depends upon the supply voltage. The reduction in voltage will have a significant impact on the mechanism of ageing as shown in Fig. 5.6.

The power consumption (PC) increases during downloads, reaching a maximum of 70 mW in Raspberry Pi and other similar protocols. Due to the equipment layout

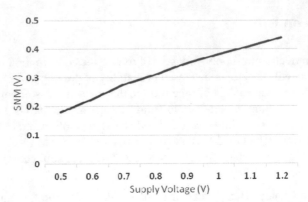

Fig. 5.4 Noise resiliency

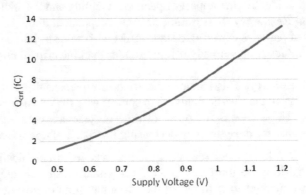

Fig. 5.5 Radiation resiliency

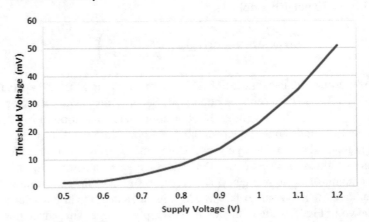

Fig. 5.6 Ageing resiliency

of these devices, the data rate decreases at a data rate of 50Mbps. The PC ranges from 0.95 W for downloading and 1.4 W for high usage. In the Raspberry Pi, or Pycom devices, the WiFi module should operate as quickly as is physically possible to conserve battery life. How much power Wireless association uses during the transmission of IoT devices, based on the bandwidth and specified duration is about 60 min allotted to every download, which is depicted in Fig. 5.7.

The maximum range of WiFi-IoT is 20 m. Packages are not misplaced within ten metres. As a result, whether other devices share the same network or bandwidth or when the transmission rate changes. WiFi-IoT does not significantly increase its current demand. The package success rate in relation to distance is depicted in Fig. 5.8.

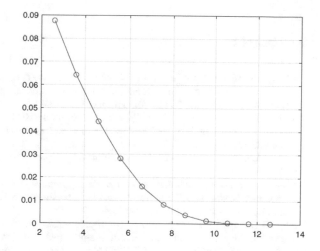

Fig. 5.7 Bandwidth utilization versus no of devices

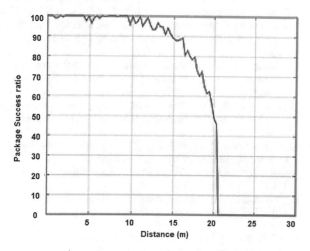

Fig. 5.8 Package success rate versus distance

Conclusion

In general, devices connected to IoT operate on batteries or depend on various sources with limited energy. Hence low power economical and portable devices are very much essential for the development of both hardware and software in applications. The main objective is to decrease the consumption of energy in IoT devices while balancing constraints in performance. This paper has given an outline of various methodologies employed for the reduction of power in IoT devices. Additionally, the issues in reliability were also discussed. Moreover, this paper will provide appropriate guidance for people who are keen on design and development of IoT devices with efficiency in energy.

References

Abdul-Qawy ASH, Srinivasulu T (2018) Greening trends in energy-efficiency of IoT-based heterogeneous wireless nodes. In: International conference on electrical, electronics, computers, communication, mechanical and computing (EECCMC)

Amrouch H, van Santen V, Ebi T, Wenzel V, Henkel J (2014) Towards interdependencies of aging mechanisms. In: IEEE/ACM international conference on computer-aided design (ICCAD), November 2014, pp 478–485

Atzori L, Iera A, Morabito G (2010) The internet of things: a survey. Comput Netw 54(15):2787–2805

Bortolotti D, Milosevic B, Bartolini A, Farella E, Benini L (2016) Quantifying the benefits of compressed sensing on a WBSN-based real-time biosignal monitor. In: Design, automation and test in Europe conference (DATE), pp 732–737

Bortolotti D et al (2014) Approximate compressed sensing: ultra-low power biosignal processing via aggressive voltage scaling on a hybrid memory multi-core processor. In: ISLPED, pp 45–50

Chandramohan S, Senthilkumaran M (2020b) SD-NFV based network optimization: an architectural framework for industrial IoT. Int J Fut Gen Commun Netw. ISSN: 2233-7857

Chandramohan S, Senthilkumaran M (2020a) Intelligent automatic guided vehicle for smart manufacturing industry. Adv Mater Manuf Eng. https://doi.org/10.1007/978-981-15-6267-9_39,pp337-343

Chandramohan S, Senthilkumaran M (2021) SDN-based dynamic resource management and scheduling for cognitive industrial IoT. Int J Intell Comput Cybernet 15(3):425–437. https://doi.org/10.1108/IJICC-08-2021-0184,August

Chandramohan S, Senthilkumaran M (2022) Adaptive computing optimization for industrial IoT using SDN with edge computing. IEEE Xplore. https://doi.org/10.1109/ICCMC53470.2022.9754048

Chatzigeorgiou A, Stephanides G (2002) Energy issues in software design of embedded systems. In: International conference on applied informatics

Da Xu L, He W, Li S (2014) Internet of things in industries: a survey. IEEE Trans Ind Inf 10(4):2233–2243

Gia TN et al (2015) Fog computing in healthcare internet-of-things: A case study on ECG feature extraction. In: International conference on computer and information technology (CIT), pp 356–363

Han J, Orshansky M (2013) Approximate computing: an emerging paradigm for energy-efficient design. In: European test symposium (ETS), pp 1–6

Lee, Lee K (2015) The internet of things (IoT): applications, investments, and challenges for enterprises. Business Horizons

Li S, Da Xu L, Wang X (2013) Compressed sensing signal and data acquisition in wireless sensor networks and internet of things. IEEE Trans Ind Inf 9(4):2177–2186

Mangayarkarasi T, Umapathy K, Sivagami A, Subitha D (1964) An IoT based safe assembly point alert system. J Phys Conf Ser 1964(7). https://doi.org/10.1088/1742-6596/1964/7/072013

Miorandi D, Sicari S, De Pellegrini F, Chlamtac I (2012) Internet of things: vision, applications and research challenges. Ad Hoc Netw 10(7):1497–1516

Muthukumaran D, Umapathy K, Boonsong W (2022) Real time data based smart Hitech classroom using IOT. In: Intelligent systems and reference library, vol 221. Springer, pp 85–92. ISSN: 1868-4408. https://doi.org/10.1007/978-3-030-99329-0

Pannu P, Sharma DK (2020) A low profile quad-port ultra wide band- multiple input multiple output antenna using a defected ground structure with dual notch behaviour. Int J RF Microw Comput Aided Eng 30(9)

Pannu P, Sharma DK (2021) Cordate-shaped UWB-MIMO antenna with notch band characteristic and high isolation. World J Eng 18(3):480–489

Pannu P, Sharma DK (2020) Miniaturize four-port UWB-MIMO antenna with tri-notched band characteristics. Microw Opt Technol Lett 63(5):1489–1498

Salman O, Elhajj I, Kayssi A et al (2015) Edge computing enabling the internet of things. In: WF-IoT, pp 603–608

Samie F, Bauer L, Henkel J (2015) An approximate compressor for wearable biomedical healthcare monitoring systems. In: CODES+ISSS, pp 133–142

Samie F, Bauer L, Henkel J (2016) IoT technologies for embedded computing: a survey. In: CODES+ISSS

Sanadhya M, Sharma DK (2022) Low power architecture of logic gates using adiabatic techniques. Indones J Electr Eng Comput Sci 25(2):805–813

Sharma R, Kumar R, Sharma DK et al (2021) Water pollution examination through quality analysis of different rivers: a case study in India. Environ Dev Sustain. https://doi.org/10.1007/s10668-021-01777-3

Tiwari V, Malik S, Wolfe A, Lee M-TC (1996) Instruction level power analysis and optimization of software. In: Technologies for wireless computing, pp 139–154

Umapathy K, Chandramohan S (2019) IOT enabled smart classroom with real time data monitoring. Int J Innov Technol Explor Eng (IJITEE) 9(2):4933–4937. ISSN: 2278-3075

Umapathy K, Sai Swaroop V, Viswam P, Balaswami Sairaja T (2020a) Counterfeit bank note detecting system. Int J Sci Technol Res (IJSTR) 9(3):1033–1035. ISSN: 2277-8616

Umapathy K, Sridevi T, Navyasri M, Anuragh R (2020b) Real time intruder surveillance system. Int J Sci Technol Res (IJSTR) 9(3):5833–5837. ISSN: 2277-8616

Umapathy K, Jagadeesh G, Lavanya P, Mouli Sree Vamsi MVS (2020c) Smart glasses for the blind. Int J Res Publ Rev 2(3):214–218. ISSN: 2582-7421

Van Santen VM, Amrouch H, Parihar N, Mahapatra S, Henkel J (2016) Aging-aware voltage scaling. In: Proceedings of the conference on design, automation and test in Europe (DATE), pp 576–581

Want R, Schilit BN, Jenson S (2015) Enabling the internet of things. IEEE Comput 48(1):28–35

Yetgin H, Cheung KTK, El-Hajjar M, Hanzo L (2015) Network-lifetime maximization of wireless sensor networks. IEEE Access 3:2191–2226

Yetgin H, Cheung KTK, El-Hajjar M, Hanzo LH (2018) A survey of network lifetime maximization techniques inwireless sensor networks. IEEE Commun Surv Tutor 828–854

Zhang Z, Xu Y, Yang J, Li X, Zhang D (2015a) A survey of sparse representation: algorithms and applications. IEEE Access 3:490–530

Zhang B, Mor N, Kolb J et al (2015b) The cloud is not enough: saving IoT from the cloud. In: USENIX conference on hot topics in cloud computing, pp 21–21

Chapter 6
Data Converter Design Space Exploration for IoT Applications: An Overview of Challenges and Future Directions

Buddhi Prakash Sharma, Anu Gupta, and Chandra Shekhar

Introduction

Data converters are a key component of "Internet of Things (IoT) devices." They are commonly utilized to bridge the analog world to the digital parts of gadgets, or vice versa. They are crucial for modern sensors including audio, biomedical, and automotive sensors, which require real-time data to be digitized for filtering, monitoring, signal processing, and analysis, as well as conversion back to the analog domain. These converters are critical for deciphering the detected data. Before the twentieth century, Kevin Ashton's concept of letting computers know everything about "things" was dubbed as IoTs. He planned to utilize computers with sensor technologies and radio frequency identification (RFID) (Ashton 2009) to collect meaningful data and identify an area without the assistance of humans. The term "Internet of Things" (Haseeb et al. 2021; Alioto 2017) refers to a network of physical objects—"things"—embedded with sensors, actuators, signal conditioning circuitry, data converters, and signal processing that allow them to remotely communicate and share data with other devices.

IoT is rapidly becoming one of the most exciting technological developments in history (Kumar et al. 2019). It has been deployed extensively in a scenario such as automotive industries, transportation, smart societies, agriculture, etc. Its uses in daily life, include sensor networks, biological records, and array signal processing (Blaauw et al. 2014; Javaid et al. 2021). The application of wireless sensor networks (WSNs) for health monitoring gives advantages over wire-line systems such as minimizing the risk of infections/failures, increasing mobility and optimizing the cost and operability. Ultra-low-power (ULP) circuit is critical for extending battery life in portable and self-contained applications. IoT is an opportunity for nations and people to better have control of their data and especially, give value to local information and data. The

B. P. Sharma (✉) · A. Gupta · C. Shekhar
Department of EEE, Birla Institute of Technology and Science, Pilani, India
e-mail: p20200414@pilani.bits-pilani.ac.in

© The Author(s), under exclusive license to Springer Nature Singapore Pte Ltd. 2023   111
D. K. Sharma et al. (eds.), *Low Power Architectures for IoT Applications*, Springer Tracts
in Electrical and Electronics Engineering, https://doi.org/10.1007/978-981-99-0639-0_6

development of data converters was primarily driven by two factors: technology and applications. The technology utilized by an electronic system is primarily determined by the system's requirements: nanoscale technologies are advantageous to speed and performance. Analog-to-Digital Converters (ADCs) and their counterpart with high precision are required in industrial process control, medical instruments, and data collection systems (10-bit or more). Speed is less important than precision in these applications because the signal bandwidth is often in the tens of kHz range.

In any case, an appropriate source of energy capable of meeting the application's requirements is necessary. Radio has the highest energy needs of any component of an IoT node. Taking care of these requirements can aid in the planning and implementation of the energy harvesting system (Davies 2021). The industrial IoT entry point of interest begins with the edge node of sensing and measuring. This is the node where the real world connects with informatics. Connected factories can detect a wide range of data that will be utilized to make critical decisions. The fundamental aspects of the various stages of IoT architecture can be explained by sensing, measuring, interpreting, and connecting data as described in Fig. 6.1 (Beavers 2021). IoT sensors are predominantly analog. IoT edge device design can look to be as difficult as squaring the circle. It has a sensor that connects to the internet. The sensor signal is sent through an amplifier or filtering circuit to an analog signal processing system. The signal is digitized by connecting the output to an A/D converter. The data is analyzed using this signal, which is delivered to the digital processing circuitry. IoT technologies are adaptable to nearly any technology that may provide its operational activity and environmental conditions.

These days, numerous businesses across a variety of industries are utilizing this technology to streamline, enhance, automate, and regulate various processes. We then demonstrate a few of the IoT's unexpectedly useful practical uses. The peculiar industrial application needs (real-time decisions) will speak about the bandwidth and dynamic range of the sensor and actuator that will be required in the analog front end (AFE) of the IoT architecture. The AFE of this chain will be part of the analog

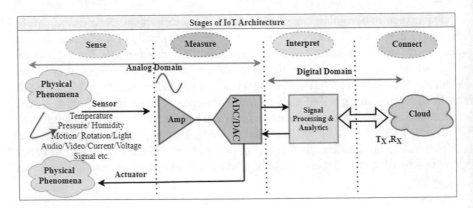

Fig. 6.1 Internet of things (IoT) sensor node

domain before sensed data is converted to a digital domain and transmitted signal to the cloud.

In most cases, signal sampling or mathematical interpretation of signal data is the most energy-intensive task for such a system shown in Fig. 6.1 To minimize the energy cost of the device at sensing and measuring nodes, strategies are being developed (Narendra et al. 2015). Thus, data converters are one of the vital elements in IoT. They are extensively used to interact with the surrounding world with the digital part of the devices. They are crucial for contemporary sensors such as audio, light, motion, biomedical and automotive sensors for which physically collected information is required to be digitized for filtering, monitoring, signal processing, and analysis enhancement. Such kinds of data converters play a critical role in understanding the sensed data.

In this chapter, we demonstrate the role of data converters in IoT, especially in the healthcare sector, and also describe the current challenges. This chapter is structured as follows: Sect. 6.2 illustrates the various data converter architectures and fundamentals. Section 6.3 introduces the trends and benchmarking summary. This section illustrates the role of specific data converters in healthcare IoT. It also gives a brief about current challenges and future directions for data converters in IoT.

Data Converter Overview

Converter Architectures

While there are many different data converter architectures available, the Successive Approximation Register (SAR) ADC, Delta-Sigma (Δ-Σ) ADC, Flash ADC, and Pipelined ADC are the most popular ones. This section also illustrates various Digital-to-Analog (DAC) topologies.

Successive Approximation Register Analog-To-Digital Converter

The fundamental blocks of a SAR A/D converter are a track-and-hold (T&H) or sample-and-hold (S&H) circuit, a comparator, digitally controlled logic and registers, and a digital-to-analog block as shown in Fig. 6.2. The first SAR ADC algorithm implementation has been traced back to 1940 at the Bell Labs (Goodall July 1947). McCreary and Gray created the charge redistribution (CR), which is the SAR ADC used today, in 1975 at the University of California, Berkeley (McCreary and Gray Dec 1975). The SAR A/D converter working principle is based on a "binary search algorithm." The conversion takes place throughout multiple clock cycles. The first step of the conversion is to sample the input voltage. The S&H function is integrated with the DAC in most of the SAR architectures. In the second step, the comparator block compares the sampled value and the output voltage of the DAC to determine

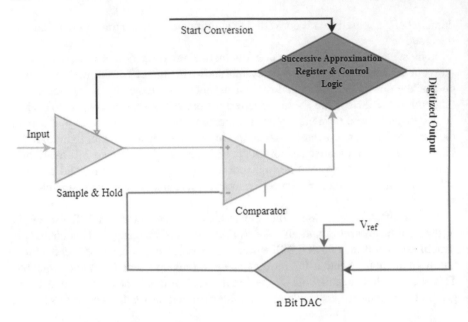

Fig. 6.2 SAR analog-to-digital converter block

the current bit. The conversion starts on each bit from the MSB-LSB by taking one bit at a time. At last, the difference between the input voltage and DAC voltages goes toward zero showing the completion of the conversion process. Therefore, N conversion steps are required for an N-bit ADC. The internal clock frequency must be at least N-fold than the sampling frequency if the SAR ADC is managed by synchronous logic. When medium–high conversion rates (about hundreds of MS/s) are needed, asynchronous logic is preferred because it does not require the same high-speed clock, hence reducing power consumption (Harpe et al. 2011).

Sigma Delta ADC ($\Sigma\Delta$ ADC)

In some applications, such as audio, instrumentation, telecommunication, healthcare, and factory automation and control, the resolution required by the ADC in the signal acquisition chain can reach up to 32 bits. In these cases, the speed of the converter is usually from tens of Hz to a few mega samples per second (MSPs) (Ahmad 2010). $\Sigma\Delta$ converters are best suited for these kinds of applications in terms of resolution and sampling rates. Theoretically, an $\Sigma\Delta$ ADC uses digital filtering, noise-shaping, and oversampling to reduce the quantization noise that exists in the signal bandwidth. The act of sampling the incoming signal more than twice its bandwidth from the Nyquist limit at a rate is known as oversampling. The sampling frequency increases as the noise level in the band of the signal decrease since the overall noise power must remain constant. The signal can be effectively converted by first converting it at

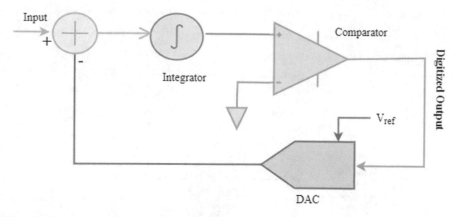

Fig. 6.3 Sigma delta analog-to-digital converter block

a high sampling rate, filtering it with a low-pass filter (LPF), and then decimating the received signal to change the sample rate back to the Nyquist criterion. Figure 6.3 depicts the structure of the sigma-delta converter. The modulator is made up of an integrator that is driven by the resultant of the input signal and the DAC output. The integrator's output is converted by an ADC before being reconverted into an analog signal by the DAC. The DAC and ADC can both be one-bit converters. A significant advantage of this type of ADC is that the data stream coming from the modulator is filtered by a digital filter. As a result, it is possible to achieve high roll-off while also having more design flexibility in the filter. $\Sigma\Delta$ ADC is the suitable choice for high resolution (larger than 12 bits) at a low-medium sampling frequency (tens of Hz to hundreds of kHz).

Pipelined ADC

The pipelined A/D converter has been introduced as a best-suited architecture for sampling rates from 10^6 to 10^9 samples per second. This ADC is working with a higher sampling rate for initial 10–12 bits and later bits are sampled with slower rates. Such resolutions and sample rates cover a broad array of applications, including digital radios, Televisions (HDTV), modems, high-speed Ethernet, biomedical imaging, digital communications, and surveillance systems. However, pipelined ADCs using a hybrid approach have progressed significantly in this decade in terms of data sample rate, precision, high speed of operation, and low energy consumption per conversion. In many applications, the data latency of pipelined ADCs is not a matter of concern (Pelgrom 2016). In Fig. 6.4, the physical world signal V_{in} first goes through a sample and hold block, the flash converter block in stage one quantizes the sampled signal, and the output is then supplied to a digital-to-analog block, where the DAC output is subtracted from the sampled signal. The desired component then gathers this "residue" and feeds it to stage 2. This built-up

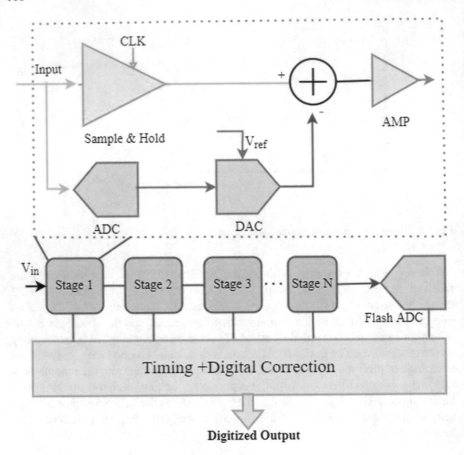

Fig. 6.4 Pipelined analog-to-digital converter block

residue is supplied into the digital error correction logic after the entire bit frame of a given sample has been time-aligned with the help of a register bank using shift registers. A stage can begin to process the next sample it receives from the sampled-and-held output embedded inside the individual stage once it has finished processing the previous sample, deciding the bits, and sending the residue to the following step. The high throughput is a result of the pipelining process.

Flash ADCs

The conversion function is simply carried out by the Flash ADC, as described in Fig. 6.5, by comparing the real-world analog signal with reference values of the resistive network of each quantization interval. The comparison gives logic high for larger non-inverting input and logic low for the high value of inverting reference input. In an n-bit flash architecture, there are 2^n regions separating the converter's full-scale

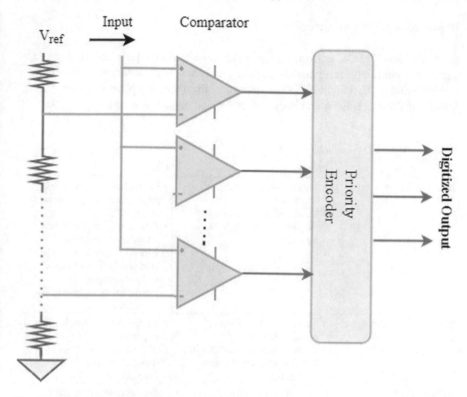

Fig. 6.5 Flash analog-to-digital converter block

range and 2^n-1 transition points. As a result, 2^n-1 comparators are required to perform the comparisons. All the comparators are activated in parallel and synchronized by a clock signal, thus the output code is generated in one clock cycle. One input of the comparator receives the signal to convert while the other terminal is connected to a reference voltage generated by a resistive divider. The outputs of the comparators form an encoder that can be translated into a digital word. Flash ADCs are mostly employed for high-speed (GHz) converter applications like radio, ultra-wide-band, and Wifi since the conversion time is equivalent to a clock period.

However, they are limited by various issues when the resolution becomes larger than 8 bits. As bits increase, the number of comparators also increases exponentially. Area and power consumption are, thus, doubled for each additional bit. Moreover, the resistance value of the unit resistance of the resistive divider is reduced to a very low value. For this reason, the output impedance of the reference voltage driving the divider needs to have a very low value in all the frequencies of operation. In a few words, this architecture is a good choice for high-speed (larger than hundreds of MHz) applications and low resolutions (lower than 8 bits).

Digital-to-Analog Converter (DAC)

A device called a DAC converts a digitized value into an equivalent analog output signal. A digital signal is represented by a digital binary code, which is an arrangement of bits 0 and 1. Various architecture exists in the literature have illustrated in the following Table 6.1. Each architecture has its design and performance benefits.

Table 6.1 Typical DAC summary

DAC type	Pros	Cons
Resistor string*	• This network contains 2^N resistors in series • This DAC architecture is simple and guaranteed to be monotonic	• For high resolution, resistors requirement is high hence increased area • Due to resistors mismatch linearity errors occurs • Parasitic capacitance limits the converter's speed since 2^N resistors are parallelly connected to achieve higher resolution
Binary weighted resistor ladder*	• Fast conversion due to N resistors in DAC • Each resistor in this network is a multiple of 2 with each descending bit	• As resistor mismatch occurs in process corner analysis, difficulties with variable resistor values arise for increased resolution
R-2R ladder*	• A modified version of the binary-weighted resistor ladder with 2N + 2 resistors • Precisely build as only two resistance values R,2R required • Stray capacitance's negative effects are eliminated by constant node voltage	• Slower conversion rate • The use of Op-AMP in structure restricts the bandwidth • Occurrence of linearity errors
Current steering*	• Useful in a high-bandwidth requirement • Without Op-AMP performance improve	• No. of current sources leads to a large glitch in the output • High power requirement • Converter's speed limit by large parasitics
Charge scaling**	• Ease of implementation with capacitors like R-2R, binary-weighted • Performance efficiency in terms of speed, and precision as technology scaling	• Op-Amp based architecture • Capacitors lead to leakages hence accuracy loss occurs after a few milliseconds

(continued)

Table 6.1 (continued)

DAC type	Pros	Cons
Oversampling**	• To increase SNR and resolution (ENOB) • The data sample rate is much higher compared to the Nyquist sample rate	• Setup and hold time issues • Higher power consumption • High cost
Charge redistribution**	• Lower complexity • Reduced switching energy and area	• Accuracy affected by sampled noise • Nonlinearity due to mismatch
Two capacitor**	• Reduce the effect of mismatch • Noise shaping improves the linearity	• Takes multiple clock cycles to generate a new sample
Switched capacitor**	• Achieve high resolution and high speed	• Higher dynamic energy consumption

Resistive DAC structure → *, Capacitive DAC Structure → **

Summary

In this chapter, various data converter architectures like a flash, SAR, Sigma delta, and Pipelined structure have been discussed as they are playing a crucial role in major IoT applications. Table 6.2 summarizes all existing converters with their design trade-offs like sampling speed, resolution, latency, accuracy, conversion time, chip area, power, cost, etc.

Figure-of-Merits

This section first addresses the various definitions, and requirement and presents state-of-the-art IoT nodes. The selection of the A/D converters for a specific circuit is based on the requirements and application of that design. For purposes of recording, visualizing, and analyzing data, the analog outputs of piezoelectric sensors, motion sensors, temperature, and displacement sensors, and more are converted to produce digital data. Important parameters are power, precision, latency, resolution, and speed. The data converter's accuracy can be specified by ENOB which can be calculated from the equation of SNDR (Murmann 2021).

$$SNDR = 6.02 * ENOB + 1.76[dB] \tag{6.1}$$

The converter's speed can be illustrated by sampling frequency (fs) and the signal bandwidth (BW). For a Nyquist converter, the sampling frequency is twice the BW. But in the case of Oversampling, BW is much lower than the sampling frequency. In summary, accuracy speed, and power can be represented in terms of figure-of-merits (FOMs) and these FOMs can be calculated with the help of

Table 6.2 Typical ADCs design tradeoffs summary

ADC architectures	Sample rate/speed (sample/s)	Resolution/bits	Latency	Accuracy	Conversion time (no. of cycles)	Area	Power	Price
Flash	High (1 Gbps-10 Gbps)	Low (6–8 bits)	Low	Low	1	High	High	High
Integrating	Up to 100	Medium (12–16 bits)	Low to moderately high	Mod. high to high	2^{N+1} dual slope 2^N single slope	Low	Low	Low
Counter	Low (1 to 1K)	Medium (10–12 bits)	Medium	Moderately high	Depends on amplitude	Low	Moderately high	Low
Pipelined	Mod. high to high (10M-5 G)	Mod. high to high (12–18 bits)	High	Moderately high	$2^{(N/2)}-1$	High	High	High
SAR	10K to 10M	Moderately high (8–20 bits)	Low	Moderately high	Variable	Low	Ultra-low to Low	Low to moderately high
Sigma Delta	Low (10 to 1M)	High (16–32 bits)	High	High	High	Medium	Low	Low to moderately high
Interleaving	Mod. high to high (100M-5 G)	Mod. High to high (12–18 bits)	Low	Moderately high	Variable	High	High	High

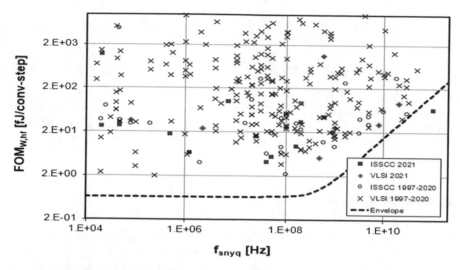

Fig. 6.6 Walden figure-of-merit versus speed

Eqs. (6.1)–(6.3). Figure 6.6 shows the Walden figure-of-merit (FOMw) and Fig. 6.7 describes Schreier's figure-of-merit (FOMs) depiction of more than two decades. These envelopes shown with dotted lines reveal the clear path for designers and show the scope of work.

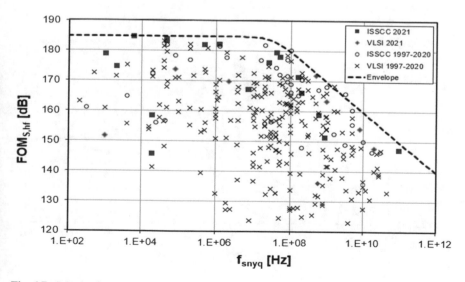

Fig. 6.7 Schreier figure-of-merit versus speed

$$FOMW = \frac{P}{f_{s,Nyquist} \cdot 2^{ENOB}} [J/Conversion - step] \qquad (6.2)$$

$$FOMS = SNDR + 10 \cdot \log\left(\frac{f_{s,Nyquist}}{2P}\right) [dB] \qquad (6.3)$$

where P: Power consumed by ADC, ENOB: Effective number of bits (Measure of accuracy), $f_{s,Nyq}$: Clock frequency at which the ADC collects and converts I/P data, SNDR: Signal-to-noise distortion ratio.

Present State-of-Art

Murmann nicely summarizes the trends in energy costs for data converters based on available data. (Murmann 2021). Figure 6.7 reveals that for low-frequency data converters, the Schreier figure-of-merit trend increased from 162 to 184 dB in the last two decades. Recent research efforts in the field of information converter architectures are depicted in Fig. 6.8 alongside typical Internet of Things (IoT) application areas. This depiction also makes it clear that SAR, which is what the majority of these applications employ, is the best data converter having high power efficiency. In the later section, various analog-to-digital converter designs for potential healthcare applications are presented.

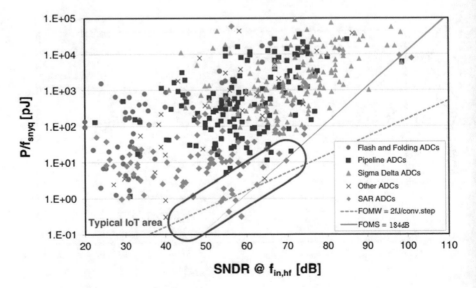

Fig. 6.8 Data converter power efficiency (energy) versus SNDR (Murmann 2021)

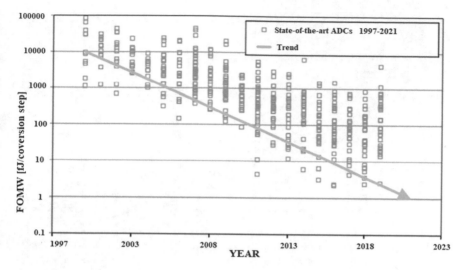

Fig. 6.9 ADC power efficiency improvement over the years (Murmann 2021)

ADC power efficiency improvement over the years is shown in Fig. 6.9. It clearly states that the current research is going on to make the IoT edge node energy efficient. In the overall review, Fig. 6.10 illustrates the energy reduction for converters based on oversampling as well as the Nyquist criteria. Similar to the design, the converter architecture with accuracy has shown in Fig. 6.11 with the trendline of the present state-of-art.

Data Converters for IoT

Data converters are found in the sensor interface and wireless receiver. Due to energy consumption limitations, these nodes are optimized for power by compromising accuracy, and speed. There are a variety of applications with varying frequency ranges and resolutions that required different converter architectures as mentioned in Table 6.2. Table 6.3 shows the numerous biomedical signals from the perspective of the internet of healthcare things (IoHT). IoT-enabled devices have altered the landscape of the healthcare industry's use of remote monitoring, releasing the perspective to keep patients healthy and granting clinicians the right to provide the best care. Patient consultations with doctors are now much simpler and more effective. In addition to reducing hospital costs and lengths of stay, remote health monitoring improves treatment outcomes. Undoubtedly, IoT is revolutionizing the healthcare business by redefining the area occupied by devices and human interaction in the delivery of healthcare solutions. In addition, it has healthcare requirements that assist patients, families, friends, relatives, medical practitioners, hospitals, physicians, and insurers.

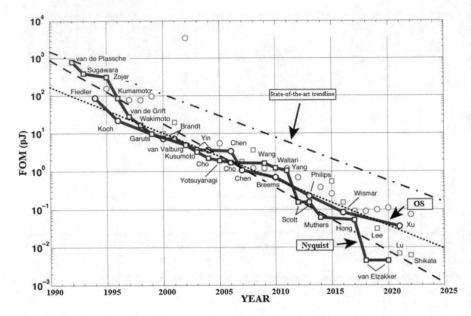

Fig. 6.10 Energy versus Trends

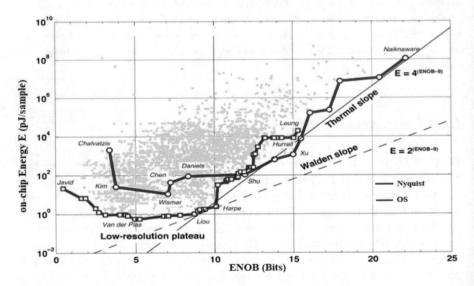

Fig. 6.11 Energy vsrsus Accuracy

Motivation

IoT is a part of routine life and exists in a variety of applications such as smart grids/houses/cities/retail/wearable, health care monitoring of plants/humans/

Table 6.3 IoT for healthcare

Signal	Frequency range	Data converters	Application	Remarks
Electrogastrogram (EGG) (Huang et al. 2008)	DC-1 Hz	Sigma delta	Motility disorder monitoring	– Requires 32-bit resolution – Requires low sampling rate
Respiratory rate (Huang et al. 2008)	0.1–10 Hz	Sigma delta	Heart monitoring	– Requires 10-bit resolution
Electroretinogram (ERG) (Huang et al. 2008)	DC-50 Hz	SAR, sigma delta	Eye monitoring	– Sampling rate 1 kHz
Blood Pressure (BP) (Huang et al. 2008)	DC-60 Hz	SAR	Blood pressure monitoring	– Requires 8-bit resolution
Electrooculogram (EOG) (López et al. 2020)	DC-100 Hz	SAR, sigma delta	Eye monitoring	– Requires 16–24-bit resolution
Electroencephalogram (EEG) (Huang et al. 2008)	DC-150 Hz	Sigma delta	Brain monitoring	– Requires 12-bit resolution
Electrocardiogram (ECG) (Huang et al. 2008)	0.01-250 Hz	Sigma delta	Heart monitoring	– Requires 16-bit resolution
Electroneurogram (ENG) (Huang et al. 2008)	250 Hz–6 kHz	SAR	Brain monitoring	– Requires 10-bit resolution
Electromyogram (EMG) (Huang et al. 2008)	20 Hz–1 kHz	SAR	Muscles monitoring	– Requires 12-bit resolution
Phonocardiogram (PCG) (Huang et al. 2008)	20 Hz–20 kHz	Sigma delta	Heart monitoring	– Requires more than 16-bit resolution
Photoplethysmogram (PPG) (Sanadhya and Sharma 2022)	0.5–5 Hz	Sigma delta	Heart rate monitoring	– Requires up to the 22-bit resolution
Positron emission tomography (PET) (Chen et al. 2022 Jan 11)	>40 MHz	Fully differential SAR	Medical imaging	– Requires 10–12-bit resolution – Low noise as well as power to enhance the dynamic range and reduce heat dissipation

(continued)

Table 6.3 (continued)

Signal	Frequency range	Data converters	Application	Remarks
Magnetic resonance imaging (MRI) (Patyuchenko 2019)	12.8–298.2 MHz	Low power multichannel pipeline	Medical imaging	– Requires 16-bit resolution – Oversampling the MR signal to achieve enhanced image – Increases SNR as well as eliminates aliasing artifacts
Ultrasonography (Chen et al. 2022 Jan 11)	1–18 MHz	SAR, pipelined	Medical imaging	– Requires high ENOB, high speed, and low THD (total harmonic distortion)
Computed tomography (CT) (Patyuchenko 2019)	0.4–20 Hz	Sigma delta	Medical imaging	– Requires 24-bit resolution
Digital radiography (X-ray) (Patyuchenko 2019)	60–100 MHz	SAR, pipelined	Medical imaging	– Requires 14–18-bit resolution – SNR level 70–100 dB – Multiple ADCs with this sampling rate

animals/agronomics, embedded industrial automation, motion/activity monitoring, and environment monitoring. In most scenarios like the Internet of healthcare things (IoHT), these IoT nodes such as wireless frontends and sensor interfaces are inaccessible, and operating renewal is not advisable. Table 6.3 shows the suitable data converter architecture according to the IoT healthcare application. Again we see the SAR ADC is the most suitable guy as it is covering maximum biomedical application areas.

This forces the IoT architecture to have a long battery life with less maintenance. Energy-efficient IoT architecture blocks enable the long autonomous operation and reduce the size of the battery or harvester used to give energy to the IoT edge node, making their incorporation into large-scale healthcare monitoring systems easier. Although the signals sensed in the real world are required to be transformed to the domain with digital information. Thus, Analog-to-Digital converters (ADCs) and Digital-to-Analog converters (DACs) form a requisite component in IoT devices.

Growth and Marketplace

Human lives are improving with the widespread use of cutting-edge digital technology like the Internet of Things (IoT). Recently, the pandemic has shown the demand for more digitally advanced IoT-based devices. International Data Corporation (IDC) forecasts that by 2025, there will be approximately 42 billion of these devices in use, capable of producing around 80 ZB (zettabytes) of data. The market segmentation of data converters is based on type, industry vertical, and geography. ADCs and DACs are the two broad categories of converters available in the market. The market is divided into aviation and security, industrial automotive, communications, electronics, healthcare instrumentations, etc. by industry vertical sector. The market for data converters is geographically dominated by North America in 2020, with a 37.5% market share. Because of the rise of the telecommunications, consumer electronics, and automotive industries, North America currently dominates the market. As a result, the Asia-Pacific area has a lot of room to grow in this sector.

From 2021 to 2026, the data converter market is expected to achieve 5.1 billion dollars, increasing at a CAGR (Compound Annual Growth Rate) of more than 5%. The market has grown due to the increasing usage of modern automatic acquisition systems and the demand for high-precision images in scientific and healthcare applications. According to IDC (International Data Corporation), the global IoT industry revenue would be around US$1.1 trillion between 2021 and 2025. The number of IoT connections is estimated to rise at a 17% CAGR from 7 billion in 2017 to 25 billion in 2025. Cars will be the fastest-growing application (30% of the M2M share by 2023) situation in recent IoT referred to M2M (mobile to mobile) connections category connected home applications (50% CAGR of the M2M share by 2023).

ADC/DAC Requirement for IoT

Sensors and industrial applications as addressed in the section, power requirement in IoT devices, IoT networks have made rapid progress in terms of system performance over the last two decades. As a result, Table 6.4 shows the power consumption of several healthcare IoT devices and applications that are currently available.

To achieve extremely energy-efficient operations, data converters with a resolution of lesser than 10 bits are extensively employed in AFE circuits. Greater resolution (≥ 10 bits) and ultra-low-power consumption are two conditions that must be met by these converters before they can be employed in high-end battery-powered devices. Higher sampling speed, Lower power consumption, lower supply voltage, and higher resolution are becoming more important to data converter designs as the channel length of the transistor shrinks (Technology scaling).

Table 6.4 Power consumption requirements for healthcare IoT (IoHT) (Sharma et al. 2021)

Application	Performance		
	Power consumption	ADC/DAC	Energy source
Heart monitoring	<10 μW	0.8–1.2 KSPS, Sigma delta ADC	Battery with more than 10 years of lifespan
Body area monitoring	<140 μW	1 KSPS, 12-bit ADC	Battery
Hearing aid	100–2 k μW	10–15 KSPS, 10–12 bit ADC	Rechargeable battery with one week lifetime
Eye monitoring	250 mW	10 KSPS, 4 bit DAC	Inductive power
Brain monitoring	1–10 mW	100 KSPS, 8–10 bit ADC	Inductive power

Challenges and Future Directions

Research into the design and development of various data converters is still ongoing, according to a literature review (Ahmad 2010; Preeti Pannu and Devendra Kumar Sharma 2021; Preeti Pannu and Devendra Kumar Sharma Dec. 2020; Pannu et al. 2020; Mouha 2021; Chung and Chiang 2019; Blaauw, et al. 2014; Kenington and Astier March 2000; Fateh, et al. 2015; Newswire and research report "Automotive IoT Market", 2020; Razavi 1995; Bashir et al. 2016; Sheingold 1986; Toledo et al. March 2021; Sisinni et al. 2018; Robertson 2015). Ultra-low energy data converter designs for the best speed and accuracy in the low to moderately high-frequency range are some research gaps that need to be filled. Most data converter implementations concentrate on improving key metrics. Precision is one of the fundamental elements requisite by plenty of IoT applications to predict and forecast the desired value. Real-time application requirements are incompatible with the capabilities of any converter circuit. As a result, a high-resolution figure-of-merit must be established for such applications.

Rapid advancements in IoT technology are forcing designers to create new designs. Signal-to-noise-distortion ratio, sampling rate, resolution, power consumption, ENOB, and spurious-free dynamic range (SFDR) are all important design characteristics. Although data converters are used in many different industries, integrating them into system-on-chips (SoCs) and field-programmable gate arrays (FPGAs) is a challenging task. It takes a lot of skill to implement FPGAs and SoCs in smart IoT devices. These factors attract professionals who are likely to contribute.

Infrastructure, agriculture, utilities, home automation, healthcare, automotive, industrial, and other applications are all possible with IoT devices. The entire spectrum of potential applications has not been considered. As more applications are addressed, the market for IoT devices will explode. There will be a lot of fresh ideas in this field, and a lot of them will originate from businesses without a history or track record in creating high-tech tools and machinery.

A single system on a chip (SoC) will be used to implement many of these new IoT innovations, which will present challenges in terms of providing the highest level of integration and chip area reduction. There may be room for customization and differentiation in high-performance analog and mixed-signal blocks. To benefit from both power and chip area savings, the majority of IoT SoC designs are implemented with technology scaling. However, due to transistor mismatch and leakage, there are significant challenges in this domain. This chapter illustrated various converter architectures for healthcare IoT, we can expect these topologies to continue pushing energy efficiency trends.

References

Ahmad I (2010) Pipelined ADC design and enhancement techniques. Springer, New York

Alioto M (2017) IoT: bird's eye view, megatrends and perspectives. In: Enabling the internet of things. Springer Nature, Cham, Switzerland

Ashton K (2009) That 'Internet of Things' thing. RFID J. http://www.rfidjournal.com/articles/view?4986. Accessed 22 June 2009

Bashir S, Ali S, Ahmed S, Kakkar V (2016) Analog-to-digital converters: a comparative study and performance analysis. In: 2016 International conference on computing, communication and automation (ICCCA), pp 999–1001

Beavers I (2021) Industrial IoT sensing and measurement: the edge node. Technical article, Analog devices

Blaauw D et al (2014) IoT design space challenges: circuits and systems, Symposium on VLSI technology (VLSI-technology): digest of technical papers. Honolulu, HI, pp 1–2

Blaauw D et al. (2014) IoT design space challenges: circuits and systems. In: Symposium on VLSI technology (VLSI-technology): digest of technical papers, pp 1–2

Chen D, Cui X, Zhang Q, Li D, Cheng W, Fei C, Yang Y (2022) A survey on analog-to-digital converter integrated circuits for miniaturized high resolution ultrasonic imaging system. Micromachines (basel) 13(1):114. https://doi.org/10.3390/mi13010114.PMID:35056279;PMCID:PMC8779678

Chung Y, Chiang M (2019) A 12-bit synchronous-SAR ADC for IoT applications. In: IEEE International symposium on circuits and systems (ISCAS), pp 1–5

Davies H (2021) Energy harvesting for edge IoT devices. Technical article

Fateh S, Bettini L et al (2015) A reconfigurable 5-to-14 bit SAR ADC for battery-powered medical instrumentation. IEEE Trans Circ Syst 62(11):2686–2694

Globe Newswire research report "Automotive IoT Market" Dublin, February 28 2020

Goodall WM (1947) Telephony by pulse code modulation. Bell Syst Tech J 26(3):395–409

Harpe PJ, Zhou C, Bi Y, van der Meijs NP, Wang X, Philips K, Dolmans G, De Groot H (2011) A 26μ w 8 bit 10 ms/s asynchronous SAR ADC for low energy radios. IEEE J Solid-State Circ 46(7):1585–1595

Haseeb K, Almogren A, Islam N, Ud Din I, Jan Z (2021) An energy-efficient and secure routing protocol for intrusion avoidance in IoT-based WSN. Energies 12:4174

Huang C-C, Hung S-H, Chung J-F, Van L-D, Lin C-T (2008) Front-end amplifier of low-noise and tunable BW/gain for portable biomedical signal acquisition, pp 2717–2720. https://doi.org/10.1109/ISCAS.2008.4542018

Javaid M, Haleem A, Rab S, Singh RP, Suman R (2021) Sensors for daily life: a review. Sens Int 2:100121. ISSN 2666-3511

Kenington PB, Astier L (2000) Power consumption of A/D converters for software radio applications. IEEE Trans Vch Technol 49(2):643–650

Kumar S, Tiwari P, Zymbler M (2019) Internet of things is a revolutionary approach for future technology enhancement: a review. J Big Data 6:111

López A, Ferrero F, Villar JR, Postolache O (2020) High-performance analog front-end (AFE) for EOG systems. Electronics 9(6):970. https://doi.org/10.3390/electronics9060970

McCreary JL, Gray PR (1975) All-mos charge redistribution analog-to-digital conversion techniques. IEEE J Solid-State Circ 10(6):371–379

Mouha R (2021) Internet of things (IoT). J Data Anal Inf Process 9:77–101

Murmann B. ADC performance survey 1997–2021. http://web.stanford.edu/~murmann/adcsurvey.html

Narendra P, Duquennoy S, Voigt T (2015) Ble and Ieee 802.15.4 in the IoT: evaluation and interoperability considerations. In: International internet of things summit. Springer, pp 427–438

Pannu P, Sharma DK (2020) A low profile quad-port ultra wide band-multiple input multiple output antenna using a defected ground structure with dual notch behavior. Int J RF Microw Comput-Aided Eng 30(9)

Patyuchenko A (2019) High performance data converters for medical imaging systems. Analog devices, vol 53

Pelgrom M (2016) Analog-to-digital conversion, 3rd edn. Springer

Pannu P, Sharma DK (2021) Cordate-shaped UWB-MIMO antenna with notch band characteristic and high isolation . World J Eng 18(3):480–489

Preeti Pannu and Devendra Kumar Sharma (2020) Miniaturize four-port UWB-MIMO antenna with tri-notchedband characteristics. Microw Opt Technol Lett 63(5):1489–1498

Razavi B (1995) Principles of data conversion system design. IEEE Press

Robertson DH (2015) Problems and solutions: how applications drive data converters (and How changing data converter technology influences system architecture). IEEE Solid-State Circ Mag 7(3):47–57. https://doi.org/10.1109/MSSC.2015.2442391

Sanadhya M, Sharma DK (2022) Low power architecture of logic gates using adiabatic techniques. Indones J Electr Eng Comput Sci 25(2), 805–813

Sharma R, Kumar R, Sharma DK et al (2021) Water pollution examination through quality analysis of different rivers: a case study in In dia. Environ Dev Sustain. https://doi.org/10.1007/s10668-021-01777-3

Sheingold D (1986) Analog-digital conversion handbook, 3rd edn. Analog devices. Prentice Hall, ISBN-0-13-032848-0 (The defining and classic book on data conversion)

Sisinni E, Saifullah A, Han S, Jennehag U, Gidlund M (2018) Industrial internet of things: challenges, opportunities, and directions. IEEE Trans Ind Informat 14(11):4724–4734

Toledo P, Rubino R, Musolino F, Crovetti P (2021) Re-thinking analog integrated circuits in digital terms: a new design concept for the IoT era. IEEE Trans Circuits Syst II Express Briefs 68(3):816–822

Chapter 7
IoT-Based Efficient and Complete Management on Street Parking

Ranjeeta Yadav and Sachin Yadav

Introduction

Conventional parking system focuses mainly on quantity. It assumes that more is always better, and it can't ever be too much. The real problem isn't the inadequate supply of parking spaces, it is the inefficient management. This inefficient management causes non-drivers to subsidise parking expenses, limit choices for transport and reduce the availability of housing.

Following are the effects of the conventional parking system.

- As per the study of PMC or Pune Municipal Corporation, Pune has over 25,00,000 documented vehicles, excluding the estimated addition of two lakh vehicles every year, but parking space for 1,800 vehicles only. Every metropolitan city like Mumbai, Delhi, Chennai and Bangalore has the same scenario these days.
- It's been reported by INRIX that normally a driver in the UK wastes about 44 h annually looking for a vacant parking slot and contributes approximately £23.3 billion to the nation. As per this report, London was declared the worst city for parking with 67 h/year spent by drivers looking for a parking space, equating to 12 min/journey. Also, on being analysed by Admiral, it was noted that 64% of drivers felt stressed while parking, while 71% stated parking spaces were scarce.
- Each UK driver spends about $6.7 billion and wastes approximately 17 h searching for parking slots.
- Searching for vacant parking slots costs Americans around $73 Billion annually.
- Every year German drivers spend about €4.4 billion and waste around 44 h looking for vacant parking slots.

R. Yadav (✉)
ABES Engineering College, Ghaziabad, Uttar Pradesh, India
e-mail: ranjeeta29@gmail.com; ranjeeta.yadav@abes.ac.in

S. Yadav
G L Bajaj Institute of Technology and Management, Greater Noida, India

© The Author(s), under exclusive license to Springer Nature Singapore Pte Ltd. 2023
D. K. Sharma et al. (eds.), *Low Power Architectures for IoT Applications*, Springer Tracts in Electrical and Electronics Engineering, https://doi.org/10.1007/978-981-99-0639-0_7

- Germany has the greatest number of parking tickets annually, summing up to €380 million.
- 30% of the traffic is created while searching for parking slots.

Despite the emerging trends of smart cities, the parking systems have observed no monumental progress in removing the stress of drivers or even reducing the time and efforts wasted by them on a day-to-day basis. Drivers waste massive amounts of time looking for a vacant parking slot, although only around 80% of spots are occupied on average. Finding a vacant parking slot has now become our beloved game of musical chairs.

IoT (Internet of Things) is the solution to the haphazard system of the traditional parking system. The term "Internet of Things" was first coined in 1985 by Peter T. Lewis.

The main terms in IoT are—"internet" and "things". IoT is an interconnection of devices over the internet. Numerous devices collect data from different positions and communicate to units involved in managing, acquiring, organising and analysing the data. The first-ever IoT device came in 1982 when Carnegie Mellon University modified a Coke machine to report to inventory and update if the newly loaded drink was cold.

The world population is 7.25 billion currently and the internet users are over 3 billion. By 2017, the count of IoT devices had reached 8.4 billion. By 2030, the number of IoT devices is estimated to be about 50 billion, thus creating an enormous network of interconnected devices connecting every device, from kitchen appliances to smartphones. For good or bad, IoT devices have already outnumbered humans, and the trend is expected to explore further. The environment of IoT comprises three components—Device, Network and Application—also called the DNA of IoT.

$$\text{Device} + \text{Controller, Sensor, and Actuator} + \text{Internet} = \text{IoT}$$
$$= \text{Internet of Things}$$

The main principle of IoT is called "3As of IoT" where the as stand for—Always, Anywhere and Anytime. IoT works with its 4 fundamental components.

- Sensors—collect data from surroundings. Collected data can be as simple as temperature or as complex as video. A device may have many sensors. Examples include GPS, camera, microphone, temperature sensors, etc. It can also convert physical data into electrical impulses. If two devices are connected, then actuators are used.
- Connectivity—Next, the collected data is transmitted to the cloud. The sensors can be connected to the cloud using various mediums like Wi-Fi, satellite networks, Bluetooth, WANs, etc.
- Data processing—When the acquired data reaches the cloud, the software process the acquired data. This can be as simple as checking temperature readings or as complex as identifying objects.

- User interface—Next, information is made available to users. This can be done by notifying them using texts or emails.

In an IoT network, one device may have both sensors and actuators, or both processors and actuators, or both sensors and processors or everything individually. As users, we are already utilising and enjoying the benefits and comforts provided by IoT devices. We preheat ovens on our way home, lock our doors remotely, track fitness on our Fitbits and book ourselves an Uber all with IoT. IoT can enhance efficiency, safety and decision-making for organisations. It can also speed up medical care, allow predictive maintenance, enhance customer care services and provide many other advantages.

In 2016 global expenditure on IoT exceeded $700 billion. It has been estimated that in the next five years, approximately $6 Trillion will be spent on IoT. However, IoT is not all about expenditure. Barcelona saves approximately $37 million annually, all contributing to smart lighting and other IoT initiatives of the city which have generated 47,000 new occupations. With 34% of IoT developers using AWS, Amazon Web Services reign the IoT market. Microsoft Azure is utilised by 23% of IoT developers, while only 20% of them use GCP or Google Cloud Platform. The networking protocols used by IoT devices are TCP (54%), Wi-Fi (48%) and Ethernet (41%).

Cisco had predicted that by 2019 IoT devices would produce data of more than 500 zettabytes annually. A ZB or a zettabyte is equal to a billion TB or a billion terabytes or a trillion GB or a trillion gigabytes. Simply saying, 1 Zettabyte has a value of 10^{21}. Another way to better understand a zettabyte is equivalent to 250 billion DVDs, HD video of 36 million years, or the volume of the Great Wall of China if you let an 11 oz cup of coffee represent a gigabyte of data. The common examples of IoT in our day-to-day lives are Voice assistants (Siri, Alexa), smart cars (Tesla), Wearable fitness trackers (Fitbits), etc.

The introduction of vehicles to the transportation sphere led to tremendous developments, including more movement of commodities and freedom in travel, along with the expansion of diverse economic spheres. Moreover, vehicles also have increased noticeable problems that steadily have progressed to the point where immediate action is required i.e. paid attention to. Emissions, environmental deterioration and noise are examples of such difficulties. Not only this, as more cars are introduced on the roads, more people and animals are vulnerable to injury, increasing traffic accidents. Vehicles also have contributed to the monetary problems related to traffic bottlenecks, which now are common almost in every city. Vehicles gradually have become a concern for city planners, particularly along the lines of guaranteeing the increasing flood of automobiles can be handled, both by highway development and sufficient parking spaces.

It is estimated that car drivers spend around 100 h per year hunting for parking slots. In India, there are about 640K paid parking spaces. Due to the lack of proper urban planning, people voluntarily park their vehicles on the road, thus magnifying the chances of their vehicles getting towed for illegal parking. Illegal parking leads to the reduced speed of traffic, which further leads to delays and congestion, and in some scenarios, even accidents. Searching for a vacant parking slot also adds to traffic generation and congestion. Approximately 40% of the roads are obstructed by parked cars on a typical working day. Indian cities are heavily congested and hence considered some of the worst options for living. These problems can be addressed if the drivers have information regarding the parking spaces' availability at their expected destination or any nearby place. Parking facilities are critical assets that form a major part of smart cities. Conventional parking system focuses mainly on quantity. Along with the advent of IoT, the making of a clever city is now achievable.

One of the major problems that smart or clever cities associate with is traffic control structures and vehicle parking facilities. In contemporary cities looking for free parking, the slot is usually hard for drivers and tends to end up tougher with an ever-growing wide variety of private drivers.

This issue could be viewed as a chance for clever cities to implement changes for improving the operation of parking assets of theirs, resulting in decreased searching time, congestion in traffic and street injuries. Institute displays growth in the number of progressive ideas associated with parking systems. In an IoT network, one device may have both sensors and actuators, or both processors and actuators, or both sensors and processors or everything individually. In 2016 global expenditure on IoT exceeded $700 billion.

Things with proprietary communication devices were the forerunners of the IoT or the internet of things. Remote computers connected to the internet can track, control and monitor devices. IoT increases Internet usage that provides network communication for objects and devices, or "Objects". We can say that IoT or the Internet of Things is a crisscross of various hardware devices, buildings, automobiles and other items—ultrasonic sensors, electronics, embedded along with software and network connectivity which makes it possible for these items to collect and exchange data. The two most important words in IoT are—"internet" and "things". The net connects a massive global network of connected servers, mobile phones, laptops and tablets using international connectivity programs and protocols. The Internet enables you to send, receive or communicate information.

The concept of building a smart city comes with the advent of IoT. Clever parking can be thought of as an application of the Internet of Things, a 1999 technology. The Internet of Things (IoT) is a concept in which a collection of things/objects connected via wireless and wired connections interact to generate new services or applications. One of the main issues related to clever cities is car management systems and car parking infrastructure. The intelligent parking system can be customised to incorporate both human and technological advancements to make more proper use of limited resources such as space, fuel and time. According to Babic et al., by ensuring that every available parking space is efficiently utilised, towns may benefit from easier, faster and denser car parking.

The intelligent parking technology is anticipated to aid city administration in reducing traffic and lowering parking management costs, among other things. Nowadays, in cities finding any free parking slot is always tough for drivers and is increasingly becoming tough with the ever-growing number of individual vehicle drivers.

The circumstances might be viewed as a chance for clever cities to enhance the efficiency of their parking spaces, resulting in shorter looking times, reduced congestion and fewer road fatalities. Parking and traffic congestion problems can be avoided if vehicles are notified ahead of time about the availability of parking spots in and around the region. Engineers may now construct new Internet of Things systems with recent advancements in low-cost, low-power embedded systems. Various urban cities have chosen to integrate various internet of things-based programs into cities along with city monitoring purposes because of developments in sensory technology.

Here intelligent parking systems work in two modes i.e. online and offline; In offline mode, it acts as a conventional parking system just with a slight difference and that is it displays the number of empty and engaged slots on the LCD display at the entrance, in online mode, there is an addition i.e. it sends this information to the customer via the internet so the customer can know beforehand about parking lots.

Literature Review

Jirge et al. (2020) presented a smart parking solution that works on IoT. It improves the parking lot connectivity as well as the whole parking management architecture. The most important thing is that it is easily applicable in malls, hospitals, etc. This model covers and solves all the parking problems like labour cost, time consumption, etc. It is a green solution with no harm to the environment saving our time and energy. This system reduces mental and physical manpower, providing easy paths to park vehicles while saving time and energy. Having reasonable cost and a simple user interface makes it simple and affordable to use. This IoT system (Priyadarshini et al. 2021c) is extremely easy to use, install and maintain. Wireless sensor networks connect most of the sensors in the searched area. These sensors are also active during use so we can live track our vehicle, vanishing our worry about the security of our asset. Along with this, their sensor network consists of PIR and ultrasonic sensors which can detect incoming light and can easily sense the presence of a human or vehicle in the nearby area. These sensors send valuable information to the controllers and enhance the control system, thus reducing the light energy consumption in the parking space and ensuring the safety of the driver as well as the vehicle. The organised parking system that follows with the pattern of parallel parking also makes people easily detect their assets with little mind-boggling.

Chaya Kumari et al. (2019) presented a solution and a plan for the problem of traffic congestion and air pollution. Most of the traffic jams and congestion is either due to less parking space or due to the use of the available ones in a very unsystematic manner. Traffic management requires much manpower (Sachan et al. 2021b) along with wastage of energy, fuel and time. They planned to give drivers a very easy-to-use and convenient plan so they could relieve themselves from the traffic stress. They used UV and IR sensors along with CCTV and Wi-Fi modules for the functioning of their model. This made their system very user-friendly, with no complications for users to understand. Just a few simple steps, which include

1. Searching for the availability of nearby parking lots
2. Browsing through those spaces and selecting which is easily accessible or preferred by them
3. Choose the time span of the parking to be used and then simply confirm your occupancy once the vehicle is parked.

This is an intelligent parking system that uses ISPA to detect vehicle number plates. Image processing is also done to make identification inexpensive and efficient. It uses mathematical computations to calculate the parking space measurements so that there is no problem in parking and the driver can know about the availability of the space and can easily choose the space which he wants to use. This solution presents a promising future for the unsystematic parking system, thereby increasing our living standards.

Moutaouakkil et al. (2019) studied the traffic systems in Casablanca and provided a solution to all the environmental, economic, safety issues which make the manual parking systems inefficient and costly to use. They took various measures into consideration like land scarcity and ineffective parking pricing. They intended to decrease the time taken to locate the parking spot, reduce the harm being done to the environment and improve the parking cum driving experience. They researched various factors affecting the problems of parking space (Singh et al. 2021) and designed their solution, keeping the factors of volume and usage as priority. They studied various areas along with different types of users like commuters, frequent visitors and intermittent visitors. It helped in reducing the time spent locating available space. The solution they designed depended on the area as per its pricing policies. So, it differed from area to area. The parking dimension, as well as management, were the key features on which this solution focused to provide better services to its user. For the parking pricing policy, they took three things into consideration—parking durations, location and pricing. The pricing policy they made intended to influence drivers' decision to have less amount to pay, and thus, solve traffic problems without spending anything in advancing the infrastructure or installation. Their solution solved the problem by quick rotation of parking spots and then combining strategic pricing to make it effective and affordable at reasonable price. This system of pricing is zone aware and traffic aware. With this case study in Casablanca, they provided a solution that is well experimented with and takes practical and useful issues into consideration, along with solving it in a better and more efficient way.

In September 2016, Shen et al. (2016) presented an intelligent management system for parking along with the pricing model so as to reduce driver's expenditure. Along with solving the problem of parking space and the number of resources that are wasted in manual work, this system also focused on cutting the extra cost that is paid in the present models. It used RTR (real-time reservations) and STR (share-time reservations) so that driver was free to book a parking space for the same time or for any time in the future. This system used MILP (Mixed-integer linear programming) to reduce the monetary costs for the drivers and efficient use of parking resources. It mainly focused on using the following to make the parking experience effortless and hassle-free.

1. Utilisation of maximum parking resources
2. Focus on an increment of parking revenue
3. Lowering the expense of drivers along with systematic spot search.

It gave the users the freedom to choose the spot according to their liking. The very thing that makes this different from all the previous models was how it allowed the drivers to reserve parking space (Priyadarshini et al. 2021b) for the future (flexible reservation) along with the real-time pricing model. The main elements of this whole model are sensors, pricing engine, data centre, a smart allocation centre and virtual message sign. Different pricing models for RTR and STR are fair for the drivers and the parking owners. It also proposes static as well as dynamic reservation that helps in maximising profit. Experiments show that it cuts the expenditure of parkers by 28%, increases utilisation by 21% and revenue by 16%, therefore, proving to be an effective solution to all the parking problems along with the reduction in expense of the driver.

We can easily see all the traffic problems which exist around us (Rastogi et al. 2018), the congestion of traffic and the shortage of parking spaces, mainly because they are not properly utilised. For the better utilisation of parking spaces, a lot of money, manpower and energy resources get wasted every day. Drivers are forced to spend more money to ensure parking space along with vehicle safety. In the year 2017 Chang et al. (2019) observed the problems in the parking systems in this technologically advanced time. They aimed to improve parking service quality and thus presented the SPA (Smart parking allocation) algorithm. This algorithm ensured that the users enjoyed the maximum benefits of a quality parking system. It could also predict a driver's behaviour and estimate parking traffic from the previous parking records. The main goal of SPA was to forecast the time taken by every vehicle from its past parking activities. SPA's three policies:

1. WF-SPA: Worst-fit
2. BF-SPA: Best-fit
3. PBF-SPA: Parking behaviour forecast to allocate the available spaces to the vehicles.

This idea achieved the following

1. Prediction of parking length for every vehicle
2. Excellent quality service
3. Improved utilisation of parking slots.

WF-SPA functioned by finding the space which had the longest idle period and further scheduling it to selected vehicles. BF-SPA functioned by finding the space which had the most appropriate time length. PBF-SPA (Parking behaviour forecast policy) predicted the future traffic based on its previous usage. It could easily forecast the time taken in parking for each vehicle in the coming days based on its past records and easily meet the user demand by scheduling vacant parking spaces. SPA can change how the traffic system works, usually with less investment and more energy conservation.

Usanavasin et al. (2018) proposed a program that preferred to benefit from another lifting program and included a new beat-up technology. This program assisted with the management and improvement of parking. The user could find information about the parking space, the number of parking spaces and all other details of the parking lot. It also had the feature of online payment, which gave the user ease of use by providing them an opportunity to pay online in app mode. The system used a computer to keep a record of the vehicle number plate in the parking lot. The user would receive a notification on his/her smartphone, thus building the confidence of the user in the whole parking experience and simultaneously enhancing security. The system would check the vehicle's number plate (Devaraj et al. 2010) and use it to notify the driver where his vehicle is parked in this for safety purposes. They proposed an algorithm that described the performance of an ultrasonic sensor in the detection of a vehicle in a parking slot. Parking slots in this system were defined as

1 = available
0 = not available

Initially, when the vehicle would be detected, the status of the slot would be checked by calculating the car's range. The camera would take a photo and the condition would be updated. Later, the range would be checked again. If the vehicle wouldn't be detected in the slot, the status would be changed for the next vehicle. When a user would want to use the app, he/she would have to register in the app which would require a username, password, mobile number and vehicle number plate. The app would provide functions in terms of job requirements and app design. The user would be able to see the availability of a parking slot and then choose a specific parking space as per his/her liking. The system would send a real-time notification to the smartphone registered with the vehicle. The timer would start to time the user in the parking lot when he/she would enter the parking lot. Upon exiting the parking lot, they would receive a notification containing the time the car spent in the parking lot. This paper proposed an intelligent parking IoT system that could provide more than just access to private information but also help the driver find available parking space to reduce traffic congestion in the parking lot.

Ahmed et al. (2019) proposed a design that included four segments and their result modified the combination of every segment. Every module was designed to perform its functions, but they were all interconnected to one another to conclude the complete process. The modules were—Main Server, Parking Centre Server, location and Android/iOS app. When an ultrasonic sensor would detect a vehicle, the camera would click a picture of the vehicle. Using the Google Cloud Vision Application interface, the processing of the image would be done to withdraw the text. The extracted text would help find the vehicle registration plate content. With the use of the Parking Centre Server updated data could be accessed. The Parking Centre server would store the information in the Parking Centre Server directory and the vehicle details would be refined along with the parking details. After tying the details to the parking centre figures, they would be forwarded to the main server, which would primarily store the details provided by the customer and Arduino/sensors. In addition, it would receive updated details from the Parking Centre Server. The customer could communicate with the server via the Android/iOS app. The user could effortlessly find his/her preferred parking space. The API would automatically suggest available parking space and its cost and access method. The ISPS system used cameras and ultrasonic sensors to aid detect parking areas and inappropriate parking. The suggested construction of the parking acquisition system will reduce search time for vacant spaces because all parking centre information will be stored on a large server and the driver would already have the directions to his/her pre-booked parking spot. The system would help the user search for parking spaces, giving preference to the user's desired parking space. The suggested system observed high power efficiency, complete automation and cost efficiency. The system could reduce congestion, human effort and most importantly the amount of carbon in the air.

The study by Harris and Karthi (2016) was not done in a conventional way. They did not evaluate the performance of parking services, did not provide any modelling system statistics and did not monitor the waiting time for each operating vehicle. They used ultrasonic sensors (a device that detects and respond to input from a physical location), Arduino Uno (ATmega328P based microcontroller), Arduino Ethernet (ATmega328-based microcontroller board) and Amazon Relational Database Service (web service that makes it simple to set up, work with and measure the database of cloud relationships). The launch part was done in the cloud-based environment and on an Android device. The type of drivers who wanted to make a reservation could be categorised as users. Parking and reservation activities would be done on the mobile app. The user would specify his/her desired parking location on the mobile app and the request would be sent to Amazon RDS to get parking status. Then the parking lot map would show the free parking spaces in the area and if the user would like to proceed with an online reservation, he/she would have to sign in and make an online payment. Once the payment would be made (Chang et al. 2019), the position of the designated area would reserve using LED lights in the parking lot. Finally, when the vehicle would enter the parking lot, the user would be verified using the OTP he/she received at the time of sign-in. This function focused on the parking system with pre-booking to overcome waiting in the queue, and so, with this prototype, the average waiting time for parking was reduced. Smart parking with a booking system (Azad et al. 2021) increased revenue for service providers, provided a diversified service for users with different needs and eliminated traffic congestion. Future upgrades could use GPS to locate and navigate parking spaces on the mobile app.

Vijayan et al. (2019) proposed the creation of a single-handed representation of slots in the parking lot. The initial phase of this smart parking plan is the discovery of a parking space. Here, they only used images recorded by the surveillance camera installed in the parking lot to detect vacant slot detection.

To locate every parking slot, a special number was given to every parking slot. The camcorder was used to capture all slot numbers in one frame. In contrast with the previous system (Priyadarshini et al. 2021a), there was no requirement for extra care to fix the camera. The only thing here needed was to make sure that the recorded image must have all the slot numbers visible. When the cars were parked in the lot, the corresponding slot number would hide the image. Now the only thing that needed to be done was to identify the available numbers. This could be done using Optical

Character Recognition (OCR) method for processing digital images. The camera would be placed in a special corner to monitor all parking lots and space numbers in one frame. There was a second and fifth delay in taking pictures with the camera. After that, the image was saved to continue working. The captured image would be processed to improve image quality. Image classification is a key method used in a system based on character recognition. The OCR-based algorithm for MATLAB was used to recognise numbers in the picture. These numbers were saved as vectors. If the car was parked, then its unique slot number would be invisible. Therefore, the slot number won't be visible in the output vector. The missing slot number would be identified as the slot taken. The numbers present in the output vector would represent vacant spaces and would be passed to the user notice section. These numbers would be visible as blank spaces in the parking lot. The parking image is processed to obtain a greyscale image and then transformed into a corresponding binary image. After proper refining, the image will only show slot numbers.

Alshehri et al. (2019) proposed a smart parking solution for the mega needs of the megacities. Their management system was built to effectively control the parking system and solve problems, thus contributing to the idea of smart cities. Their smart parking system provided reservation parking slots and displayed statistics with the assistance of the IoT (Internet of Things). With the assistance of sensors used to detect parking availability and recognition to monitor the access mechanism, all this was made possible. They figured that pre-booking a parking spot would help to save the driver's time (Sahu et al. 2021), effort and fuel spent searching the parking lot in real time. Not only did their model consist of the basic features, but they also had an automatic number plate recognition camera for access control. There were sensors in each parking slot that controlled the slot state by detecting a vehicle's presence. The user may use the application to reserve a parking space, cancel the reservation, make an online payment, edit personal data or display statistical reports. When he/she makes a reservation, the user will receive a note. The camera would catch the vehicle's number plate upon hitting the parking slot. The gate or barrier will only be opened if the number plate had a registered reservation. This will regulate the flow of the car in the parking lot, thus making the parking space for the driver hassle-free.

khan et al. (2018) and Vo et al. (2021) highlighted the fact that India is getting motorised day by day as people are preferring to have their own private vehicles rather than using public transport. Hence, the number of private vehicles is increasing exponentially and so is the need for a systematic parking system. To deal with this, they decided to digitise the process of finding a vacant parking slot. They created an application that would help the driver to find the nearest parking. The driver would register with basic details like username, number plate of the vehicle, mobile number and a connected wallet (PayTm, PhonePay, UPI, Amazon pay, etc.). The app was implemented using different search algorithms, like max–min algorithm or genetic algorithm (Nguyen et al. 2015). It added dynamic locating and guiding to the parking spaces in real time. It was basically intended to maximise time and distance. For sensing the vacant parking spots, they deployed sensors in each parking slot. When the user would request a vacant parking space, then the request would be passed to the nearest node. If there would be a parking space available within 30 m radius, then the user will be notified along with the directions and address, else the request would be forwarded to next node. This project totally focused on providing an agile and smooth parking experience to drivers.

An integrated smart parking system was proposed by Nait-Abdesselam et al. (2018) and Sachan et al. (2021a) to provide a mobile application for real-time driver interaction with the infrastructure of the car parking in a way that minimised the driver's time looking for a vacant parking spot. The main aim of their parking system was to distribute drivers' available parking spaces properly along with reducing their time for testing. The main feature of this project was that, based on gaps in duration between sending and receiving a signal, it regularly checked the condition of the parking spots. An image was submitted to the device until the adjustment was identified, thereby identifying incorrectly parked vehicles (Rastogi et al. 2018). It lacked, however, a proper way of measuring free parking spots easily. Then, to aid the drivers in finding a vacant parking slot near their destination, Mejri et al. suggested a parking reservation system known as "ROSAP". Reducing the on-foot distance from the parking slot to the destination was the key feature of this scheme. But ROSAP's biggest downside was the privacy issues of drivers who were unwilling to disclose their destination. Since the smart parking system architecture consists of databases, data collection is inevitable.

Belinova et al. (2018) and Ghanem et al. (2021) shed light on the issue of inadequate parking spaces faced today by many cities. They proposed the notion of sharing the car park with more than one organisation (Sharan Sai et al. 2018). They predicted that this concept could save 20–40% of the parking spaces. They witnessed the introduction of a smart parking project in Uherske Hradiste, Czech Republic. There are around 25,000 inhabitants in this city. There are five types of parking areas in Uherske Hradiste that have paid parking lots. The purpose of this is to optimise the turnover of cars in the lot and to compel drivers who park their cars to use the allocated parking space for a longer time period. In paid parking district, there are about 1600 spaces. The emphasis of this parking management system was that smart methods should take advantage of existing smart technology in order to upgrade the existing parking system for better and more effective use. Parking spaces may, according to them, be divided into two types: parking spaces in isolated areas and street parking spaces. The model they offered consisted of 2 main components:

1. Geographical localisation and definition of parking units and systems
2. Localisation above the Street Net network of parking units and unit networks

The first component concentrated on the information and geographical location of all the parking vehicles. The relationship between the parking vehicles and Street Net in the database was defined by the second component of the data model. ArcGIS Geodatabase was used in the physical model implementation and the last step was to show the required information on the app or website. The governments can experiment with this model and as per the needs of each country, this system can be modified.

Smart Parking System

Motivation to use Smart Parking:

Parking optimisation—Users find the best available spot, saving time, resources and effort. The parking lot fills quickly, and commercial and corporate entities can make good use of the available space.

Reduced traffic—As fewer cars are required to drive around looking for an open parking space, traffic flow increases.

Reduced pollution—Looking for parking consumes approximately one million barrels of oil per day. An optimal parking solution will significantly reduce driving time, lowering daily vehicle emissions and, ultimately, the global environmental footprint.

Real-Time Data and Trend Insight—Over time, a smart parking solution can generate data that reveals user and lot correlations and trends. These trends can be extremely useful to lot owners in terms of determining how to adjust and improvements to drivers.

In our proposed smart parking system, the user will be easily able to get to a vacant parking spot without wasting time and resources. The parking lot entrance will have an LED display displaying the total occupied and vacant parking spots in the parking. It will be followed by a barrier that will not open in case the parking lot is full, thus saving the driver from unnecessary stress. Inside the parking lot, each parking spot will have IR sensors for detecting the presence of a vehicle and two LEDs lights. The green LED at the parking spot will indicate the vacant parking spot, while the red LED will indicate the occupied parking spot. The IR sensors will be connected to the barrier the LED display at the entrance and the LED lights at their parking spots via the cloud. As soon as the driver enters the parking lot, he/she will be able to spot the vacant spots easily. This will save the driver from the hassle of going through each row of cars and wasting fuel and time (Fig. 7.1).

The entire workflow of the presented prototype as shown in Fig. 7.2. It elaborates on the working of the prototype. IR sensor transfers the results to Arduino Uno, which is displayed on the LCD screen as a visual output near the prototype. It uses a Wi-Fi module esp8266 module to transfer the data and make it visible remotely on the Blynk application. Further, the block diagram has been divided into two parts for better understanding (Fig. 7.3).

The Block diagram represented in Fig. 7.4 shows that the power supply is given to the IR sensor, Arduino Uno and LCD display after which the IR sensor senses the presence of the car and then gives it to the Arduino microcontroller which further displays it on the LCD display. The Arduino module is connected to Wi-Fi. Arduino transmits data to be displayed on the app. The smart device helps in providing internet connectivity. Then the data through the Wi-Fi module is shown on the Blynk app.

In the latest smart parking system, the user will be easily able to get to a vacant parking spot without wasting time and resources. The parking lot entrance will have an LED display displaying the total, occupied and vacant parking spots in the parking. It will be followed by a barrier that will not open in case the parking lot is full, thus

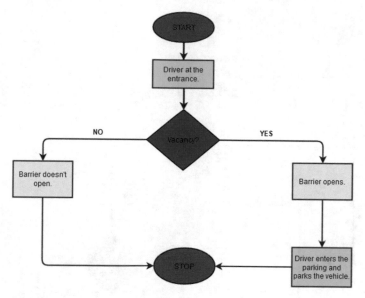

Fig. 7.1 Flowchart of driver's POV

saving the driver from unnecessary stress. Inside the parking lot, each parking spot will have IR sensors for tracking the presence of a vehicle and LED lights. The red light will be on when there is no parking in the provided slot. Therefore, on the screen on the selected slot, it will display an "N" character which is the symbol that the slot is totally empty. While, when any car occupies the slot, there will be two lights emitting is green and red which shows that the IR sensor has detected something, and the IR sensor transmitter and receiver are working properly. Since the light is glowing then on the screen, we will be seeing the "Y" sign on the selective slot. Hence,

- "Y" character on the screen means that the slot is occupied.
- "N" character on the screen means that the slot is empty.
- This information will be automatically updated in the Blynk app as well. And on the selective slot, it will show "1" to the occupied slot and "0" to the slot which is not occupied. Therefore, in the Blynk app:
- "1" means the slot is occupied on the app.
- "0" means the slot is not occupied yet.
- This will save the driver from the hassle of going through each row of cars and wasting fuel and time. In the future, if we must make a real-world app then what we can offer to our customers in the app so that parking can be as smooth as possible. These are the possible features
- Login/Signup features so that users can register themselves.
- The layout of the parking slot which will be visible to the customer through our app.

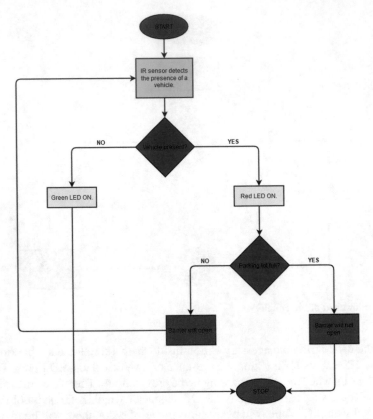

Fig. 7.2 Flowchart of sensor's working

- Video of the car parking in case of security reasons as proper surveillance will be installed in the parking system.
- Discount on the registered user which will attract the customers.
- A warning people about the mental illness which is caused the drivers (Fig. 7.5).

Working

Arduino microcontroller is the main component of this system. Car Parking Slots Monitoring System based on IoT using Arduino, Node-MCU ESP8266 wi-fi module. There are two floors in the parking lot. There are five slots on each floor. Each parking spot has one infrared sensor. As a result, we have a total of ten infrared sensors. Each sensor is used to sense whether a vehicle is present in the spot. Arduino is connected to these infrared sensors. When a car is parked in the slot, the Arduino transmits a signal to the Node-MCU ESP8266 Wi-fi module, which then sends it to the Blynk

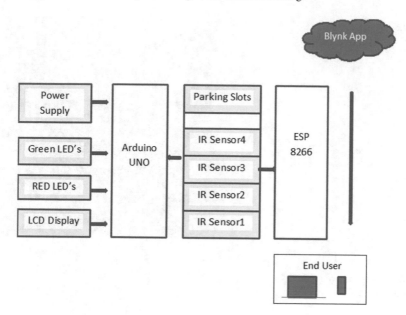

Fig. 7.3 Block diagram—smart parking system

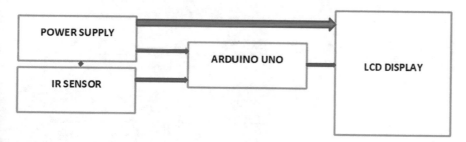

Fig. 7.4 Block diagram showing parking monitoring and sensing

app. The Node-MCU ESP8266 wi-fi module allows us to monitor parking spaces from anywhere in the world. The real-time data are displayed on the app.

All the pins are carefully labelled. Never power the Node-MCU ESP8266 Wi-Fi module with the Arduino's 5 V. If you use the Arduino's 5-V power supply to power this module, it will keep resetting. The user can access the data on the Blynk app on their smartphone (Fig. 7.6).

Fig. 7.5 Smart parking
model

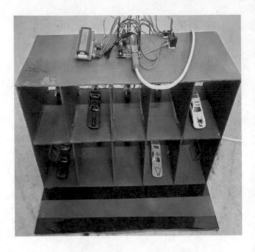

Fig. 7.6 Flow chart of smart
parking system

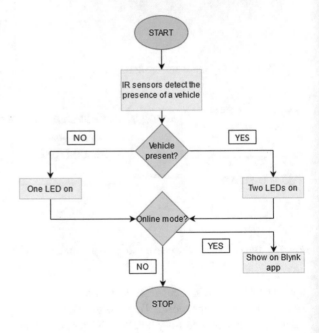

Results

The turning on the message of the prototype is shown in Fig. 7.7. After 3 s of
displaying the message Smart Parking System, it starts to find the Wi-Fi network
using the esp8266 module. During the time while the Wi-Fi connection is established
the LCD screen shows a message of connecting as shown in Fig. 7.4 (Figs. 7.8 and
7.9).

Fig. 7.7 Turning on LCD message

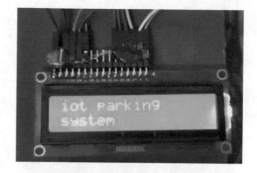

Fig. 7.8 Connecting to WI-FI

Fig. 7.9 Display on LCD SCREEN when ALL slots are occupied

This system will show "Y" on every slot, then it means that it has been fully used and the Blynk app will also throw a message stating that the slots are full and cannot be used further.

In case, we tend to make it real then we will not use the Blynk app because it has its restrictions. Therefore, we will provide and make an application by ourselves that can provide SIGNUP and SIGNOUT features and the feature we want to give to our people. In case there are not enough slots filled then we will see "N" on the slot number and "Y" on the slots where the parking has been occupied. Module ESP 8266 plays a crucial role in the connection between the device and hardware. First, you

Fig. 7.10 All slots are not full

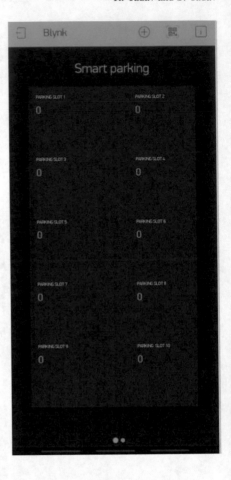

must rename your Hotspot as provided by the Blynk app and changes the password as well so that the hardware can be connected to the software easily. After that only we must run the Blynk app, and it will automatically fetch data through ESP 8266 and update the slot's details of being used or not. Remember, it is very crucial to restart the system if it shows an error that is unpredictable. In this way, we can reduce the time to find parking for a particular diver (Figs. 7.10 and 7.11).

Conclusion

The desire for a well-organised and hassle-free parking system has been the dream of every driver. With today's technologically advancing world, this dream is coming true. The drastic boom in the IoT domain has brought technology to each aspect of our life. From an air conditioner at home to even our cars, IoT is everywhere.

Fig. 7.11 All slots are occupied

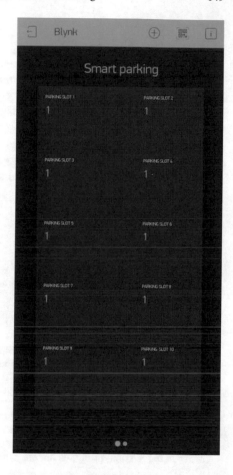

Thus, with the implementation of IoT in parking lots, the lives of drivers are going to become a lot easier. From reduced time and fuel wastage to keeping the stress of finding a vacant parking spot at bay, this smart parking system will make the parking experience smooth.

The smart parking system's demand is growing exponentially. Users can now include real-time access to the parking space. The current system in the world does not contain parking reservations and checking parking availability. The previous technology was a vision-based monitoring system that calculated the number of incoming and exiting vehicles to estimate the number of parking spaces available in the region, which took a long time and effort. The upcoming technology includes a sensor-based system that uses ultrasonic sound waves to detect vehicle detection and then two-line parking using the concept of more than one parking vehicle. The result of this smart car parking program aims to connect the parking lot to the rest of the world to save time and money for the user effectively. This system reduces the fuel consumption of a car used in car searches.

Future Scope

Smart houses have always been a pipe dream. Over the last few years, some work has been made toward making the goal of a smart city an actuality. Cloud technology and the IoT have opened new possibilities for smart cities. Smart parking has long been at the heart of smart city development. The technology delivers process and parking information in real time. This increases efficiency by saving consumers time when looking for a parking spot. It contributes to the alleviation of the growing problem of traffic congestion. Users will be able to book a parking spot from a remote GPS position in the future, and a license plate scanner will be deployed.

References

Ahmed MT, Nitu ZF, Ahmed S, Al Maruf MA, Roy A (2019) A proposed model of integrated smart parking solution for a city. In: International conference on robotics, electrical and signal processing techniques (ICREST)

Alshehri S, Nollily S, Farooqi N, Alqurashi G, Alrashedi A, Najmi L (2019) UParking: developing a smart parking management system using the Internet of Things. In: Sixth HCT information technology trends (ITT)

Ansari U, Kazi S, Mane D, Khan S (2018) Smart parking based system for smarter cities. In: international conference on smart city and emerging technology (ICSCET)

Azad C, Bhushan B, Sharma R et al (2021) Prediction model using SMOTE, genetic algorithm and decision tree (PMSGD) for classification of diabetes mellitus. Multimedia Syst. https://doi.org/10.1007/s00530-021-00817-2

Chang C-Y, Chen G, Chen S-Y, Lin J (2019) SPA: smart parking algorithm based on driver behavior and parking traffic predictions. IEEE Access 7

Chaya Kumari HA, Chandan G, Aniruddh MC, Chandana M, Fathima A (2019) A study on smart parking solutions using IoT. In: International conference on intelligent sustainable systems (ICISS)

Devaraj JDD, Voon YV, Al-Absz HRH, Sebastian P (2010) Vision-based automated parking system. In: 10th international conference on information science, signal processing, and their applications (ISSPA)

Ghanem S, Kanungo P, Panda G et al (2021) Lane detection under artificial colored light in tunnels and on highways: an IoT-based framework for smart city infrastructure. Complex Intell Syst. https://doi.org/10.1007/s40747-021-00381-2

Harris P, Karthi M (2016) Smart parking with reservation in cloud based environment. In: IEEE international conference on cloud computing in emerging markets (CCEM)

Jirge V, Tiwari A, Ashok D (2020) Smart parking system using IoT technology. In: international conference on emerging trends in information technology and engineering (ic-ETITE)

Moutaouakkil F, Jioudi B, Medromi H, Sabir E (2019) Congestion awareness meets zone-based pricing policies for efficient urban parking. IEEE Access 7

Nait-Abdesselam F, Djahel S, Melnyk P (2019) Towards a smart parking management system for smart cities. In: IEEE international smart cities conference (ISC2)

Nguyen DB, Deng D-J, Pham TN, Dow C-R, Tsai M-F (2015) A cloud-based smart-parking system based on Internet-of-Things technologies. IEEE Access 3

Priyadarshini I, Kumar R, Sharma R, Singh PK, Satapathy SC (2021a) Identifying cyber insecurities in trustworthy space and energy sector for smart grids. Comput Electr Eng 93:107204

Hlubuckova K, Belinova Z, Langr M, Ruzicka J, Silar J (2018) Smart parking in the smart city application. In: smart city symposium prague (SCSP)

Priyadarshini I, Kumar R, Tuan LM et al (2021b) A new enhanced cyber security framework for medical cyber physical systems. SICS Softw-Inensiv Cyber-Phys Syst. https://doi.org/10.1007/s00450-021-00427-3

Priyadarshini I, Mohanty P, Kumar R et al (2021c) A study on the sentiments and psychology of twitter users during COVID-19 lockdown period. Multimed Tools Appl. https://doi.org/10.1007/s11042-021-11004-w

Rastogi P, Gupta A, Jain S (2018) Smart parking system using cloud based computation and Raspberry Pi. In: International conference on I-SMAC (IoT in social, mobile, analytics and cloud)

Sachan S, Sharma R, Sehgal A (2021a) Energy efficient scheme for better connectivity in sustainable mobile wireless sensor networks. Sustain Comput: Inform Syst 30:100504

Sachan S, Sharma R, Sehgal A (2021b) SINR based energy optimization schemes for 5G vehicular sensor networks. Wirel Pers Commun. https://doi.org/10.1007/s11277-021-08561-6

Sahu L, Sharma R, Sahu I, Das M, Sahu B, Kumar R (2021) Efficient detection of Parkinson's disease using deep learning techniques over medical data. Expert Syst e12787. https://doi.org/10.1111/exsy.12787

Sharan Sai GN, Domma HJ, Borra KY, Kodali RK (2018) An IoT based smart parking system using LoRa. In: International conference on cyber-enabled distributed computing and knowledge discovery (CyberC)

Shen Y-C, Kotb AO, Huang Y, Zhu X (2016) IParker: a new smart car-parking system based on dynamic re-source allocation and pricing. IEEE Trans Intell Transp Syst 17

Singh R, Sharma R, Akram SV, Gehlot A, Buddhi D, Malik PK, Arya R (2021) Highway 4.0: digitalization of highways for vulnerable road safety development with intelligent IoT sensors and machine learning. Saf Sci 143:105407. ISSN 0925-7535

Usanavasin S, Nambut K, Lookmuang R (2018) Smart parking using IoT technology. In: 5th international conference on business and industrial research (ICBIR)

Vijayan P, Athira A, Kurian B, Lekshmi S (2019) Smart parking system based on optical character recognition. In: 3rd international conference on trends in electronics and informatics (ICOEI)

Vo MT, Vo AH, Nguyen T, Sharma R, Le T (2021) Dealing with the class imbalance problem in the detection of fake job descriptions. Comput, Mater Contin 68(1):521–535

Chapter 8
UM5 of Rabat to Deep Space: Ultra-Wide Band and High Gain Only-Metal Fabry–Perot Antenna for Interplanetary CubeSats in IoT Infrastructure

Fouad Omari, Boutaina Benhmimou, Niamat Hussain, Rachid Ahl Laamara, Sandeep Kumar Arora, Josep M. Guerrero, and Mohamed El Bakkali

Introduction

Small spacecrafts and CubeSats have become emerging tools to explore space technology and then to perform inexpensively related science (Bakkali 2020; Popescu 2017). CubeSats are frequently used and have become more ambitious due to their low costs, short development time, simplicity, and, most importantly, low power consumption as compared with other conventional satellites. However, going from

F. Omari · B. Benhmimou · R. A. Laamara · M. E. Bakkali
Faculty of Sciences, University Mohammed Five in Rabat (UM5R), B.P. 1014, Agdal, Rabat, Morocco
e-mail: fouad.omari@um5r.ac.m

B. Benhmimou
e-mail: boutaina.benhmimou@um5r.ac.ma

R. A. Laamara
e-mail: r.ahllaamara@um5r.ac.ma

M. E. Bakkali
e-mail: mohamed.elbakkali1617@gmail.com

N. Hussain (✉)
Department of Smart Device Engineering, Sejong University, Seoul 05006, South Korea
e-mail: niamathussain@sejong.ac.kr

S. K. Arora (✉)
School of Electronics and Electrical Engineering, Lovely Professional University, Phagwara, Punjab, India
e-mail: sandeep.16930@lpu.co.in

J. M. Guerrero (✉)
Center for Research on Microgrids (CROM), Department of Energy Technology, Aalborg University, 9220 Aalborg East, Denmark
e-mail: joz@et.aau.dk

© The Author(s), under exclusive license to Springer Nature Singapore Pte Ltd. 2023
D. K. Sharma et al. (eds.), *Low Power Architectures for IoT Applications*, Springer Tracts in Electrical and Electronics Engineering, https://doi.org/10.1007/978-981-99-0639-0_8

LEO to GEO orbits and due to the amount of data transmitted to Earth (from Kbits to Mbits), the CubeSat's communication systems are preferred to be improved as high as possible in order to fully support science and make these missions more accessible for space partners (Rivera and Boyle 2013; EU 2012). The CubeSat's communication subsystem is crucial, as it provides transmission with earth stations and hence a high-data-rate communication subsystem is required in order to transfer high-resolution images and perform other tasks scheduled by the CubeSat mission. Moreover, CubeSats require antenna systems with specific characteristics to realize various functions such as telemetry, tracking, earth observation, global positioning system (GPS), global satellite navigation systems, and inter-satellite cross-link communications (Bakkali 2020; Rodríguez-Osorio and Ramírez 2012; Wu et al. 2014). CubeSat antennas can work at a wide range of frequencies and realize various tasks similar to conventional satellites (Rahmat-Samii et al. 2017). After the CubeSat is deployed into the targeted orbit, its reorientation must be applied in order to define the transmission links with earth stations as per the areas of that CubeSat missions and performances of both CubeSat antennas and ground stations on earth. Henceforth, CubeSats require high-performance antenna designs for establishing communication with earth stations and so accomplishing the CubeSat Mission (Babuscia 2020).

However, despite various antennas designed can be placed on the CubeSat body, the design and implementation of CubeSat Subsystems present strict limitations of weight and dimensions (Bakkali 2020; Jiang et al. 2017). Antenna performances will be, therefore, affected by closely adjacent antennas and hence limits the effectiveness of multiple-antenna designs for one CubeSat mission. From another hand, the use of very high-frequency (VHF) ultrahigh-frequency (UHF) monopole and dipole antennas used on CubeSats is incapable to meet capabilities of high-data-rate transmission and so long lifetime CubeSat mission despite their length of hundreds of millimeters and the need of deployment operation after the CubeSat lunch. Particularly, mainly taking into consideration both gain, size, and stiffness, planar antennas present the best choice and more especially at high working frequencies (Bakkali et al. 2021).

Moreover, Single-feed planar antennas have been widely used because of their low profiles, lightweight, and simplicity in design. However, their inherent drawbacks of narrow impedance, low-temperature stability, and low gain limit their suitability for use on small spacecrafts and CubeSats. To transact with these challenges, this research work introduces a new small spacecraft antenna approach based on the use of Fabry–Perot configurations for interplanetary CubeSats.

The proposed Fabry–Perot antenna approach falls under the endeavors of the Mohammed Five university of Rabat in order to target emerging space technologies and furthermore open doors to understanding how the universe works. These features are targeted due to its rank as the oldest Moroccan university and first research organization established after achieving independence from France (Mohammed Five University of Rabat). In this antenna approach, both strips of the proposed Fabry–Perot are slotted using two arrays of square cells and are optimized in order to obtain the highest gain possible with suitability for interplanetary CubeSats. In addition to that, the impedance bandwidths are preferred to be ultra-wide as much as possible.

This paper is summarized through the following sections: Geometrical analysis of approach is presented in detail in Sect. 8.2. The achieved performances are introduced and discussed in Sect. 8.3. Section 8.4 concludes the proposed study.

Antenna Design Geometrical Description

The proposed Fabry–Perot antenna is designed using ANSYS HFSS for use on 6U CubeSat configurations at Ku-band. It is lightweight and is developed without the use of any dielectric material; refer Figs. 8.1, 8.2, and 8.3. It consists, therefore, of only metal high gain Fabry–Perot antenna structure optimized using a quasi-Newtonian method which is a part of HFSS packages (ANSYS HFSS simulator). The source antenna is a 50Ω probe excited circular patch ring antenna. It has a physical size of 23×23 mm^2 and is made of copper. The excitation probe is shifted by 1.5 mm from the antenna center in order to achieve the highest gain possible with good impedance matching around an operating frequency of 13.40 GHz. The aim of the presented study is to open doors for use of only metal Fabry–Perot antennas on deep Space environments where the temperature is too high and antenna peak gain should be as high as possible. Henceforth, the proposed Fabry Perot is optimized using QNM in order to achieve a peak gain bigger than 15.0 dBi with high return loss and total size suitable for 6U CubeSats.

The Fabry–Perot strips have a total size of 154×154 mm^2, are separated by an air gap distance of 1.2 mm, and are placed at a distance of 26 mm above the source antenna. They are made also of copper metal and are welded with the CubeSat chassis using four metallic screws of Aluminum.

In terms of geometry, weight, size, cost, stiffness, and power consumption, the proposed metallic Fabry–Perot antenna is very suitable for use in Deep Space CubeSats.

Fig. 8.1 3D HFSS model of the proposed antenna system

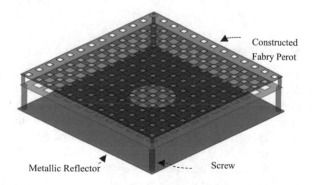

Constructed
Fabry Perot

Metallic Reflector   Screw

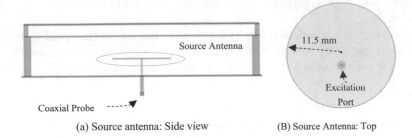

(a) Source antenna: Side view   (B) Source Antenna: Top

Fig. 8.2 Geometry of proposed source antenna

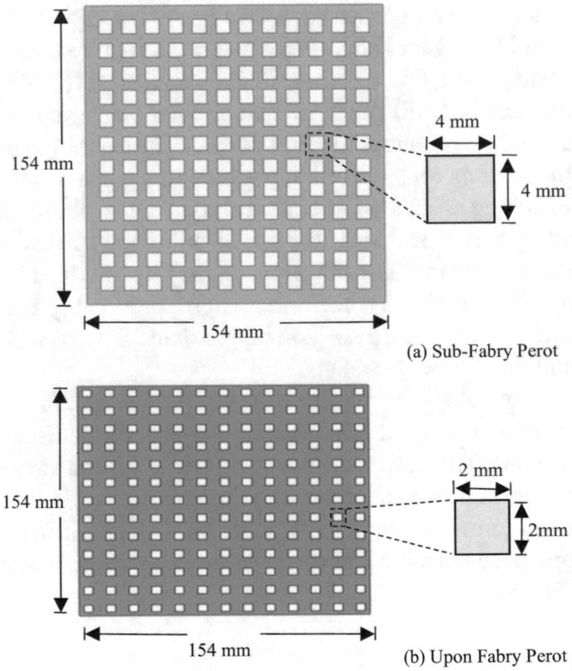

Fig. 8.3 Geometry of
developed Fabry Perot

(a) Sub-Fabry Perot

(b) Upon Fabry Perot

Results and Discussion

As it is mentioned above, the constructed only metal Fabry–Perot antenna is designed
and optimized for operation at Ku-band. Figures 8.4 and 8.5 show both the reflection
coefficient and VSWR of the source antenna alone and the optimized configuration
of the Perot antenna. It is observed that the first one gives a low reflection coefficient
(high return loss) and VSWR close to one around our targeted working frequency
of 13.40 GHz. It presents ultra-wide impedance bandwidth ranging from 13.05 to
14.70 GHz with a high return loss of about 32.41 dB at 13.48 GHz. The second one,

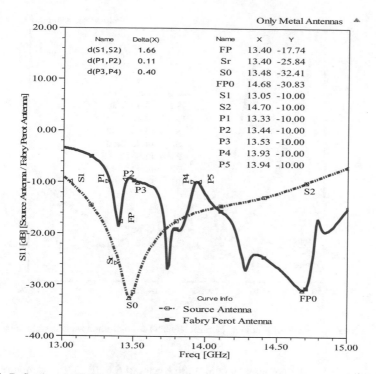

Fig. 8.4 Reflection coefficient of proposed antenna configurations versus frequency

Fabry–Perot configuration, gives similar results of |S11| and VSWR coefficients with bandwidth enhancement around the same operating frequency.

The metallic Fabry–Perot antenna highlights, therefore, an ultra-wide band with a good reflection coefficient for use by Deep Space CubeSats. These results can be translated to a low electric power being forwarded back to the excitation port and hence the maximum quantity of excitation power being radiated outside the CubeSat body.

2D radiation pattern and 3D gain plots of the source antenna alone and 2D gain plots of both metallic antenna structures are given in Fig. 8.6. It is shown that the source antenna alone achieves a high gain of about 9.2 dBi with unidirectional radiation pattern and wide beamwidth angle at 13.40 GHz. This very small metallic antenna configuration is, hence, very suitable for all CubeSat configurations although it gives away much space on the CubeSat body for solar panels and other satellite devices.

Due to the long distances introduced by deep space missions, higher results of gain are preferred because they limit requirements of deep space earth station antennas for earth-deep Space CubeSat links and hence the cost of the overall space mission. Figure 8.7 proves the effectiveness of implementing Fabry–Perot structures above the proposed metallic source antenna on the peak gain at our resonant frequency of 13.4 GHz.

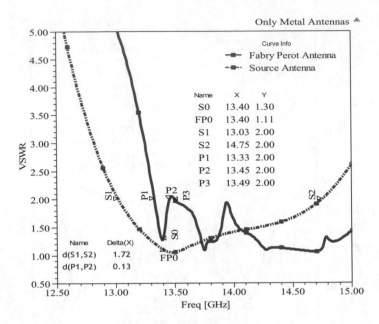

Fig. 8.5 VSWR coefficient of proposed metallic antenna configurations versus frequency

We show that they increase the peak gain by about 6.5 dBi at the same operating frequency and using the same excitation power used by the source antenna alone and hence increase the suitability of the proposed metallic antenna configuration for Deep Space missions.

This means that both Fabry–Perot strips get excited through electromagnetic coupling with the source antenna and then increase radiated power in the z-direction outside the CubeSat. By adding the Fabry–Perot strips, the final metallic antenna design becomes suitable for Deep Space CubeSat missions with the use of a suitable earth station in the transmission chain. To complement our study, in Tables 8.1, 8.2, and 8.3, our antenna is compared to similar CubeSat antenna designs in terms of frequency bands, materials, stiffness, weight, cost, and suitability for both uplink and downlink transmissions using CubeSats. It is found that our antenna design presents the lowest volume, and lowest cost, and achieves the best gain for deep space satellite missions using CubeSats.

Through this study, it is proved that low power consumption, lightweight, low cost, and simple configuration of metallic Fabry–Perot antenna can overtake gain of 15.50 dBi with ultra-wide impedance bandwidth at Ku-band. Henceforth going from LEO CubeSat missions to interplanetary uses can be easily obtained using metallic Fabry–Perot antennas (Omari et al. 2022; Benhmimou et al. 2022).

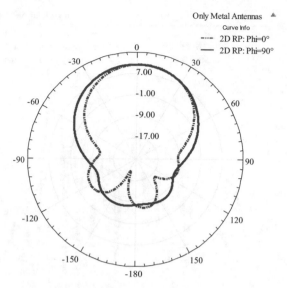

(a) E-field and H-field of proposed source antenna

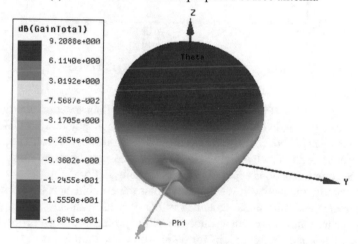

(b) 3D Gain of proposed metallic source antenna

Fig. 8.6 2D radiation pattern and 3D gain plots of proposed source antenna alone at 13.4 GHz

Conclusions

A high gain Only-Metal Fabry–Perot antenna is proposed for deep orbit CubeSat missions in this research work. The presented study shows that both the source antenna and the Fabry–Perot configurations achieve peak gains higher than 9.0 dBi at Ku-band and hence both antennas can be used for CubeSat missions that require

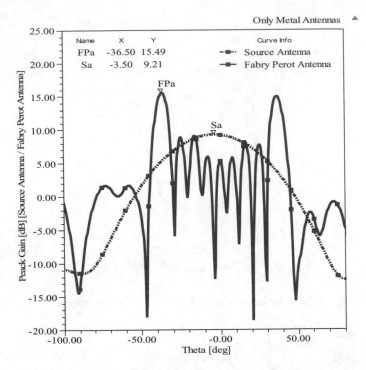

Fig. 8.7 Peak gain of proposed metallic antennas at Ku-band (13.4 GHz)

a lifetime bigger than 100 years. In addition to that, both antenna configurations present ultra-wide bandwidths around an operating frequency of 13.4 GHz with a gain enhancement of about 6.50 dBi using the constructed Fabry–Perot. The proposed Fabry–Perot antenna, which is lightweight and low cost, can be, therefore, used for deep space communications using 6U CubeSat configurations.

Consequently, the achieved results prove that the combination between Fabry–Perot structures and only metal antennas offers very high antenna peak gains and wide impedance bandwidth with advantages of low profile, low power consumption, and low-cost antenna configurations for deep orbit CubeSat missions.

Table 8.1 Brief comparison with literature works at C/X/Ku-band: Fabry–Perot antennas

Reference	Frequency	Materials	Approach	Return loss (dB)	Gain (dBi)	CubeSat	Stiffness	Weight
Bakkali et al. (2019)	Ku-band (13.9 GHz)	Rogers RT Duroid 5880	Parasitic elements	~35.0	8.8	All structures	High	Low
Abdulkarim et al. (2020)	Ku-band (12.5 GHz)	FR4	Metasurface	~43.0	~2.5	×	Medium	Medium
Ren et al. (2018)	Ku-band (10.7 GHz)	FR4	P. converter + PRS + AS	~30.0	~10.0	All structures	Medium	Medium
Cao et al. (2018)	Ku-band (15.0 GHz)	Rogers RT/duriod 5880	PRS + MEDA + FP	~17.0	~5.0	1U CubeSats	Medium	Low
Calleau et al. (2019)	Ku-band (15.0 GHz)	HF51 foam	PRS + HIS + FP	>10	~13.0	×	Medium	Medium
Our work	Ku-band (13.4 GHz)	No dielectric	FP	~20.0	15.5	3U and 6U	High	Low

Table 8.2 Brief comparison with literature works based on Roger RT 5880 Material

Reference	Frequency	Materials	Approach	Return loss (dB)	Gain (dBi)	CubeSat	Stiffness	Weight
Sumathi et al. (2021)	C-band (6.85 GHz)	Roger RT Duroid 5880	LCAM + multi layers	~33.0	~8.0	×	Very low	Medium
Qin et al. (2015)	X-band (10.0 GHz)	Roger RT Duroid 5880	2 layers PRS + FP	~40.0	~14.0	3U and 6U CubeSats	Low	Medium
Our work	Ku-band (13.4 GHz)	No dielectric	FP	~20.0	15.5	3U and 6U	High	Low

Table 8.3 Brief comparison with literature works based on FR4 Material

Reference	Frequency	Materials	Approach	Return loss (dB)	Gain	CubeSat	Stiffness	Weight
Chen and Zhang (2019)	X-band (10.5 GHz)	FR4	AMC + CPCM + FP	~17.0	~8.0 dBi	All structures	Medium	Medium
Naik and Vijaya Sri (2018)	X-band (13.67 GHz)	FR4	Parasitic elements	~40.0	~8.0 dBi	×	High	Low
Cheng and Dong (2020)	C-band (5.0 GHz)	FR4	PRS + FP	~22.0	14.8 dBic	6U	Medium	High
Yang et al. (2020)	C-band (5.1 GHz)	Liquid metal + FR4 + PMMA	Liquid–metal PRS + FP	~18.0	~8.5 dBi	All structures	Medium	High
Our work	Ku-band (13.4 GHz)	No dielectric	FP	~20.0	15.5 dBi	3U and 6U	High	Low

Acknowledgements The authors would like to thank Prof. Gurjot Singh and Prof. Alexander Kogut, Prof. Nancy Gupta, and Prof. Yadgar Ibrahim Abdulkarim for their valuable support in preparing this research work.

References

Abdulkarim YI, Awl HN, Muhammadsharif FF, Karaaslan M, Mahmud RH, Hasan SO, Işık Ö, Luo H, Huang S (2020) A low-profile antenna based on single-layer metasurface for Ku-band applications. Int J Antennas Propag 2020:8. Article ID 8813951. https://doi.org/10.1155/2020/8813951
EU (2012) An international network of 50 CubeSats Project

Babuscia A (2020) Telecommunication systems for small satellites operating at high frequencies: a review. Information 11(258):2–13. https://doi.org/10.3390/info11050258

Bakkali ME, Tubbal F, Gaba GS, Kansal L, Idrissi NEAE (2019) Low-profile patch antenna with parasitic elements for CubeSat applications. In: Luhach A, Jat D, Hawari K, Gao XZ, Lingras P (eds) Advanced informatics for computing research. ICAICR 2019. Communications in computer and information science, vol 1076. Springer, Singapore. https://doi.org/10.1007/978-981-15-0111-1_12

Benhmimou B, Hussain N, Gupta N, Laamara RA, Guerrero JM, El Bakkali M, Arpanaei F, Alibakhshikenari M et al (2022) Miniaturized transparent slot antenna for 1U and 2U Cube-Sats: CRTS space missions. In: 13th international conference on computing, communication and technologies (13th ICCCNT), 3–5 Oct 2022, pp 1–6

Calleau A, García-Vigueras M, Legay H, Sauleau R, Ettorre M (2019) Circularly polarized Fabry–Perot antenna using a hybrid leaky-wave mode. IEEE Trans Antennas Propag 67(9):5867–5876. https://doi.org/10.1109/TAP.2019.2920266

Cao W, Wang Q, Jin J, Li H (2018) Magneto-electric dipole antenna (MEDA)-fed Fabry-Perot resonator antenna (FPRA) with broad gain bandwidth in Ku band. IEEE Access 6:65557–65562. https://doi.org/10.1109/ACCESS.2018.2878054

Chen Q, Zhang H (2019) High-gain circularly polarized Fabry-Pérot patch array antenna with wideband low-radar-cross-section property. IEEE Access 7:8885–8889. https://doi.org/10.1109/ACCESS.2018.2890691

Cheng Y, Dong Y (2020) Bandwidth enhanced circularly polarized Fabry-Perot cavity antenna using metal strips. IEEE Access 8:60189–60198. https://doi.org/10.1109/ACCESS.2020.2983062

El Bakkali M (2020, July) Planar antennas with parasitic elements and metasurface superstrate structure for 3U CubeSats. Thesis, Sidi Mohamed Ben Abdellah University, City of Fez, Morocco

HFSS, High Frequency Simulation Software, Ansys Products, HFSS v. 18.0 (2018)

El Bakkali M, Bekkali ME, Gaba GS, Guerrero JM, Kansal L, Masud M (2021) Fully integrated high gain S-band triangular slot antenna for CubeSat communications. Electronics

Jiang JH, Yue Q, Reising SC, Kangaslahti PP, Deal WR, Schlecht ET, Wu L, Evans KF (2017) A simulation of ice cloud particle size, humidity and temperature measurements from the TWICE CubeSat. J Earth Space Sci 4(8):574–587

Mohammed Five University of Rabat, Agdal, Rabat, UM5R (2022). http://www.um5.ac.ma/um5/

Naik KK, Vijaya Sri PA (2018) Design of hexadecagon circular patch antenna with DGS at Ku band for satellite communications. Prog Electromagn Res M 63:163–173. https://doi.org/10.2528/PIERM17092205

Omari F, Hussain N, Benhmimou B, Gupta N, Laamara RA, Abdulkarim YI, El Bakkali M et al (2022) Only-metal ultra-small circular slot antenna for 3U CubeSats. In: 13th international conference on computing, communication and technologies (13th ICCCNT), 3–5 Oct 2022, pp 1–6

Popescu O (2017) Power budgets for CubeSat radios to support ground communications and inter-satellite links. IEEE Access 5(X):12618–12625

Qin F et al (2015) Wideband circularly polarized Fabry-Perot antenna [antenna applications corner]. IEEE Antennas Propag Mag 57(5):127–135. https://doi.org/10.1109/MAP.2015.2470678

Rahmat-Samii Y, Manohar V, Kovitz JM (2017) For satellites, think small, dream big: a review of recent antenna developments for CubeSats. IEEE Antennas Propag Mag 59(2):22–30

Ren J, Jiang W, Zhang K, Gong S (2018) A high-gain circularly polarized Fabry-Perot antenna with wideband low-RCS property. IEEE Antennas Wirel Propag Lett 17(5):853–856. https://doi.org/10.1109/LAWP.2018.2820015

Rivera M, Boyle A (2013) Space for all: small, cheap satellites may one day do your bidding. NBC NEWS, Innovation, 14 July 2013, 5:11 am ET

Rodríguez-Osorio RM, Ramírez EF (2012) A hands-on education project: antenna design for inter-CubeSat communications [education column]. IEEE Antennas Propag Mag 54(5):211–224. https://doi.org/10.1109/MAP.2012.6348155

Sumathi K, Lavadiya S, Yin P et al (2021) High gain multiband and frequency reconfigurable meta-material superstrate microstrip patch antenna for C/X/Ku-band wireless network applications. Wirel Netw 27:2131–2146. https://doi.org/10.1007/s11276-021-02567-5

Wu S, Chen W, Zhang Y, Baan W, An T (2014, August) SULFRO: a swarm of nano-/micro-satellite at SE L2 for space ultra-low frequency radio observatory. In: The AIAA/USU conference on small satellites, Logan, UT

Yang X, Liu Y, Lei H, Jia Y, Zhu P, Zhou Z (2020) A radiation pattern reconfigurable Fabry-Pérot antenna based on liquid metal. IEEE Trans Antennas Propag 68(11):7658–7663. https://doi.org/10.1109/TAP.2020.2993310

Chapter 9
A Shared Patch MIMO Antenna for NB-IoT Applications

Sneha, Praveen Kumar Malik, and Ahmed Alkhayyat

Introduction

In the Present era of digitization where everybody has to become an IT incumbent in some manner. For the last few decades, somehow, we are all depending on Technology and it plays an important role in our everyday life. This combination of devices and wireless network connectivity forms the Internet of Things. Narrow Band Internet of Things technology is one of the latest advancements and most useful technology of IoT. NB-IoT provides a wide range of wireless network services that can help to improve IoT Services. It is a low-power, wide-area technology that consumes very little power in data communication. The bandwidth is a requirement for wireless communication systems with high data rates (Sneha et al. 2022). The indoor wireless connectivity degrades due to multipath fading and this can be resolved using MIMO technology (Kumar et al. 2019; Sundar et al. 2020; Zhuo et al. 2020). As the MIMO technology helps in improving the signal quality, this technology is widely used in designing the indoor antenna these days. Initially, the planar monopole antenna was proposed for ultra-wideband application, with the orthogonal polarization which is achieved by designing the multiple patches which are arranged orthogonal to each other (Ren et al. 2014; Kiem et al. 2014; Huang et al. 2015; Tripathi et al. 2015; Tao and Feng 2016). But the problem with these antennae is, that the size of the antenna is increased as the same antenna is placed sometimes. As the patch is placed nearby

---

The original version of this chapter has been revised. The affiliation for author "Praveen Kumar Malik" has been changed. The correction to this chapter can be found at https://doi.org/10.1007/978-981-99-0639-0_15.

Sneha (✉) · P. K. Malik
Department of Electronics and Communication, Lovely Professional University, Phagwara, India
e-mail: snehabhardwaj13@gmail.com

A. Alkhayyat
College of Technical Engineering, The Islamic University, Najaf, Iraq
e-mail: ahmedalkhayyat85@iunajaf.edu.iq

165

D. K. Sharma et al. (eds.), *Low Power Architectures for IoT Applications*, Springer Tracts in Electrical and Electronics Engineering, https://doi.org/10.1007/978-981-99-0639-0_9

to each other, some isolation techniques are required to improve the isolation of the antenna (Shin et al. 2020). Similarly, the fractal antenna provides a good bandwidth at a very low frequency as it resembles with large resonant length helps in decreasing the size of the antenna (Elijah and Mokayef 2020; Schnabel et al. 2013; Metz et al. 2001). In this article, we have proposed the Fractal patch MIMO antenna which can be utilized in NB-IoT applications. The proposed antenna is designed on an FR4 substrate of $\varepsilon_r = 4.4$, and excitation is provided using a lumped port. It is designed to cover the B1(2100), B3(1800), and B5 (800) bands of NB-IoT. The designed antenna is of dimension 20 mm × 10 mm. It is resonating at 2 GHz and provides a good bandwidth of 135%. The antenna is designed and simulated using HFSS.

Antenna Design and Analysis

The patch design steps which is used to evolve the fractal patch are shown in Fig. 9.1 in steps. The slant line is at 45° and the fractal shape is iterated in three steps in the last steps the fractal line is shaped into a polygon with five sides. The patch antenna is fed by two microstrip line which is placed orthogonally which helps in reducing the size of the antenna as compared with a conventional MIMO antenna. The mutual coupling between the port and patch is improved by increasing the distance between antenna ports. The substrate provides mechanical support to the patch antenna. here we used Flame retardant FR4 material which has a dielectric constant $\varepsilon_r = 4.4$ and substrate thickness is 1.6 mm, the patch antenna is designed on top of the substrate size of $20 \times 10 \, \text{mm}^2$, and the ground is designed on the other side or considered as the bottom of the substrate with the defected ground concept that helps in increasing the effective size of the grounds. The patch antenna is excited with a lumped port through the two microstrip feed line placed complementary to each other as mentioned in Fig. 9.2.

We aim to design a planar antenna for NB-IoT Applications. To achieve the required resonating frequency of the antenna we need to increase its resonating length in a very small dimension antenna so, we have the fractal technology and improve the signal quality reception we have used multiple input multiple output technology (Kaur and Malik 2021; Malik et al. 2020, 2022; Rahim and Malik 2021).

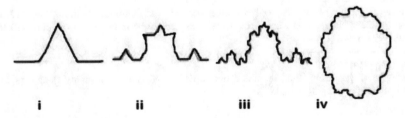

i   ii   iii   iv

Fig. 9.1 Design steps involved in the patch design

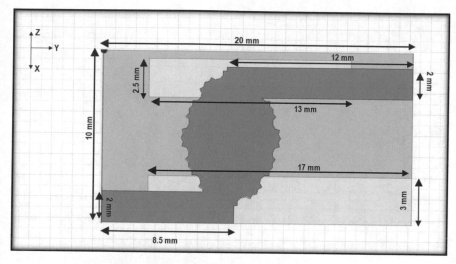

Fig. 9.2 The dimension of the patch antenna

The ground is designed in such a way that it helps in improving the isolation between two ports and improves mutual coupling. The antenna sideline is designed in three iterations in fractal design with skew angle zero and slat angle forty-five, so the fractal unit in the polygon has the size of 0.268 mm, after the third steps mention in the figure,1 the five-side polygon is designed as a radiator. For our NB-IoT application, the B1(2100), B3(1800), and B5 (800) bands are covered using this design. The radiator patch behaved as a shared patch between two feed lines of length.

Result and Findings

Here in the result section, To study the effect of the designed prototype we have studied its various parameter which is analyzed after stimulation of the designed antenna in HFSS. The reflection coefficient, S11 parameter is mentioned in Fig. 9.3 of the final designed antenna the antenna is resonating at 2.05 GHz and has an impedance bandwidth of 2 GHz. The values of through power are extracted from the voltage standing wave ratio (VSWR) according to the equation given below. This deduces that reflected power is only 10% from the radiating patch. The VSWR of the antenna is mentioned in Fig. 9.4.

Gain is one of the basic parameters of an antenna that measures the power delivering capability of the radiator from the transmitter side to the target. Gain depicts the maximum intensity of radiation caused by the radiating element when compared with the lossless isotropic antenna which is provided with the same amount of power. An antenna with a gain of 2 implies that the effective power delivered is twice when compared to an isotropic radiator, As the dimension of the antenna is very less so, the

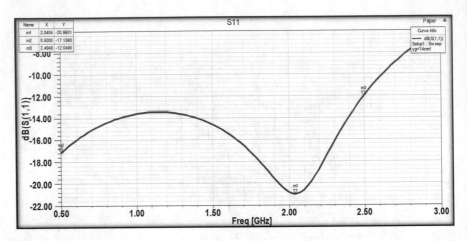

Fig. 9.3 Reflection coefficient of final designed antenna resonating at 2.09 GHz

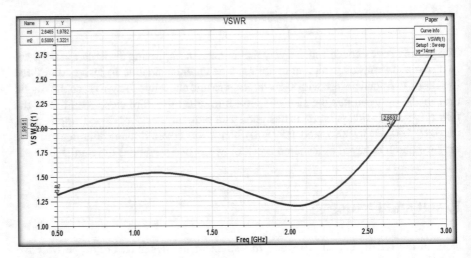

Fig. 9.4 The simulated VSWR of the final prototype

antenna gain is very less at low frequency and shows 2.15 dBi of gain around 4 GHz. The 2 D radiation pattern also mentioned the co polarization and cross-polarization of the antenna and it is mentioned in Fig. 9.5. A parametric study is also performed on the design concerning the feed length and feed width just to find the exact matching of port with feedline and antenna so that the efficiency of the antenna improves by reducing the reflection loss. Figure 9.6 shows the parametric study in which the width of feed (wf) is varing from 0.5 to 5 mm. As shown in figure the resonance is shifted from left to right with the increment in feed width. Figure 9.7 shows the variation in the reflection coefficient with respect to the length of feed. Table 9.1 is a

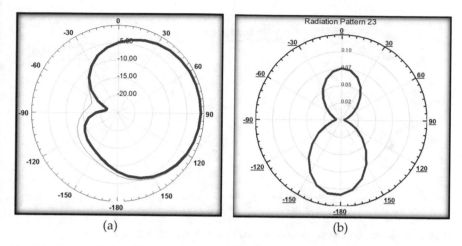

Fig. 9.5 2D Radiation pattern of the antenna in Phi plane (**a**) and Theta plane (**b**) of the antenna

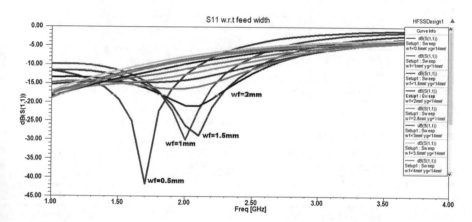

Fig. 9.6 Reflection coefficient variation with respect to the width of feed (wf)

brief comparison of our final antenna with the previously designed antenna by other authors which is published.

Conclusion

In this work, a noble compact two-port fractal antenna is designed for narrowband IoT applications. The patch is common between two feeds and the microstrip feed lines in orthogonal polarizations. The shared patch MIMO antenna is very small in size as compared to the conventional patch MIMO antenna in which two antenna is designed on a substrate. The antenna has bandwidth of 2 GHz covering 3 bands of

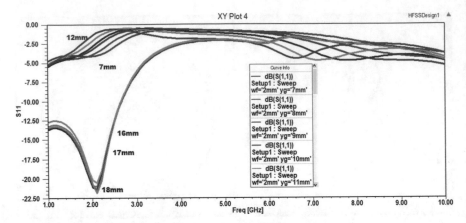

Fig. 9.7 Reflection coefficient variation with respect to length of feed (yg)

Table 9.1 Comparison of the final designed antenna with another available antenna for IoT technology

References	Antenna technology	Material of substrate	Operating frequency	Application	Size (mm³)
Giay and Alam (2018)	Antenna with array	FV	2.4 GHz	IoT	55 × 40 × 1.56
Pandey and Nair (2020)	Patch with DGS	FR4	871 MHz	LoRa	55 × 67 × 1.6
Sonawane et al. (2020)	Flexible printed antenna	Polyimide	868 MHz	IoT	23.9 × 23.5 × 0.19
Ta et al. (2017)	Rectangular patch with slot	FR4	915 MHz 2.45 GHz	IoT	56 × 40 × 3.2
Mushtaq et al. (2020)	Patch antenna	FR4	433 MHz	IoT	210 × 164 × 1.6
Duong Thi Thanh et al. (2017)	MPA with the stepped feed line	Taconic RF-35	5 and 10 GHz	IoT	2.70 × 3.74 × 5.36
ul-Haq and Kozieł (2017)	UCA & UIT design	FR-4	868 MHz	IoT	34 × 80 × 0.8
Trinh et al. (2017)	Folded antenna	Copper (PEC)	868 MHz	IoT	28 × 10 × 5
Lizzi and Ferrero (2015)	Ring-based slotted structure	FR-4	915 MHz 2.45 GHz	IoT	25 × 60 × 1
Mung et al. (2019)	Foldable and non-foldable structure	FR4	2.4 GHz ISM	IoT	56 × 60 × 3.2
Proposed antenna	Fractal design with MIMO	FR4	2.1 GHz	NB-IoT	10 × 20 × 1.6

NB-IoT, B1(2100), B3(1800), and B5 (800). The designed antenna is of dimension 20 mm × 10 mm. It is resonating at 2 GHz and provides a good bandwidth of 135%. The final fractal design is achieved in four iteration stages of the line and its slant line is at 45° angles. The designed antenna is fed by two complimentary placed microstrip lines and it is designed and simulated using HFSS. The DGS concept is used to improve the resonance and isolation in two-port antennae. The bandwidth and gain of the antenna can be further improved with other substrate materials and by introducing the metamaterial concept.

Acknowledgements This research work and paper would have been possible without the support of my supervisor. His knowledge and zest toward research keep us motivated toward work. This research work was supported by Lovely Professional University, Phagwara, Punjab, India.

References

Elijah AA, Mokayef M (2020) Miniature microstrip antenna for IoT application. Mater Today: Proc. https://doi.org/ https://doi.org/10.1016/j.matpr.2020.05.678

Giay Y, Alam BR (2018) Design and analysis 2.4 GHz microstrip patch antenna array for IoT applications using feeding method. In: 2018 international symposium on electronics and smart devices (ISESD). IEEE, Bandung, pp 1–3

Huang H, Liu Y, Zhang S-S et al (2015) Compact polarization diversity ultrawideband MIMO antenna with triple band-notched characteristics. Microw Opt Technol Lett 57(4):946–953

Kaur A, Malik PK (2021) Multiband elliptical patch fractal and defected ground structures microstrip patch antenna for wireless applications. Progr Electromagn Res B 91:157–173. ISSN:1937-6472. https://doi.org/10.2528/PIERB20102704

Kiem NK, Phuong HNB, Chien DN (2014) Design of compact 4 × 4 UWBMIMO antennae with WLAN band rejection. Int J Antennas Propag 1–11. https://doi.org/10.1155/2014/539094

Kumar P, Ghivela GC, Sengupta J (2019) Optimized N-sided polygon shaped microstrip patch antenna for UWB application. IEEE

Lizzi L, Ferrero F (2015) Use of ultra-narrow band miniature antennas for the internet of things applications. Electron Lett (IET Publisher) 51(24):1964–1966

Malik PK, Wadhwa DS, Khinda JS (2020) A survey of device to device and cooperative communication for the future cellular networks. Int J Wirel Inf Netw (Springer) 27:411–432. https://doi.org/10.1007/s10776-020-00482-8

Malik P, Lu J, Madhav BTP, Kalkhambkar G, Amit S (eds) (2022) Smart antennas: latest trends in design and application. Springer. ISBN 978-3-030-76636-8. https://doi.org/10.1007/978-3-030-76636-8

Metz C, Grubert J, Heyen J, Jacob A, Janot S, Lissel E et al (2001) Fully integrated automotive radar sensor with the versatile resolution. IEEE Trans Microw Theory Tech 49(12):2560–2566

Mung SWY, Cheung CY, Wu KM, Yuen JSM (2019) Wideband rectangular foldable and non-foldable antenna for internet of things applications. Int J Antennas Propag 2019:1–5

Mushtaq A, Gupta SH, Rajawat A (2020) Design and performance analysis of LoRa LPWAN antenna for IoT applications. In: 7th International conference on signal processing and integrated networks (SPIN)

Pandey A, Nair MVD (2020) Inset fed miniaturized antenna with defected ground plane for LoRa applications. Sci Direct Procedia Comput Sci 171:2115–2120

Rahim A, Malik PK (2021) Analysis and design of fractal antenna for efficient communication network in vehicular model. Sustain Comput: Inform Syst (Elsevier) 31:100586. ISSN 2210-5379. https://doi.org/10.1016/j.suscom.2021.100586

Ren J, Hu W, Yin Y et al (2014) Compact printed MIMO antenna for UWB applications. IEEE Antennas Wirel Propag Lett 13:1517–1520

Schnabel R, Hellinger R, Steinbuch D, Selinger J, Klar M, Lucas B (2013) Development of a mid range automotive radar sensor for future driver assistance systems. Int J Microw Wirel Technol 5:15–23

Sneha MPK, Bilandi N, Gupta A (2022) Narrow band-IoT and long-range technology of IoT smart communication: designs and challenges. Comput Ind Eng 172:108572. https://doi.org/10.1016/j.cie.2022.108572

Shin G, Park TR, Park J, Lee SK, Kim G, Yoon IJ (2020) Sustaining the radiation properties of a 900-MHz-Band planar LoRa antenna using a 2-by-2 thin EBG ground plane. IEEE Access 8:145586–145592

Sonawane S, Pathak H, Mistry S (2020) Design and analysis of FPC (Flexible Printed Circuit) antenna for LoRa frequency: 865–867 MHz application. Int J Sci Res Publ 10(5)

Sundar PS, Kotamraju SK, Ch SK, Madhav B, Srikanth Y, Babu N (2020) Pentagon shaped microstrip antenna for wireless IoT applications. J Critical Rev 7(14). ISSN-2394-5125

Ta SX, Choo H, Park I (2017) Broadband printed-dipole antenna and its arrays for 5G applications. IEEE Antennas Wirel Propag Lett 16:2183–2186

Tao J, Feng QY (2016) Compact isolation enhanced UWB MIMO antenna with band-notch character. J Electromagn Waves Appl 30:2206–2214. https://doi.org/10.1080/09205071.2016.1217173

Tiwari P, Malik PK (2021) Wide band micro-strip antenna design for higher "X" band. Int J e-Collaboration (IJeC) 17(4):60–74. https://doi.org/10.4018/IJeC.2021100105(ISSN:1548-3673)Oct2021

Trinh LH, Nguyen TQK, Phan DD, Tran VQ, Bui VX, Truong NV, Ferrero F (2017) Miniature antenna for IoT devices using LoRa technology. In: International conference on advanced technologies for communications, pp 170–173

Tripathi S, Mohan A, Yadav S (2015) Compact octagonal fractal UWB MIMO antenna with WLAN band-rejection. Microw Opt Technol Lett 57(8):1919–1925

ul-Haq MA, Kozieł S (2017) Design optimization and trade-offs of miniaturized wideband antenna for the internet of things applications. Metrol Meas Syst 24(3):463–471

Zhuo L, Han H, Shen X, Zhao H (2020) A U-shaped wide-slot dual-band broadband NB-IoT antenna with a rectangular tuning stub. In: IEEE 4th information technology, networking, electronic and automation control conference (ITNEC 2020)

Chapter 10
Development of Laser Beam Cutting Edge Technology and Iot Based Race Car Lapse Time Computational System

B. Thiyaneswaran, E. Ganasri, A. H. Hariharasudan, S. Kumarganesh, K. Martin Sagayam, Hien Dang, and Ahmed Alkhayyat

Introduction

The objective of racing contest is to determine the winner of the race. The participant who completes the race with pre-determined number of lapses in a shortest time will be announced the winner of the race. Racing was originated during 1920–1930s in Europe in order to entertain people. The basic set of rules for formula 10.1 racing was formed by FIA standardized racing in 1946. Other than the world championship series, many other non-championship races were also held after 1983. Every race has 4 drivers where they can switch the drivers if it is a long race and along with this the support staff of each team will also be present who plays the vital role in the team's success.

Each formula one racing has its unique characteristics. It depends on iconic tracks or it may be street circuits, it has different pre-determined set of lapses, it may have any specific distance. The number of lapses will be decided according to the length

B. Thiyaneswaran (✉) · E. Ganasri · A. H. Hariharasudan
Department of ECE, Sona College of Technology, Salem, Tamilnadu, India
e-mail: thiyanesb@yahoo.co.in

S. Kumarganesh
Department of ECE, Knowledge Institute of Technology, Salem, Tamilnadu, India

K. M. Sagayam
Department of ECE, Karunya Institute of Technology and Sciences, Coimbatore, Tamilnadu, India

H. Dang
Department of Computer Science, University of Massachusetts Boston, Boston, MA, USA
e-mail: hiendt@tlu.edu.vn

Faculty of Computer Science and Engineering, Thuyloi University, Hanoi, Vietnam

A. Alkhayyat
College of Technical Engineering, The Islamic University, Najaf, Iraq
e-mail: ahmedalkhayyat85@iunajaf.edu.iq

© The Author(s), under exclusive license to Springer Nature Singapore Pte Ltd. 2023
D. K. Sharma et al. (eds.), *Low Power Architectures for IoT Applications*, Springer Tracts in Electrical and Electronics Engineering, https://doi.org/10.1007/978-981-99-0639-0_10

of the racing circuit. At present Rx transmitter and receiver are used for calculating the lapse time in a race which high cost for fabrication, it can be used for multi car racing but in single car racing this project can be used where it has an advantage over the pre-existing system. One major advantage of using embedded systems is, it can be connected to the internet and can transfer data to various devices via internet all over the data.

In this research the lapse count, race starting time, race ending time, time taken for each lapse and their starting and ending time can be calculated using embedded systems and can be uploaded to the cloud via internet. Thus, the devices can communicate over the internet and it is known as the internet of things. As mentioned before time is a very important factor in racing and it should be sensed accurately. For sensing time, here we use LiDAR (light detection and ranging) sensor and it is also known as laser sensing.

At present, the race car lapse calculation techniques will have 2 sensors in it. One in the car and the other on the track. The exact position of the vehicle is estimated using the Global positioning system (GPS). Unique sensors on the vehicle enables a signal back again each time the when the vehicle crosses the start-finish line. There is a special type of sensors which is embedded on the track of the racing on the start-finish line which in turn signal computes to reset the duration timing of the lapse and increments the lapse count by 1. This is how the lapse and lap times are measured for a car.

Every car running on the track would have similar sensors on board. This gives the relative position of the cars. On track, sensors estimate the lap times. But this is cost prohibitive and for individual race car lapse calculations, investing large amounts is unnecessary. This ideology is different from the others as it uses a distance calculating sensor to calculate the lapse and it is also precise. Also, the fabrication cost is low for this project. LiDAR is a sensing technology which uses air as medium which helps in the fast collection of data and it has high accuracy.

The values are not influenced by the amount of light present, it gives exact value even in presence of dark and bright light. If you are trying to detect something moving quickly, the fast update rate will allow you to detect those targets as well. This system along with the instant display it also has the added advantage of updating the collected data to the cloud. The data can be updated instantly to the cloud and people from various places can view the data without any huge delay time. Thus, using LiDAR and embedded technology in racing is efficient.

Literature Review

A vehicle identification framework based on light detection and ranging sensor was proposed by Jian et al. (2022). This shows that the system has good stability under simple working conditions and it is cost efficient. Zhang et al. (2020) have proposed method that the vehicle speed is a key variable for detection and validation. LiDAR technologies have significant potential in quick detection of fast-moving objects. It proposes a tracking framework from roadside LiDAR to detect and track vehicles with the aim of accurate vehicle speed estimation. Deng et al. (2021) have proposed a paper that deals with path planning and vehicle control of racing car and realizing the safe driving of the car using LiDAR technology. The result of the actual experiment shows that the thesis can quickly detect the target of the racing car.

Chaari and Al-Rahimi (2021) have proposed a paper that deals with the idea of wirelessly charging internet of things (IOT) devices. It gives the solution to power up sensors and devices wirelessly via radio frequency (RF) energy. The breathing level monitoring process used the embedded system proposed by Thiyaneswaran et al. (2020a). The way of receiving data may useful for developing proposed system. Changyoung et al. (2020) have proposed that wireless power transmission can be achieved through various method but it is important to focus on power transmission distance and efficiency. This paper deals with multi antenna design which focus on the efficiency of power transmission.

The automatic observation and manipulation of automated vehicle tracking system with time-lapse was proposed by Dong et al. (2018). It works on the safety of vehicles and lapse calculation in racing. Kenneth et al. (2018) have proposed a paper that studies about the feasibility of time-lapse ground penetrating radar in deep excavation works and it helps to identify differences which are usually not notable by naked eye but by signal processed image. Park et al. (2018) have proposed a paper which deals with the problem that the fast-moving object cannot be calculated in time series as a solution to it taking pictures in time-lapse concept has been a great advantage. It periodically captures images of specific point over an extended period and replays it quickly (Thiyaneswaran et al. 2020b).

Vo et al. (2021) have proposed that autonomous vehicle has widely developed with radars, camera, and LiDAR technology in recent days, however, accuracy of measuring data is important when concerned about the safety of riders. Q-learning based gaussian mixture model can achieve a promising solution for lidar fault tolerant. The accuracy, false acceptance rate and other metric parameters are elaborated for testing out the system by Thiyaneswaran et al. (2023) and Kumarganesh et al. (2016). Sachan et al. (2021a) have stated that determining the distance between objects their shape and size in practical aspects with accuracy in current technologies is one of the challenging tasks. To overcome this LiDAR system uses the principle of measuring the time of flight of an optical signal to calculate the distance between the sensor and the object in an effective manner.

Ghanem et al. (2021) have stated that the advancement of autonomous driving and vehicular ad-hoc networks it is important to have vehicle to vehicle communication in an effective manner. Sharing traffic information collected by sensor with each improves driving safety, in this paper to increase the performance LiDAR technology is used in v2v communication. Sachan et al. (2021b) have stated that most of the existing vehicle detection models are single-modal based either LiDAR or camera. In this paper to increase the performance of vehicle detection multi-modal-based LiDAR-camera fusion is used. This multi-modal system works only in the presence of day light and only Lidar works in the absence of day light.

Azad et al. (2021) have proposed that autonomous driving has become remarkable in industry and private uses. Using a greater number of LiDAR's in order to reduce the blind spot of the LiDAR is cost effective. So, based on the kinetic behavior of the vehicle, dynamic analysis was performed and the angle of LiDAR detection changes with the rotation of the steering wheel. Priyadarshini et al. (2021b) have proposed that the autonomous driving vehicles have been commercialized so it is important to promote more efficient and safer autonomous driving technologies. LiDAR technologies is one of the most effective sensors in lane detection of roads and road curbs. To reduce the trade of between time consumption and object detection LiDAR technologies can be used.

Priyadarshini et al. (2021c) have proposed that LiDAR is one of the important technologies used in autonomous vehicle. Thus, as a critical sensor lidar needs to work in terrible weather condition such as rain, fog, snow, etc. using popular near-infrared (NIR) ToF LiDAR it shows that the sensor gives accurate results in extreme weather conditions also. Singh et al. (2021) have proposed that the fault detection algorithm in LiDAR sensor used in autonomous driving vehicle. Here an automotive LiDAR sensor is used to calculate the deviation between the actual distance and the ideal plane representing the target.

The lane information is an essential part of high-resolution traffic data was proposed by Sahu et al. (2021). Usage of high-density on board LiDAR cannot be used to process low-density road side data. Using ground recognition and lane marking point extraction low-density data can also be measured in autonomous driving. Zubaca et al. (2021) have proposed the system that state the capabilities of the algorithm can be applied to any race track, regardless of their curves, shape of the track, gate position, width, etc. It also has the advantage of low computational effort, which enables fast tuning during racing events.

Liniger and Lygeros (2019) have stated three different aims of racing are proposed to avoid collision accidents. In the first game the collision avoidance constraints are only followed by the follower. In the second game both the players are conscious about the collision constraints. The third game is designed to promote blocking. This research shows that the presented games can have different racing behaviors and generate interesting racing situations. Huang (2022) has proposed this paper which shows about the LiDAR-based simultaneous localization and mapping (LiDAR-SLAM) uses the sensor to build the map of the surrounding environment by observing the environmental features. Localization with high accuracy and practicability is a complex and hot issue in recent years.

Proposed Method

This project is applicable when one car is raced individually and its lapse count need to be calculated. It can also be used to calculate the speed of the racing car. This system has an advantage over other systems in terms of accuracy and fast detection of objects as we use LiDAR technology. The data which is acquired from the racing can also be displayed instantly and it can be updated in the cloud instantly for people to access and view the data from various places. LiDAR technology has an advantage over other pre-existing techniques like manual calculation of lapse in racing, ultrasonic sensors, fully automatic timing (FAT), Radio frequency identification (RFID), IR transmitter and receiver. The race car lapse cutting-edge calculation using laser beam is more efficient than the other technologies. Laser lights are not like other types of light forms such as flashlights. The beam stays focused and it will not spread out. Thus, laser beams are very narrow, bright and can travel for very long distances. The laser's light waves travel together with their peaks all lined up, or in phase.

Block Diagram

The developed system block diagram is shown in Fig. 10.1. The microcontroller used for this project is Arduino UNO board which is an open-source platform used for building embedded projects by Thiyaneswaran et al. (2022). It has Integrated Development Environment (IDE) along with a physical programmable circuit (Priyadarshini et al. 2021a). The sensor used for tracking the car is LiDAR (Light Detection and Ranging) sensor. It measures the time difference between the transmitted and reflected pulse and with this time difference the distance which is in between the obstacle and the sensing sensor can be calculated. LiDAR is one of the important components in this project because it emits a laser beam which has less expansion with travel distance. The sensor transmits and receives laser pulse in nano seconds of time so a very large amount of data can be fetched in a very short period of time which is one of the major benefits of using this sensor in racing.

$$D_s = c \times \frac{T}{2} \tag{10.1}$$

D_s is the distance between sensor and object
c is the speed of light in vacuum
T is the measured time between emitting and receiving the signal.

The LiDAR sensor is a famous sensing method which enables the user to know the exact distance of the object which is present in the surface of the earth. The LiDAR follows a basic principle in which it emits the laser light into the environment at an obstacle on the surface of the earth and calculates the time duration it takes to return to the receiver part of the LiDAR sensor. The distance can be calculated using the Eq. (10.1). The working of the sensor depends on the speed at which the light travels which is about 186,000 miles per second, the process of measuring the exact distance through LiDAR seems to be unbelievably fast than any other existing technologies.

The operating range of the LiDAR sensor is 0.1–12 m. It needs a supply voltage of minimum 5 V. The frame rate of this sensor is 10–1000 Hz. This sensor can be used in obstacle detection, obstacle avoidance, assisted landing, terrain following,

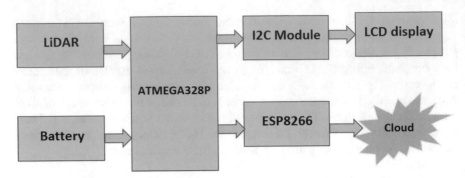

Fig. 10.1 Block diagram of developed system

vehicle position sensing, etc. It is compact in size and it is light weight. An LCD display is used to display the output in this project, if this is furnished in real entity then TFT display or any other large display can be used. The data is also uploaded to the google cloud so that people from various places can access the data with systems.

The lidar sensor starts working and gets the input, when the car cuts the laser beam the lapse count gets incremented this will continue until it reaches the total number of lapses required to complete the race. Once when this is completed, the LCD displays as the race is completed. Initially two push button switches are used in order to get the total number lapse count needed to complete the race.

The flow chart of the system developed system in Fig. 10.2 which one control switch when turned on, the other switch starts taking input and each time it is pressed, the lapse count value gets incremented. Once when we have done with giving the total number of lapse count, now turn off the Control switch. Now the microcontroller will have the total number of lapse count needed to complete the race by the car.

Simulation of Proposed System

The simulation system of proposed system is shown in Fig. 10.3. It shows the circuit diagram of the system which gives the simplified representation of the components of an electrical circuit. It also shows the relative position of all the elements and their connections to one another. Arduino UNO is the central unit of the circuit which is the microcontroller used in this system. A LiDAR sensor is connected to the system which is used to measure the distance of the car from the sensor. An LCD display along with the I2C module is also interfaced to the microcontroller board (Arduino UNO). Two switches are used to get the input from the user and a 9 v batter is used as the power supply for the system.

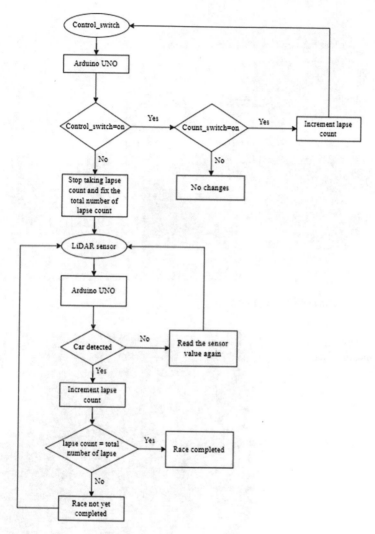

Fig. 10.2 Flow chart of the system

Results and Discussion

The developed system is tested in the practical environment before releasing the system into the market to ensure error free working of the system.

The hardware of the system shown in Fig. 10.4 has two switches for getting the final lapse count that is needed to end the race. The switches the connected with the resistor for regulating the power supply. The Arduino UNO board is used as a microcontroller and a LCD display is connected with the I2C module. I2C module is used to establish communication between two or more IC's. This display overcomes

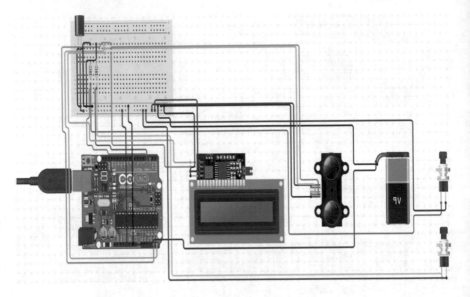

Fig. 10.3 Simulation of developed system

Fig. 10.4 Hardware
implementation of the
system

the drawback of LCD 16 × 2 parallel LCD display in which you will waste about 8 pins on your Arduino for the display for the display to get working.

The display progress of the developed system is shown in Fig. 10.5. Initially the system initiates the user to give the total lapse count as shown in Fig. 10.5a. The user starts entering the lapse count by pressing the push button switch. After the user enters the count, it gets incremented and the total lapse count is displayed for reference. The test system shows the entered values as 7 as shown in Fig. 10.5b. When the car starts moving the system starts calculating the lapse count. Every time a lapse

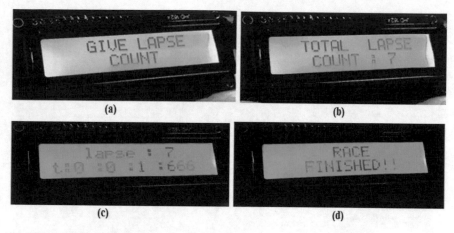

(a)

(b)

(c)

(d)

Fig. 10.5 Display of progress of developed system

is completed it is displayed on the LCD along with the duration of that lapse. Once the lapse count gets incremented and reaches the final count the race gets completed. Figure 10.5c shows the display of 7th race lapse. Now the race completion status is displayed on the LCD display. Figure 10.5d shows the race finished status in LCD display. Once the system is restarted this procedure takes place again from the start.

Figure 10.6 shows the data of the race which is acquired using race car lapse cutting edge using laser beam. These data are uploaded to cloud preferably google sheets for ease of access. It contains the date and time at which the race took place, the race lapse count, its starting and finishing time, and the duration of each lapse is also uploaded instantly.

Each trail is set with a specific lapse count. The graph is plotted between time in minutes and lapse count. Figure 10.7 represents the lapse count and time taken for each lapse in three different trails.

Table 10.1 shows the comparison between manual calculation, ultrasonic sensor, and LiDAR sensor. Through which we can conclude that LiDAR technology has an benefit over the other two methods in means of time delay, accuracy, and maximum distance coverage. This data is instantly uploaded to the cloud without any huge time delay and a link will be created by which the people even not in the racing region can view these race details precisely.

Using ultrasonic sensor in racing lapse calculation is not an effective idea. As the ultrasonic sensor works on the principle of emitting sound waves at a very high frequency in which one cannot hear it and receives them back. The time gap in between transmitting and receiving the signal is used to compute the distance between the sensor and the object. Here since it is a sound wave there will be a time delay in order to overcome this LiDAR sensors are used where it emits laser beam to calculate the distance between sensor and the object in nanoseconds of time delay.

Another method used in vehicle tracking is IR ID chip which acts as the key of IR sensor as it has the car identification number. Every IR sensor is fitted in the car

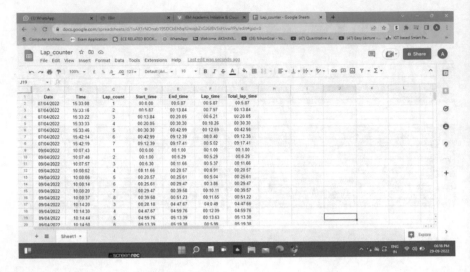

Fig. 10.6 Output in google spread sheet

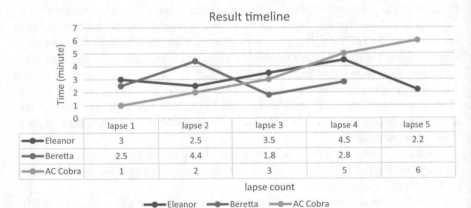

Fig. 10.7 Sample timeline and table of results

Table 10.1 Comparison between manual, ultrasonic and LiDAR lapse technology

	Manual calculation	Ultrasonic sensor	LiDAR technology
Max distance coverage	Not accurate	4 m	12 m
Time delay	More than a second	20–50 ms	1–10 ns

Table 10.2 Comparison between IR transmitter and LiDAR technology in lapse calculation

Lapse count	Lap time using IR transmitter (min)	Time delay (s)	Lap time found using LiDAR technology (min)	Time delay (ns)
1	2:30.18	0.1	2:30.17	0.1
2	3:42.11	0.2	3:42.09	0.2
3	4:11.23	0.2	4:11.21	0.2
4	5:21.33	0.1	5:21.32	0.1
5	6:18.09	0.2	06:18.07	0.1
6	7:37.17	0.1	07:37.16	0.1

and it is embedded with one IR ID chip which has the identification number of the vehicle. It also has a RF transmitter fitted to the car and it frequently transmits the RF signal toward its moving direction through the antenna. The receiver which is fitted in the control unit at specific point in the race track accepts the signal which is transmitted by the transmitter and sends the data to the system present in the nearby control room for getting the full details such as lapse count, lapse time, etc.

This system has an advantage when it comes to multiple car tracking but while single car is raced this system will not be accurate and cannot sense fast-moving vehicles. In LiDAR technology only have nano seconds of delay time. Table 10.2 shows the comparison between the IR transmitter and LiDAR technology in lapse calculation for racing. To be noted that the LiDAR technology gives the time delay in nanoseconds whereas the lapse time calculated using the IR transmitter and receiver has the time delay in seconds difference.

Table 10.3 shows the comparison between the recent technologies and LiDAR technologies and why LiDAR technologies has an advantage over the other two technologies. An RFID tag is a microchip which is attached to the car to track the position of the vehicle. The tag picks the signal from an RFID reader and scanner and then returns the signal, usually with some additional information such as start and finish time of the racing vehicle. The main disadvantage of this system is it cannot track the fast-moving vehicle like race cars. From the given information it is known that the LiDAR technology has more advantages over the other technologies for detecting fast-moving objects like a racing car with less amount of time delay.

Figure 10.8 represents the comparison between the different technologies that is used in lapse calculation for racing. The time delay, the minimum time that the object should be present in the sensor range so that the sensor can track its present and accuracy of the object are represented in the chart given below. The Radio Frequency Identification (RFID) is the advanced technologies that use wireless transformation of data between the tag or car and a reader or device to automatically trach or identify the physical location of each object. The system's transmission range is restricted to a few meters from the reader and the tag should be in a clear line of sight.

Table 10.4 shows the sample set of values obtained while using this system. The date at which the event occurred, time, lapse count, start time of each lapse, end time

Table 10.3 Comparison between recent technologies and LiDAR technology

Features	Radio frequency identification (RFID)	IR transmitter and receiver	LiDAR technology
Reader range (m)	0–2	0–5	0–12
Integration	Difficult	Difficult	Easy
Memory storage	No	Yes	Yes
IOT enabling	No	Yes	Yes
Response	Identification	Identification + positioning	Identification + positioning + speed
Cost of fabrication	Expensive	Expensive	Affordable

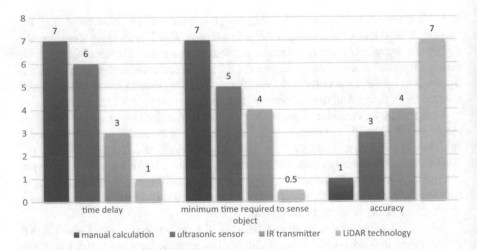

Fig. 10.8 Comparison between different technologies available in lapse calculation

Table 10.4 Information that was obtained with this system

S.no	Date	Time	Lap count	Start time	End time	Lap time	Total lap time
1	17/10/2002	15:33:08	1	00:0.00	00:5.87	00:5.87	00:5.87
2	17/10/2002	15:33:16	2	00:5.87	00:13.84	00:7.97	00:1.84
3	17/10/2002	15:33:22	3	00:13.84	00:20.05	00:6.21	00:20.05
4	17/10/2002	15:33:33	4	00:20.05	00:30.30	00:10.26	00:30.30
5	17/10/2002	15:33:46	5	00:30.30	00:42.99	00:12.69	00:42.98
6	17/10/2002	15:42:14	6	00:42.99	09:12.39	08:0.40	09:12.38

of each lapse, duration of each lapse, and the total race time was calculated with this system.

This system was tested against the fully automatic timing (FAT) system to check its accuracy and efficiency. Fully automatic timing (FAT) is a famous type of racing

Table 10.5 Accuracy of the system when compared against FAT

Lapse count	FAT	LiDAR technology
1	00:5.11	00:5.11
2	00:6.45	00:6.45
3	00:4.98	00:4.97
4	00:5.21	00:5.21
5	00:6.11	00:6.10
6	00:5.55	00:5.55
7	00:6.32	00:6.31

timing system that helps to get the race results that are accurate to 0.01 of a second. This system needs a start signal, running time, and capture device to be digitally synchronized to ensure accuracy. This system is designed in such a way that it is activated automatically by a initiation signal, rather than manual initiation. In this the start signal is generated by the start sensor which is integrated with a gun which is used to start the race. The finish time must also be recorded electronically to remove any human error. The finish signal is generated by the ribbon or string. The sample readings that have been acquired in this system is shown in Table 10.5. The readings in the table shows that LiDAR technology can be accurate and it does not need any external activation system for initiation like FAT.

The common issue of difficulty in lapse calculation is directed in this paper in an efficient manner. This system enables uninterrupted monitoring and storing of race-related information. This data is displayed through LCD display for instant viewing. It is cost friendly, efficient, and accurate in terms of time measurements.

Conclusion

The proposed system was developed and hardware configuration was implemented. The laser beam-based LiDAR was suitably utilized in the developed system. The ATMEGA328 controller was used to access the LiDAR technology. The perfect triggering was performed to activate the LiDAR when racing element crossed the beam. The race car lapse cutting edge using laser beam had fabricated and tested. The results of this system were accurate and even nano seconds of differences can be calculated and this was compared with the precision model which is the fully automatic timing (FAT) system. There are no huge differences which states that the system is accurate. The data was also uploaded to cloud using internet of things (IOT). LiDAR technology has many advantages in racing sector where fast-moving objects can be detected effectively. The developed system can able to track the maximum of 12 M track width with maximum 10 ns computation.

References

An C, Ryu HG (2020) Multiple antennas design for the RF wireless power transfer system. In: IEEE wireless power transfer conference (WPTC)

Azad C, Bhushan B, Sharma R et al (2021) Prediction model using SMOTE, genetic algorithm and decision tree (PMSGD) for classification of diabetes mellitus. Multimed Syst. https://doi.org/10.1007/s00530-021-00817-2

Chaari MZ, Al-Rahimi R (2021) Energized IoT devices through RF wireless power transfer. In: International symposium on electrical and electronics engineering (ISEE)

Deng C, Liu G, Jia A, Wen X, Ma K, Ying B (2021) Study on LiDAR obstacle detection for FSAC racing car. In: 4th international conference on intelligent autonomous systems (ICoIAS)

Dong S, Liu X, Lin Y, Arai T, Kojima M (2018) Automated tracking system for time lapse observation. In: IEEE international conference on mechatronics and automation (ICMA)

Ghanem S, Kanungo P, Panda G et al (2021) Lane detection under artificial colored light in tunnels and on highways: an IoT-based framework for smart city infrastructure. Complex Intell Syst. https://doi.org/10.1007/s40747-021-00381-2

Huang L (2022) Review on LiDAR-based SLAM techniques. In: International conference on signal processing and machine learning (CONF-SPML)

Jin X, Yang H, Li Z (20222) Vehicle detection framework based on LiDAR for autonomous driving. In: 5th CAA international conference on vehicular control and intelligence (CVCI)

Kenneth PAKCW, Ren G, Li J, Lai WW-L (2018) Feasibility study of time lapse ground penetrating radar as monitoring measures for deep excavation works. In: 17th international conference on ground penetrating radar (GPR)

Kumarganesh S, Suganthi M (2016) An efficient approach for brain image (tissue) compression based on the position of the brain tumor. Int J Imaging Syst Technol 26(4): 237–242. https://doi.org/10.1002/ima.22194

Liniger A, Lygeros J (2019) A noncooperative game approach to autonomous racing. IEEE Trans Control Syst Technol 28(3)

Park K-W, Choi D, Jeon W-J (2018) Applying time-lapse concepts onto storage system for long-term system trace analysis: technical challenges and blueprints. In: IEEE first international conference on artificial intelligence and knowledge engineering (AIKE)

Priyadarshini I, Mohanty P, Kumar R et al (2021a) A study on the sentiments and psychology of twitter users during COVID-19 lockdown period. Multimed Tools Appl. https://doi.org/10.1007/s11042-021-11004-w

Priyadarshini I, Kumar R, Tuan LM et al (2021b) A new enhanced cyber security framework for medical cyber physical systems. SICS Softw Inensiv Cyber-Phys Syst. https://doi.org/10.1007/s00450-021-00427-3

Priyadarshini I, Kumar R, Sharma R, Singh PK, Satapathy SC (2021c) Identifying cyber insecurities in trustworthy space and energy sector for smart grids. Comput Electr Eng 93:107204

Sachan S, Sharma R, Sehgal A (2021a) Energy efficient scheme for better connectivity in sustainable mobile wireless sensor networks. Sustain Comput: Inform Syst 30:100504

Sachan S, Sharma R, Sehgal A (2021b) SINR based energy optimization schemes for 5G vehicular sensor networks. Wirel Pers Commun. https://doi.org/10.1007/s11277-021-08561-6

Sahu L, Sharma R, Sahu I, Das M, Sahu B, Kumar R (2021) Efficient detection of Parkinson's disease using deep learning techniques over medical data. Expert Syst 12787. https://doi.org/10.1111/exsy.12787

Singh R, Sharma R, Akram SV, Gehlot A, Buddhi D, Malik PK, Arya R (2021) Highway 4.0: digitalization of highways for vulnerable road safety development with intelligent IoT sensors and machine learning. Safety Sci 143:105407. ISSN 0925-7535

Thiyaneswaran B, Bhuvaneshwaran V, Dharun M, Gopu K, Gowsikan T (2020a) Breathing level monitoring and alerting by using embedded IOT. J Green Eng 10(6):2986–2994

Thiyaneswaran B, Anguraj K, Kumarganesh S, Thangaraj K (2020b) Early detection of melanoma images using gray level co-occurrence matrix features and machine learning techniques for effective clinical diagnosis. Int J Imaging Syst Technol 31(2):682–694

Thiyaneswaran B (2022) IOT based smart cold chain temperatur monitoring and alert system for vaccination container. Przeglad Elektrotechniczny 1(8):208–210. https://doi.org/10.15199/48.2022.08.38

Thiyaneswaran B, Kumarganesh S, Martin SK, Dang H (2023) An effective model for the iris regional characteristics and classification using deep learning alex network. IET Image Processing 17(1):227–238. https://doi.org/10.1049/ipr2.12630

Vo MT, Vo AH, Nguyen T, Sharma R, Le T (2021) Dealing with the class imbalance problem in the detection of fake job descriptions. Comput Mater Continua 68(1):521–535

Zhang J, Xiao W, Coifman B, Mills JP (2020) Vehicle tracking and speed estimation from roadside Lidar. IEEE J Sel Top Appl Earth Obs Remote Sens 13

Zubaca J, Stolz M, Watzenig D (2021) smooth reference line generation for a race track with gates based on defined borders. In: IEEE intelligent vehicles symposium (IV)

Chapter 11
IoT-Based Solar-Assisted Low-Cost Ceramic Water Purification in Rainwater Harvesting System

Ramesh Chandra Panda and Md. Safikul Islam

Introduction

Water scarcity is a well-known issue around the world. According to the 2016 World Economic Forum, the greatest global threat for the next ten years is water scarcity (ahead of climate change, the food crisis, people migration, weapons of mass destruction, etc.). In areas where rain falls frequently, rainwater collecting and strong rainwater for conversion into drinking water aid to reduce drinking water scarcity. People in developing countries have been known to have trouble finding safe drinking water, especially during the summer. A natural IoT-based system for collecting and storing rainfall that turns it into drinking water has been presented as a solution to this problem. Water management is one of the Sustainable Development Goals (SDG). One of the water crisis management approaches is to build the ability to store rainwater and convert it to drinking water. Water quality is determined by its physical, chemical, and biological qualities. Each of these three sorts of characteristics has its own set of standards for water quality. Physical entities are color, odor, turbidity, temperature, and conductivity while the chemical parameters for water quality assessment are pH, acidity, alkalinity, hardness, solid harmful chemicals, chlorides, sulfates, iron, nitrates, heavy metals, and pesticides. One of the factors of water quality is temperature. If rainwater is gathered and stored for future use, it is supposed to be one of the sources of potable water (free of chemical pollution). This invention is based on the use of temperature to increase the quality of collected

R. C. Panda
Research Development Cell, Synergy Institute of Engineering and Technology, Dhenkanal, Orissa, India

Md. Safikul Islam (✉)
Dr. Ambedkar International Centre (DAIC), Ministry of Social Justice and Empowerment, New Delhi, India
e-mail: safik.delhi@gmail.com

Department of Geography, Jamia Millia Islamia, New Delhi, India rainwater. In this process, the required components are (i) solar heater as per the capacity (ii) PVC pipe as per the capacity (iii) temperature-controlled solenoid valve with appropriate capacity (iv) storage as per the capacity (v) ceramic material to filter the water inside the PVC pipe.

Major Traditional Rainwater Harvesting Systems in India

Any approach intended to address the challenge of water scarcity in India must include water conservation as a crucial component. The government of India has started investigating ways to resuscitate the nation's historic water collection systems because rainfall patterns are changing practically every year (Pal 2016). Given that most of these techniques are straightforward and environmentally friendly, they are not only very useful for the individuals who rely on them but also beneficial for the environment.

- Direct raindrop harvesting took place. They gathered water from rooftops, stored it in tanks constructed in their courtyards, and then used it. They gathered rainwater from open community lands and kept it in man-made wells.
- When it rained during the monsoon season, they harvested monsoon runoff by collecting water from overflowing streams and storing it in various types of water bodies.
- The flooded rivers were used to capture water.

Talab

These are reservoirs (Centre for Science and Environment no date) where rainwater is collected and stored for use in drinking and domestic purposes. They could be man-made, like the lakes in Udaipur, or they could be natural, like the *Pokhariyan* ponds near Tikamgarh in the Bundelkhand region. Small lakes are referred to as *Talais*, medium-sized lakes as *Bandhis*, and larger lakes as *Sagars* or *Samands*. Talais have an area of less than five bighas.

Taanka

This is a primitive method of collecting rainwater that was first used in Rajasthan's Thar desert. Rainwater from roofs, courtyards, or intentionally created catchments runs into a cylindrical, paved subterranean pit called a Taanka. The water in a Taanka can be fully filled once, and it can provide a household of 5–6 people for the whole of the dry season. Taankas, a crucial component of water security in these desert areas, can spare families from the daily hardship of obtaining water from far-off sources.

Johads

Small earthen check dams called Johads are one of the earliest methods of groundwater conservation and recharge. They collect and store rainwater. Excavated earth is used to make a storage pit, which is then utilized to build a wall on the fourth side, in a location with three sides that are naturally elevated. There are instances when numerous Johads are joined by deep channels, with a single outlet leading into a nearby river or stream. This guards against structural damage to the water pits, also known as *Pemghara* in Odisha and *Madaka* in Karnataka.

Kund

A kund is a circular subterranean well in the center of a jug-shaped catchment area that gently slopes in that direction. Rainwater collection for drinking is its main objective. Western Rajasthan and Gujarat's drier regions are covered in Kunds. Although many contemporary Kunds have been built simply out of cement, historically these well-pits were covered in hygienic lime and ash.

Baoli

The characteristic features of these magnificent stepwells include lovely arches, carved designs, and perhaps rooms on the sides. Groundwater is collected from the bottom while rainwater is collected from above of the well. Baolis are frequently employed as a clue as to their purpose by their locations. Baolis were primarily utilized in villages for social gatherings and daily-use purposes. It was common practice to stop in Baolis along trade routes to rest. Water was directed into the fields via drainage systems in stepwells that were only utilized for agriculture.

Eri

One of the earliest water management systems in India is the Eri (tank) system used in Tamil Nadu. Eris, which are still frequently employed in the state, serve as flood-controlling mechanisms, stop soil erosion and runoff waste during the time of heavy rains, and help rehydrate the groundwater. Eris can either be a system Eri, which receives its water through canals that redirect river water, or a non-system Eri, which receives its water only from rainfall. The tanks are connected to make it possible to reach the farthest village and to maintain a steady water level in the event of an oversupply. Without the Eri method, paddy farming in Tamil Nadu would not have been viable because it allows for the full utilization of river water for irrigation.

Nadi

Nadis are village ponds that collect rainfall from surrounding natural catchment regions and are located close to Jodhpur in Rajasthan. The site of a Nadi is selected after careful consideration of its catchment and runoff characteristics since the location of a Nadi has a significant impact on its storage capacity. Nadis rapidly silted because they frequently acquired heavy deposits of sand from the irregular, torrential rainfall that provided their water source. In order to stop siltation, an area nonprofit organization called the *Mewar Krishak Vikas Samiti* (MKVS) has been pushing afforestation of the drainage basin and installing systems like spillways and silt traps on old Nadis.

Zabo

The Zabo method, which means "impounding run-off," integrates water conservation with farming, forestry, and animal care. Zabo, commonly referred to as the Ruza method, is a practiced in Nagaland. Rainwater from forested hilltops is collected via canals, and the runoff water is then deposited in pond-like structures built on the terraced slopes. Before eventually wandering into rice fields at the base of the hill, the channels also pass-through cattle yards where they gather the manure and urine of the animals. The fish are raised in ponds made on the paddy field, and medicinal plants are also encouraged to flourish there.

Recent Rainwater Harvesting System

It is made up of a collection region (the roof), conveyance (guttering, downspouts, pipework, and first flush), filtration, storage, and distribution. Rainwater is moved from the roof to the storage container using guttering. Guttering typically attaches to the structure or bamboo hut beneath the roof and collects rainwater as it drips from the roof.

Primary flushing system: The roof of a structure or another collection location will gather debris, dirt, dust, and animal droppings. This undesired material will be washed into the tank when the first rains come.

Filtration setup: When rainwater enters a tank, the sand-charcoal-stone filter is frequently employed to filter the water. Silt and other suspended solids can be removed from the water using dividers and settling tanks.

Storage system: Both natural and artificial storage devices (tanks) can be used to recharge underground water aquifers. They can come in a variety of shapes and sizes and be fashioned of a variety of locally accessible materials. Consequently, their price fluctuates. Two different types of rainwater storage systems could exist: a straightforward rooftop system and one powered by geothermal energy.

Advantages of Harvesting Rainwater

- Enhancement of ground water quality
- An increase in water levels in dry bore wells and wells with wells.
- Reducing the consequences of the drought
- An ideal response to water issues in regions with insufficient water resources 5.
- A decrease in soil erosion as a result of less surface runoff
- Offers soft, low-mineral water of excellent quality.
- Lowers the expense of pumping ground water.

Necessity for Purification of Rainwater

Fresh water can only be obtained naturally through rain. In general, 5–20% of total precipitation is used to replenish ground aquifers. Only a small portion of the precipitation from surface runoff may be stored in topsoil. Without substantial input to the aquifer system, a significant amount of rainwater eventually makes its way to lakes, ponds, etc. through streams.

Rainwater may be contaminated with one or more of the following substances, making it dangerous to drink without first purifying it.

- as raindrops travel to the earth's surface, they pick up dust, dangerous chemicals, smoke, and other airborne pollutants.
- When it reaches the earth's surface, it becomes mixed with dead insects, sand, algae, twigs, and other debris.
- E. coli, microbes, and other potentially life-threatening germs proliferate in the contaminated water.
- Rainwater from specific older roof types may have dissolved asbestos, a fibrous-silic material that is a carcinogen (a substance that may become a leading cause of cancers).

Methods of Purification for Harvested Rainwater

A private company named "Chaitanya" dealing with rain harvest products revealed a couple of methods of purification for harvested rainwater (Converting Rainwater into Potable Drinking Water—Methods and Benefits 2018). According to the company, the ideal approach to use rainwater for drinking purposes is to set up a system at home for collecting it and filtering it before using it. The following are a few equipment and naturally based techniques for turning rainfall into drinkable water reserves:

Equipment Based Method

Before rainfall enters the conveyance system, the water from the catchment regions must pass-through the first flush devices to remove visible and big contaminants including leaves, twigs, bird droppings, and sand, among others (distribution pipes). The gutter screens can be fitted alongside first flush devices at the catchment area's outside edges. As a result, the conveyance system's obstruction will be lessened, lowering the cost of maintenance. To keep pollutants confined to the bottom of the water storage tanks, filters are required. A screen filter, a paper filter, and a carbon or charcoal filter are examples of filtration systems.

Naturally Based Methods

Although filters are excellent in removing obtrusively large contaminants from rainwater harvesting, they cannot get rid of all contaminants. Filtration techniques that result in the elimination of soluble contaminants are necessary for high-quality drinking water.

Chlorine treatment: Mostly, chlorination is the primary method of disinfection in the public water system. Cholera, typhoid, dysentery, and hepatitis are just a few of the waterborne illnesses that chlorine is good in curing. However, caution must be exercised because chlorine is very reactive and can mix with a variety of different organic substances that are found in nature, potentially leading to dangerous combinations that could be damaging to human health.

Using Ultra Violet (UV) lights: The genetic makeup of water can be disrupted by ultraviolet radiation, which prevents microorganism cells from reproducing. Water must go through the filtration system before being exposed to UV rays for treatment.

Using membrane filtration: Membrane filtration is another option to traditional filtration techniques. Reverse osmosis (RO), microfiltration, ultrafiltration, and nanofiltration are a few examples of membrane technologies that operate under pressure. Reverse osmosis, when compared to other membrane technologies, is the most popular. Radium, natural organics, pesticides, cysts, germs, and viruses, as well as other tiny particles like 0.001 microns in size, are all things they can get rid of. However, because a significant amount of water is drained out during the process of eliminating pollution, RO systems waste water. Despite being small and best suited for domestic use, RO systems are still available.

Distillation: The easiest way to purify water is Distillation method. In order to evaporate the pollutants from the water, it is first heated to a boil. The cleaned water that condenses is then collected in containers. Evaporation causes the loss of 5–10% of the water. Except for volatile organic compounds (VOCs), the distillation process may almost eliminate all contaminants from water. VOC removal may be aided by the use of carbon filters in a distillation system.

Recognized Research on IoT-Based Rain Water Harvesting

There have been found few recent research on IoT-based rainwater harvesting, drawing the development in the concerned field. In 2018, Vinoj and Gavaskar (2018) proposed a smart centralized rainwater harvesting solution that included more sensors (rainwater sensor, ultrasonic sensor), as well as Arduino (microcontroller), to save the rainwater process. After one year of this study, another study (Gannoju et al. 2019) looked into the role of IoT in addressing climate change and improving energy efficiency. In comparison to other survey articles, the authors of this research examine IoT architecture and technical aspects. In the very next year, a couple of studies have been found in employing smart approaches for harvesting rainwater. The first study looked at how to effectively monitor rainwater and evaluate information using IoT in order to design rainwater harvesting systems for catchment areas (Chandrika Kota et al. 2020). The second study has tried to find not only the way of water harvesting but also the improving the quality of harvested water with the help of IoT-based smart technology (Ranjan et al. 2020). The present study has applied solar energy during the purification of harvested water, which is identical to the study of Chandrika Kota et al. (2020) who used a solar panel to charge the battery through charging the controller. But, any of the aforesaid studies have not used ceramic pot for filtering the water. This study has invented this inexpensive purification of harvested water through IoT-based solar-assisted medium.

Working Principle

The most pressing issue confronting the twenty-first century is acute water scarcity. The best way to deal with the water crisis is to use it properly by collecting rainwater and consuming it effectively and responsibly. Rooftops, land surfaces, and rock catchments are all options for collecting rainwater. Rainwater harvesting is a sustainable method with no negative consequences, which is one of its most important features. Individual places only require a small amount of water; hence a large quantity of water is not required. Local water harvesting systems, on the other hand, are often small and thus ineffective. Effective options for cleaner and less expensive rainwater harvesting systems will be of the highest relevance in areas affected hard by clean water shortages due to geographical regions, socio-economic values, and industrial waste per unit.

The study on IoT-based solar-assisted ceramic-based water purification for natural rainwater harvesting primarily intends to offer cleaner and drinkable water for practically every household, as well as on a large scale when needed.

The idea behind IoT-based rooftop rainwater harvesting is to collect and store rainfall in a tank that is ideally located on the roof and let it flow to a directed thin glass tank using gravity (Fig. 11.1). Rainwater accumulated in the glass tank will be covered at an angle by a slanted glass layer. After reaching a sufficient temperature, the sun's rays fall on the stored water via the glass surface, killing the majority of the hazardous germs. When the water inside the glass tank reaches a particular temperature, the droplets form on the inner surface of the slanted glass layer and begin to evaporate. This water droplet will be gathered through a tube that will be put just beneath the thin glass layer and will lead to an IoT sensor-equipped outlet valve that will collect the evaporated water. The water will be passed via a temperature sensor with a digital display before being filtered. The initial phase in the process is filtering, which should remove roughly 60% of the dangerous bacteria and other organisms. The evaporated water collected in a secondary tank is permitted to run through a ceramic vessel for secondary filtration, which removes any remaining dangerous organisms and pollutants.

Ceramic water filters are a traditional water filtration technology. This process, developed by Henry Doulton in 1827, involves passing water through a porous ceramic media to remove bacteria, parasites, and other microorganisms. It's a low-cost, versatile water filtration system that may be placed in homes or used as a supplementary transportable filtering device. Ceramic filters on the pot allow the stored water to travel via a network of small pores measuring roughly half a micron

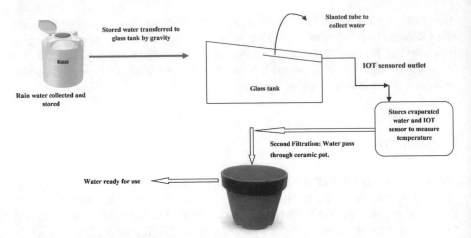

Fig. 11.1 Fundamentals of rainwater harvesting system

in diameter. As the water travels through these pores, the contaminants are trapped, making the water safe to drink and useful for a variety of other reasons. Bacteria, sediments, and turbidity are all removed from the water using ceramic pots. The water obtained from the second step of filtering through the ceramic pot can be used for a variety of reasons, including domestic use, gardening, sanitation, and cleaning.

Flowchart of Harvesting Water

A flow chart of the rainwater harvesting system has been portrayed for a better understanding of innovation (Fig. 11.2).

Steps

i.   The collected rainwater is stored in the Primary Storage (Sintex).
ii. The collected rainwater is transferred to a glass container by the principle of gravity.
iii. Adjust the lid of the glass container slanted at a certain angle (say 30°).
iv. As the sun rays fall on the glass container, the water droplets formed by evaporation shall be collected through a glass tube fitted beneath the slanted lid of the glass container.
v.   These vaporized water droplets are allowed to pass-through an IoT sensors outlet valve that is adjusted at certain specifications. If not, the IoT specifications should be adjusted again.
vi. Once Specifications are at par, the stored evaporated water droplets are transferred to third storage with an attached temperature-controlled solenoid valve. This allows for measuring the temperature adequately.

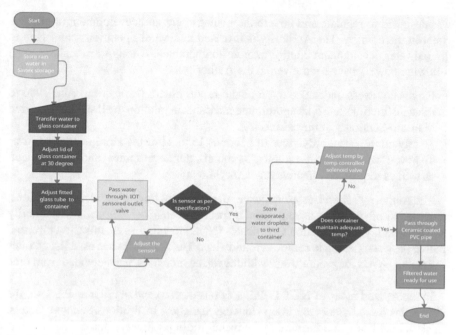

Fig. 11.2   Detailed flow chart of harvesting water with the application of IoT

vii.   Once the adequate temperature is reached killing around 60% of waterborne pathogens, it is passed through a porous ceramic-coated PVC pipe.

viii. This second stage of filtration ensures to kill remaining harmful bacteria and any other chemicals, pathogens making it efficient for drinking purposes.

ix.   The filtered water shall be used for testing its chemical properties like alkaline value, pH value, chlorides, sulfates, nitrate, iron, pesticides, etc.

Policy for Educational Institutions Against Rain Water Harvesting System

Surplus monsoon runoff that flows into the sea must be preserved and recharged in order to augment rapidly depleting groundwater reserves. The Central Ground Water Board (CGWB), a constituent office of India's Ministry of Water Resources, is the National Supreme Authority charged with gathering empirical contributions for the management, research, surveillance, analysis, enhancement, and regulation of the country's groundwater resources. The Central Ground Water Authority (CGWA) was established on 14th January 1997, according to an order of the Hon'ble Supreme Court of India, under sub-Section (3) of Section 3 of the Environment (Protection) Act, 1986, to regulate groundwater management and development in the country. It was designed to regulate and govern the management and development of ground-water in the country. The Authority is involved in several operations connected to groundwater development control in order to guarantee its long-term viability. The following powers have been given to the Authority:

- Exercise powers under Section 5 of the Environment (Protection) Act, 1986 to issue instructions and take appropriate measures in relation to all subjects referred to in sub-Section 3 of the said Act.
- To rely on the penal provisions of Sections 15 to 21 of the aforementioned Act.
- To govern and regulate the country's groundwater development and management, as well as to provide effective regulatory directions.

The Authority supervises groundwater development through advice, instructions, notices, and other means as and when a specific scenario develops. The Authority has been issuing No Objection Certificates (NOC) to enterprises, infrastructure, and mining projects seeking to remove groundwater. The Authority has established rules for issuing NOCs for groundwater withdrawals, which have been updated from time to time.[1]

In recognized areas of NCT Delhi, sections of Haryana, and Uttar Pradesh, the CGWA has issued orders to Group Housing Societies, Institutions/Schools, Hotels, Industrial facilities, and farmhouses to install rooftop rainwater harvesting systems as a regulatory action.

The Central Ground Water Board has issued Directions to all Residential Group Housing Societies/Institutions/Schools/Hotels/Industrial Establishments falling in the over-exploited and critical areas (except in water-logged areas) in the country to adopt Roof Top Rain Water Harvesting Systems in their premises via Public Notice dated 8.10.2009.

Directions were sent through a letter dated 8.8.2006 to Chief Secretaries in 12 states and administrations in two union territories with over-exploited blocks to take the appropriate actions to encourage artificial recharge to groundwater/rainwater collection.

Because water is a state concern, state governments/UTs must establish legislation for groundwater development and regulation. The Union Government, on the other hand, has distributed a Model Bill to the States and Union Territories for them to implement appropriate legislation for groundwater development management and control. The bill was first circulated in 1970, and it was re-circulated for enactment in 1992, 1996, and 2005.

State governments are making some efforts to improve rainwater collecting efficiency and artificial groundwater replenishment. The Central Government supports state governments' efforts by providing technical and financial help through a variety of initiatives and programs. Rainwater harvesting has been made compulsory in several states and union territories by establishing legislation, establishing laws and

---

[1] http://cgwb.gov.in/CGWA/Documents/Approved%20Guidelines%20for%20evaluation%20of%20proposals.pdf.

regulations, including provisions in building bye-laws, or through relevant government directives. Rainwater harvesting has been implemented in the states of Andhra Pradesh, Gujarat, Haryana, Himachal Pradesh, Kerala, Madhya Pradesh, Maharashtra, and Tamil Nadu. Ranchi Regional Development Authority, Bombay Municipal Corporation, Pimpri-Chinchwad Municipal Corporation, Municipal Corporation of Ludhiana, Improvement Trust, Jalandhar, Jaipur Municipal Corporation, and Mussoorie Dehradun Development Authority, to name a few, have made significant progress in rainwater harvesting development. Furthermore, the Union Territories of Delhi, Daman & Diu, and Puducherry have made rainwater harvesting system installation obligatory in their development bye-laws. Andaman and Nicobar, Lakshadweep, and Karnataka have all taken steps in this direction. The Orissa government is actively considering the creation of comprehensive water laws. As and when necessary, the Law will take the required steps to make rooftop rainwater collecting mandatory.

Interventions from Government Nodal Agencies

Recently[2] The University Grants Commission also issued a circular instructing all affiliated colleges and institutions to install Rain Water Harvesting Structures (RWHS) on their campuses as part of the National Water Mission's 'Catch the Rain' campaign, which aims to conserve water, reduce waste, and ensure more equitable distribution both across and within states. The National Water Mission's 'Catch the Rain' program was launched to encourage states and stakeholders to prepare rainwater harvesting infrastructure before the monsoon season begins, with a focus on gathering rain as it falls, where it falls. Apart from rainwater harvesting structures, educational institutions must also organize activities such as moves to build water harvesting pits, rooftop RWHS, check dams, and other water harvesting structures; removal of obstructions in the channels that bring water to them from catchments, and so forth.

Even the National Assessment and Accreditation Council (NAAC) guidebook for self-study reports of institutions emphasizes Institutional Values and Social Responsibilities under its assessment Criterion VII. It examines and grades institutions based on their sensitivity to topics such as climate change and environmental issues. Furthermore, if the institute follows environmentally friendly practices and takes the appropriate steps, such as energy-saving, rainwater harvesting, garbage recycling, and so forth.

---

[2] https://www.ugc.ac.in/pdfnews/8615255_Catch-the-Rain.pdf.

Conclusions

Traditional harvesting systems for collecting rainwater are the initial effort for rainwater harvesting in response to use the water for irrigation and daily necessities but, it is not drinkable in this form. As the drinkable surface water is becoming scarce on daily basis, there is felt a cost-effective innovation to purify the harvested rainwater. A smart technology-based rainwater harvesting system is not applicable everywhere in the country due to its high-priced nature. There is a clear distinction between rural and urban areas in terms of affordability. Therefore, this low-cost rainwater harvesting system and purification of the harvested water can be accessed anywhere in the world irrespective of region. This system will eliminate the use of artificial energy (thermal) by replacing solar energy and will increase the level of groundwater in order to reduce the scarcity of water during a crisis. This invention will certainly benefit especially the poor population residing in the rural areas.

References

Centre for Science and Environment (no date) Traditional water harvesting systems. https://www. cseindia.org/traditional-water-harvesting-systems-683. Accessed 6 Nov 2022
Chandrika Kota VSP et al (2020) Smart approach of harvesting rainwater and monitoring using IoT. J Adv Res Dyn Contr Syst 12(2):91–100. https://doi.org/10.5373/JARDCS/V12I2/S202010011
Converting Rainwater into Potable Drinking Water—Methods and Benefits (2018) Chaitanya. https://www.chaitanyaproducts.com/blog/converting-rainwater-into-potable-drinking-water-methods-and-benefits/. Accessed 8 Nov 2022
Gannoju R et al (2019) Automated rainwater harvesting using IoT. J Appl Sci Comput 6(1):298–307
Pal S (2016) Traditional water conservation systems of India, The Better India. https://www.thebet terindia.com/61757/traditional-water-conservation-systems-india/. Accessed 6 Nov 2022
Ranjan V et al (2020) The Internet of Things (IOT) based smart rain water harvesting system. In: 2020 6th international conference on signal processing and communication, ICSC 2020, pp 302–305. https://doi.org/10.1109/ICSC48311.2020.9182767
Vinoj J, Gavaskar S (2018) Smart city rain water harvesting (Iot). Int J Sci Dev Res (IJSDR) 3(8):1–6

Chapter 12
Leveraging Blockchain Technology in Industry 4.0 and Industrial Internet of Things (IIoT) Scenarios

Shraiyash Pandey, Abhik Kumar De, Shrishti Choudhary, Bharat Bhushan, and Surbhi Bhatia

Introduction

Blockchain is a highly trending topic, especially in the Information Technology sectors and the business world. The concept of Blockchain came into the spotlight with the launch of Bitcoin (Nakamoto 2008) in 2008. Bitcoin is a digital currency that is established as a peer-to-peer payment network. It allows individuals or big companies to pay one another without an external medium such as a central bank. This eliminates the problem known as double-spending (Zhang and Lee 2019). In layman's terms 'Blockchain', or chain of blocks, is a system that strictly prevents intruders from changing, hacking, or cheating recorded information. A system that takes privacy into its own hands. Blockchain can be referred to as a set of multiple nodes connected in a way that forms a chain of networks. In this, each node is used to verify information via the public key attached to its data in the node. In other words, an individual or group with a public or private key can access the data being shared from one end to another. However, there is the use of a private deciphering key used to decipher the message. The concept behind these keys was found back in 1976 by Diffie and Hellman (Gan et al. 2013). These two individuals achieved a milestone

S. Pandey (✉) · A. Kumar De · S. Choudhary · B. Bhushan · S. Bhatia
School of Engineering and Technology, Sharda University, Greater Noida, India
e-mail: shraiyash.pandey@gmail.com

A. Kumar De
e-mail: 2020525333.abhik@ug.sharda.ac.in

B. Bhushan
e-mail: bharat.bhushan@sharda.ac.in

S. Bhatia
e-mail: Sbhatia@kfu.edu.sa

College of Computer Science and Information Technology, King Faisal University, Hofuf, Saudi Arabia in asymmetric cryptography. With the help of this asymmetric cryptography, two individuals or a group can share data over a public network and establish a secure connection. After the connection has been successfully established, the individuals or the group can send and retrieve data. Both private and public keys are interrelated, which means they are used together as a combo through the help of an algorithm. This algorithm sets an exclusive bond between the pair of keys. In terms of confidentiality, public keys are allowed to be shared amongst others, while private keys are not and must be kept secret.

A central bank has access to a lot of data, too much is not an issue, however, some find this situation very upsetting. These individuals want more transparency and enhanced security without the use of a central bank as an external medium to share data or money. Blockchain solves this issue since it has no external medium for individuals and companies to deal with. As well as provides instant traceability, increased speed and efficiency, as well as enhanced security which all parties require. Blockchain technology protects data in a structural form with extreme security. The foundation is built upon the concept of cryptography, consensus, and decentralization (Saxena et al. 2021; Bonneau et al. 2015). All these concepts provide verifiability in transactions. In most DLT's, the structural form of that data is represented in blocks. These blocks are all connected using a cryptographic chain. No intruder can tamper with data if the blocks are stored in such a form. Consensus mechanism handles the validity of all transactions which ensures if a transaction is valid or not. Decentralization is enabled using blockchain technology for all members within a network.

Miners play a crucial role in blockchain technology. By analyzing cryptographic puzzles and then solving them as well as attaining agreement, the miners validate the data in a network (Bonneau et al. 2015). Such procedure results in the security of blockchain. A transaction is documented each time a miner deciphers any puzzle. Several Bitcoins are earned after a puzzle is solved. This is known as the reward approach where miners have the incentive to solve puzzles. Now, a miner with a greater number of resources can solve the puzzle at a faster pace compared to a miner with a fewer number of resources (Bhushan et al. 2021). Whenever a new miner arrives, it is provided with access to a blockchain for the first time, however, the miner has access to the whole blockchain. That includes everything from the genesis to the biggest block. Supporting the valid blockchain, the genesis is the first block created that is strongly embedded into the client software. Since miners are assigned the task to solve puzzles, also referred to as proof-of-work (PoW) (Tang et al. 2017; Wang et al. 2019), a new block is initiated and created from where it is then added into the pre-existing blockchain, only then will the new transaction be valid. The major contributions of this work can be enumerated below.

- This paper highlights the evolution of the industrial revolution from the first to the fourth industrial revolution and all the nine pillars that structure Industry 4.0.
- This paper presents the Overview of Blockchain that consists of its predefined structure, the working of multiple chains of blocks, and all sorts of characteristics acquired in Blockchain.

- This paper presents the evolution of technology over such a long period of time that led to the 4th industrial revolution where such technologies including Blockchain that plays a major role in Industry 4.0.
- This paper highlights sectors such as Robotics and Artificial Intelligence, Cyber-security, IoT, Cloud database, and Virtual Reality which are various smart tools and kits subcategorized from overall drivers and enablers in Industry 4.0.

The remainder of this paper is organized as follows. Section 12.2 explains the evolution that has taken place in terms of industrial revolution and innovation of new and enhanced technologies. As well as providing an overview of Industry 4.0 and the nine pillars of it. Section 12.3 presents the overview of the blockchain that consists of the different types of blockchain, the working of blockchain and its characteristics. Section 12.4 analyzes the different sectors of Industry 4.0 that are subcategorized from overall drivers in Industry 4.0. Section 12.5 presents the recent advancements in Blockchain and Industry 4.0. Finally, the paper concludes itself in Sect. 12.6 highlighting the major open research directions and future discussion.

Industry 4.0

Klaus Schwab, Founder of the World Economic Forum, is the reason Industry 4.0 became so popularized back in 2015. Rapid change in industries, technology, processes and societal patterns was conceptualized by Industry 4.0 due to the increase in smart automation and interconnectivity in the twenty-first century (Chen et al. 2018).

The innovation of new technologies, especially in areas such as Cloud Computing and analytics, AI and Machine Learning, and Internet of Things (IoT) has led to a massive transformation in the world of industry over the past decade. All these technologies are shown in Fig. 12.1. To represent the fourth revolution in the industry, we call it Industry 4.0 (Dallasega et al. 2018). It showcases the extent of recurrence in manufacturing which is so compelling.

Fig. 12.1 Industry 4.0

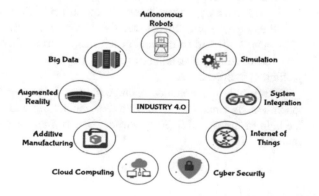

Fig. 12.2 Industrial
revolution

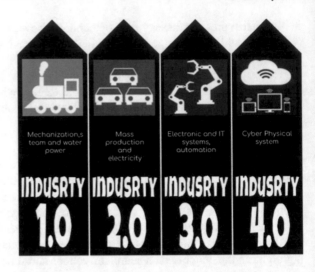

Enhancing the third revolution which includes automation and the adoption of computers with the help of new autonomous systems leads to the fourth industrial revolution. The fourth industrial revolution consists of all innovations from the third, as well as the new enhancements that revolve around the industry. The evolution of the industry is portrayed in Fig. 12.2.

To allow for better decision-making, the smart factories of the twenty-first century are equipped with robotics, advanced sensors, and new embedded software. When operational data from ERP, customer service, and supply chain is combined with data from production operations, a higher value is generated to create a higher level of insight and visibility from previous industrial revolution.

To improve the quality and productivity, the use of high-tech IoT devices is implemented in smart factories. The manufacturing errors are reduced, and money is saved along with time by replacing manual inspection with AI-powered investment. To monitor manufacturing processes from anywhere, a smartphone can be connected to the cloud by a quality control personnel, yet all of it is done with minimal investment. Errors usually found at later stages of development, can be very difficult to repair and more expensive, however, manufacturers can detect them immediately with the help of algorithms of machine learning. A new level of responsiveness and efficiency is offered to customers with the help of these digital technologies that have led to self-optimization of process improvements, increased automation, and predictive maintenance.

To improve maintenance management and the overall performance of regular machines, they need to be converted to self-learning and self-aware machines with the help of industry 4.0. To construct a smart manufacturing platform is the aim of Industry 4.0.

Nine Pillars of Industry 4.0

Big Data and Analytics

To support real-time decision-making, the compressive evaluation and collection of data from various enterprises and customer management as well as sources of production equipment will likely become standard. Big Data Consists of four dimensions: Value of Data, Velocity of generation of new data and analysis, Variety of Data, and Volume of Data according to forester's definition (Erboz 2017). To identify threats that occurred earlier in the previous industry, we keep track of previous data analysis as well to help forecast any new issues or any solutions that helped to solve any of those issues.

Autonomous Robots

A time will come soon when robots work safely side by side and interact with one another, as well as learn from each other. Day by day, robots are becoming more flexible and autonomous. In places where human workers are restricted to work, robots are used to precisely perform tasks and autonomous production methods. Features like versatility, safety, and performing the task precisely within a given time are strictly of an autonomous robot (Erboz 2017).

Simulation

To replicate the actual world in a virtual reality model, simulations are to be used in certain operations that can be used to grip any real-time data. In the virtual model, it consists of humans, machines, and products. For the simulation of ergonomic or consumption aspects of the production facility, virtual commissioning can be used (Erboz 2017). Reduction of failures in the start-up phase is caused by using simulations of the processes of production. It can also shorten the time and change it. With the help of simulations, decision-making can be enhanced easily.

System Integration

There are two major mechanisms which are used in the industrial organization: self-optimization, and Horizontal and Vertical System Integration (Sethi et al. 2020). There are three dimensions of integration that outline the paradigm of Industry 4.0.

Cooperation along standardized processes and automation of communication are the results of automation and integration of manufacturing processes.

The Industrial Internet of Things

Industrial Internet of Things (IIoT) is the system of IoT that collects data from every sensor in every single production device (Sethi et al. 2020). To connect machines to other machines for data management, IIoT is implemented. It allows productivity and optimization to make smart factories. IIoT distinguishes the past offering interconnected devices and sensors that run along the maintenance and production to the fourth industrial revolution. Continuously sending data for processing and devices connected to a central server, IIoT enables automation on an unpredictable scale.

Cyber Security and Cyber Physical Systems (CPS)

The odds of data breaches go up since Industry 4.0 relies so heavily on data transfers. Therefore, protecting these systems against cyber threats is very important. Perpetrators can take advantage of systems for intellectual property, IP leakage, production sabotage or even industrial espionage (Sethi et al. 2020). Cyber security protects against any attacks or malicious data code injection as well as controlled physical access to the system.

To revolutionize how companies share information and automate processes, cyber-physical systems combine digital networks and physical components. The cost of an expanded attack and surface that requires both OT and IT defenses is what comes with the smart factory's combination of physical and virtual systems that make real-time and interoperability capability possible. To have a successful Industry 4.0 journey, the organization has to carefully consider the security implications as a result.

Cloud Computing

To store, manage and process data, Cloud Computing uses a set of remote servers. Manufacturing businesses can bring their own knowledge and intelligence to all sales situations and introduce a faster development process for products.

Additive Manufacturing

3D printing is best known for additive manufacturing. To make small batches of products that are customized according to the customer's needs is the perfect use of 3D printing. Faster prototyping of products is enabled by the significant price reduction of 3D printers and digital scanners. Allowing more complex parts to be made in less time, 3D printing is used in production by many large companies.

Cutting the resource waste and producing less waste is what additive manufacturing is best known for. To test, produce, and make any changes without a lot of trouble, 3D printing is best since its cost, and prototyping are lower. It's a benefit compared to traditional manufacturing processes that are not able to meet the requirement of multiple production steps or handle complex designs. As a result, it increases both the time required to assemble and create the different parts, and labor and material costs.

Augmented Reality (AR)

The way information is used, accessed, and exchanged is revolutionized by Augmented Reality (AR). Information that broadens users' perception is what's known as augmented reality. Allowing others to interact with information, this technology maximizes the perspective experience (Sethi et al. 2020). AR has the potential to actively contribute to the transformation of industrial production processes and the overall success of it. It becomes more meaningful when data is provided with context. Therefore, AR comes into place which can be implemented in many ways. Selecting parts based on requirements, and streaming repair instructions as applications, the AR tech holds the potential to increase human efficiency. A perfect example of it can be delivering food in remote places such as Africa.

Blockchain

Implementation of the Merkle Tree and cryptographic hash function was done by Stuart and W. Scott to store certified documents in a single block (Zhou et al. 2019). However, blockchain technology was brought into the spotlight after the launch of Bitcoin, a digital currency that is established as a peer-to-peer payment network (Banerjee et al. 2019; Vishakha et al. 2021; Bhushan and Sharma 2020; Jogunola et al. 2019). After Bitcoin became a very successful digital currency in the market for cryptocurrencies, it motivated other industries to make use of Blockchain as well. Two terms are used in the keyword, "block" and "chain". The term "block" defines the collection of data that includes different sets of transactions and related information. Whereas the term "chain" represents the link between different sets of blocks using cryptographic hash code. All the links help the blockchain technology become more secure.

Structure of Blockchain

The three main components of Blockchain – Block header, List of transactions, and Miners—are discussed in the subsections below. A complete structure of a Blockchain or a chain of blocks is shown in Fig. 12.3.

Block Header

The block header consists of three components: hash code of the previous block, to create a block mining statistic are used, Markle Tree. The hash code of the previous block is supposed to link with the current block to the previous one. Mining statistics (Qin et al. 2018): used to create the block Markle tree.

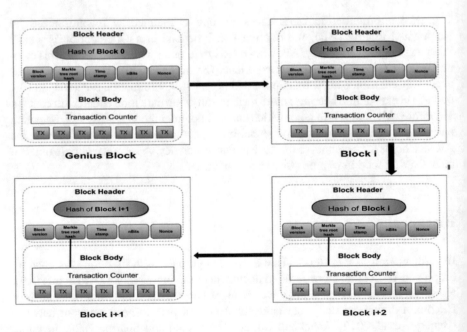

Fig. 12.3 Chain of blocks

List of Transactions

Transaction size and block size is the dependency of the list of transaction. Using asymmetric cryptography (Plos et al. 2013), the process of authentication and authorization of the transactions are to be completed. A transaction cannot be removed once it has been included in the chain of blocks (Abururab 2014). Each block consists of a hash of the previous block from which a chain of blocks is formed. A computational hash generated using the mining procedure determines if the block is to be accepted into the chain (Chenaghlu et al. 2016). The hash checks its validity and its proof of work. All blocks succeeding to a block that has been modified will have to be recomputed. An extremely secure hashing technique that includes several hash pointers helps ensure the modifiability of any blocks previously.

Miners

A list of transactions that are in line to be added are the ones that miners try to mine blocks on their own with. Once a block has been mined, then for verification it is broadcasted to all the other nodes in the network (Calders and Goethals 2007). The block that records the highest consensus will be the one to be accepted and join the chain of blocks in order. While other blocks are labeled as orphan blocks. Some transactions are thrown in for further mining process because they have already been added. Though only added, most of them have yet to be considered.

Working of Blockchain

To initiate a transaction, a private key cryptography-based signature is used at a specific node considering that digital assets are transferred between peers in a network as a data structure (Baliga 2017). Gossip pool is used to generate transactions in the network. Whereas an unconfirmed pool is used to store such transactions. From a concept of war, most generals prefer to retreat, however, some may prefer to attack. In this concept, an agreement is found, otherwise, a major failure is more likely to take place if most generals are not ready to attack but a few of them are ready. This kind of agreement is defined as consensus. It's difficult to reach a consensus agreement since the network is mostly disturbed. It's not possible to use an existing central node and verify the disturbed nodes for identical ledgers. However, it's possible using a protocol. The protocol ensures the consistency of all the nodes present in the network. With the use of the consensus mechanism of Blockchain, it's easy to eliminate the problems of Byzantine generals and double-spending. The working of blockchain is shown in Fig. 12.4.

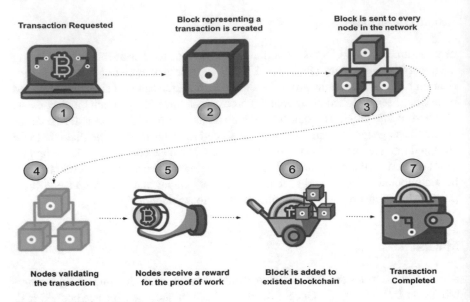

Fig. 12.4 Working of Blockchain

Overview of Characteristics

Four different characters are involved in the implementation and blueprint of Blockchain. All these characteristics are enhanced to an extent to create a working system that consists of a chain of blocks. The characteristics are discussed in the subsections below.

Auditability

To respectively validate and record all transactions, a digital timestamp and a digital distributed ledger are used. Previous records are easily traced and audited if any node in the network has been accessed. For instance, take Bitcoin for example, all transactions can be iteratively traced which makes it easier for the data state to be transparent and auditable. Though, if the money has tumbled upon various accounts, it's very difficult to trace its origin.

Persistency

Assuming there are 20 blocks in a block of chains (Blockchain), the last block in the chain, 20th block, holds the information used to create a new block, and includes the previous block's hash (Baliga 2017). Thus, all blocks are linked together. With this process, the current transaction is connected to the previous one. A block's hash is changed if any transaction is updated. In fact, all the previous blocks must be changed if any information has been updated. To add more, other users in the network must confirm after a new generation of a block by a miner. Of course, modifying the information of previous transactions to confirm the generation of a new block by the users, it requires a lot of work.

Decentralization

Trust, fail-over, lift resilience, availability, and fail-over are all required in a conventional centralized system to validate transactions. Although, by creating a centralized peer-to-peer Blockchain architecture, a better solution can be found. However, a transaction can be conducted by two peers in the Blockchain network without the help of a central agency. Through this process, using consensus procedures we can reduce the trust (Azaria et al. 2016).

Anonymity

A user having multiple random generated addresses can interact with a Blockchain network to avoid highlighting its identity. User's private information is not recorded or monitored by a central authority. Transactions between members and their identities should remain anonymous (Kurtulmus and Daniel 2018). However, anonymity cannot be achieved through just this. The mechanism must also not prevent from verifying the transaction.

Types of Blockchains

There are three different types of blockchains. Private blockchains, public blockchains, and Consortium blockchains. In public blockchains, an anonymous participant is allowed to enter the public blockchain network, whereas in private blockchains, identification is used to confirm if the individual is part of the private blockchain or not. A Consortium blockchain network consists of a preselected set of points or nodes by a preselected number of stakeholders to implement a consensus process. All types of blockchains are discussed in the subsections below as well as shown in Table 12.1.

Public Blockchain

In a public blockchain (Vukolic´ 2015), there is an open-source environment where transactions can be verified and checked by anyone that's included in the Blockchain

Table 12.1 Types of Blockchain

Comparison parameters	Public/Permissionless	Private/Permissioned	Consortium
Governance type	Public	Single node	Set of nodes
Throughput	Slow	Fast	Fast
Nodes's identity disclosure	Not revealed	Revealed	Revealed
Energy efficiency	No	Yes	Yes
Protocol	PoW, PoS, PoET		PBFT, PoA, Tendermint
Permission	Without permission		With permission
Example	Bitcoin, Ethereum, Ripple		Multichain, Hyperledger
Attack (Double Spending)	Yes	Difficult	Yes
Transaction validation	Any node can be miner		List of authorized node
Scalability	High	Low/Medium	Low/Medium
Infrastructure	Decentralized	Decentralized	Distributed
Censorship/Regulation	No	Yes	Yes

network. Anyone is allowed access to participate and use this open-source environment. In simple terms, without a set of restrictions applied to anyone, they all are allowed to participate in this permission-less blockchain network. A few examples of public blockchains are well-known cryptocurrencies such as Ethereum, Litecoin, and Bitcoin.

Private Blockchain

Private Blockchain (Vukolic´ 2017) is the second type of blockchain, also referred to as permissioned blockchain, which provides a closed network where participants are picked as well as their roles in the network. This kind of blockchain is used for private commercial use or by industries. A blockchain where restrictions are set to who can access blockchain data is known as Private Blockchain. Such users are permitted to access specific data. In other words, a node being a user in the network is strictly restricted from accessing data. A few examples of private blockchains are Monax, Oracle Blockchain Platform, Bankchain, Database management, Multichain, etc.

Consortium Blockchain

The third and last type of blockchain is called Consortium Blockchain (Li et al. 2017), also referred to as Hybrid Blockchain. From the word hybrid, one may assume it's a mixture of Private and Public Blockchains, which is correct, however, not entirely. In this blockchain, the number of participants is defined as having control over the read and write data. Usually implemented by firms or groups of organizations. In fact, to carry out tasks, they work in a restricted environment where they have restricted access to data. A few examples of this blockchain are Hyperledger and R3CEV.

Drivers

Some of the very familiar drivers are supply chains, smart factories, smart solutions, and smart products (Leng et al. 2021). To develop blockchain technology many new enablers have been employed to provide specific services, especially in industrial sectors. Robotics and Artificial Intelligence, Cybersecurity, IoT, Cloud database, and Virtual Reality are various smart tools and kits that have been subcategorized from overall drivers and enablers. All cryptocurrencies are used to comprehend specific future needs; it is all embraced by blockchain (Biswal and Bhushan 2019; Lu 2018). Blockchain has developed dramatically over the past few years. This blockchain technology has validated the block and collected data by forming a chain of information. To serve as a registry for buildings, vehicles and houses, the public sector is seeking to implement blockchain. Blockchains can be very useful in the public sector since they can improve back-office functions, facilitate voting, and reduce fraud (Sajid et al. 2021). Its focus, however, comes on transactions in businesses, decision making and data management.

Data can become a major asset without the requirement of an external agent which helps to create more trust and a special bond between the customers and stakeholders. If a supply chain placed on the blockchain is particularly different, then all stakeholders can achieve consensus (Bhushan et al. 2022a). To establish a coordination process amongst various factories, one must make use of the mechanisms available. Overall, blockchain technology improves efficiency and accountability in the supply chain. The requirement and need for Blockchain have grown rapidly in automotive sectors over the past years. The supply chain will be populated in many countries and industries over the next few years (Bhushan et al. 2022b).

Recent Advancements

Qu et al. (2021) proposed jointly using blockchain and federated learning on comprehensive data-driven cognitive computing to solve the "data island" problem. Blockchain provides support towards attacks and incentive mechanisms. Lahbib et al. (2021) proposed the use of requester sensitive attributes and policies for shared access control to ensure strong privacy. Since the verification process remains public and transparent, a privacy layer is added for encapsulating sensitive attributes. Bhatt et al. (2021) highlighted the importance of identifying recent technological trends and breakthroughs in the field of blockchain as well as studying the patent publication trends. Garrocho et al. (2021) proposed a blockchain based technology on access control architecture that is directly deployed onto edge devices positioned close to other devices that require access control. When carried out at a practice in a mining environment, the architecture showed severe enhanced performance.

Shukla et al. (2021) suggested a six-layered architecture that forecasts CNC tool wear detection using a technique based on AdaBoost and random forest models and soft-voted prediction model. Wu et al. (2021) suggested that to enable scalable and secure infrastructures, the converging of edge computing paradigms and blockchain should be implemented. Moschou et al. (2020) came up with a novel methodology that was useful to blockchain practitioners for designing future solutions via measuring the performance of such two transactional processors presented, evaluated, and deployed in the Hyperledger Sawtooth environment. Cheng and Shaoqin (2020) suggested the combination of IoT, Radio Frequency Identification (RFID) technology and blockchain technology to integrate a blockchain based lightweight password security authentication mechanism of the smart factory RFID system.

Kuperberg (2020) proposed a novel that suggested using a tree based of context chains, an architecture for blockchain consensus and ledger can be created. Hasan et al. (2022) showcased an IoT model based on blockchain that is capable of monitoring price hikes and corruption from Industry 4.0 perspective that includes production and packaging of products and their subsequent purchase by wholesalers and retailers. Bodkhe et al. (2020) presented a review that consisted of blockchain related solutions in various applications of Industry 4.0. Hossain et al. (2020) suggested a stable operation of smart grids of SCADA systems that analyzed the scope of blockchain application in the system's data acquisition. Feld et al. (2014) focused on collecting network distribution, size of the network, and number of clients to reduce novel insights related to P2P network that focuses especially on the distribution of network amongst other systems.

Fujimura et al. (2015) proposed in terms of the development of management system that is decentralized for an application of blockchain technology which illustrated the results of trial implementation. Anish Dev et al. (2014) proposed an idea that would result in faster mining by mining bitcoin on non-customer hardware. The use of both illegal and legal mining networks and the usage of computing elements gave such results. Zyskind et al. (2015) suggested the implementation of protocols that transform blockchain into a control manager by passing the requirement of reliability on a third party. Zhang and Wen (2015) (Begam et al. 2020) proposed to observe the paid data on IoT with the help of P2P trade and transaction of small property in an IoT based E-business model and redesign E-business models with the use of blockchain principles and smart contracts. Barkatullah and Hanke (2015) (Thanh et al. 2020) analyzed that Coin Terra's first-generation Bitcoin mining processor's implementation and architecture were used as a precursor in designing a much more complete mining machine called Terraminer IV. Decker and Wattenhofer (2013) (Nguyen et al. 2020) analyzed that through network and ledger replicas, it was possible to propagate transactions in Bitcoin and interpret multi-hop broadcast's use as well.

Di Battista et al. (2015) (Jha et al. 2019) suggested when and how the Bitcoin's flow mixes well with other flows for high level analysis in a transaction graph. Giaglis (2015) (Sharma et al. 2019) analyzed the concept of smart money and its various potential uses highlighting M2M money and smart contracts to Money-over-IP. Lee et al. (2014) (Sharma et al. 2020a) suggested that to achieve productivity and transparency, transform the manufacturing sector in the fourth industrial revolution using Blockchain and Big Data and analyzed how to manage big data using smart predictive informatics tools. Kong et al. (2021) (Dansana et al. 2020) suggested exploiting a Blockchain with the help of proof-of-stake consensus to achieve a mechanism that verifies the immutable and aggregation dissemination of performance records. Allian et al. (2021) (Malik et al. 2021) proposed that a trustworthy interoperability requires a set of essential requirements in the fourth industrial revolution. Faz-Mendoza et al. (2020) (Sharma et al. 2020b) proposed a study that constructs a bibliometric and conceptual result of quantified production in Knowledge Intelligence and Management and identifies the main authors and such research areas. King et al. (2020) (Dansana et al. 2021) highlighted current literature regarding the fourth Industrial revolution when considered from a business model perspective. A review was conducted to explore current research at the intersection of the research domains of Industry 4.0 and the Business model. The major advances in blockchain based Industry 4.0 applications are summarized in Table 12.2.

Table 12.2 Major blockchain based Industry 4.0 advancements

Reference	Year	Major contribution
Qu et al. (2021)	2021	Solved "data island" problem using blockchain and data-driven cognitive computing
Lahbib et al. (2021)	2021	To ensure strong privacy introduced the use of requester sensitive attributes and policies for shared access control
Bhatt et al. (2021)	2021	Identified recent technological trends and breakthroughs in the field of blockchain
Garrocho et al. (2021)	2021	Proposed a blockchain based technology on the access control architecture
Shukla et al. (2021)	2021	Suggested a six-layered architecture using a novel ensemble technique
Wu et al. (2021)	2021	Proposed an idea to enable scalable and secure infrastructures, the converging of edge computing paradigms and blockchain should be implemented
Moschou et al. (2020)	2020	Proposed a novel methodology that was useful to blockchain practitioners for designing future solutions

(continued)

Table 12.2 (continued)

Reference	Year	Major contribution
Cheng and Shaoqin (2020)	2020	Suggested the combination of IoT, Radio Frequency Identification (RFID) technology and blockchain technology to integrate a blockchain based lightweight password
Kuperberg (2020)	2020	Suggested using a tree based of context chains to create an architecture for blockchain consensus and ledger
Hasan et al. (2022)	2022	Showcased a IoT model based on blockchain that is capable of monitoring price hikes and corruption from Industry 4.0
Bodkhe et al. (2020)	2020	Presented a review that consisted of blockchain related solutions in various applications of Industry 4.0
Hossain et al. (2020)	2020	Suggested for a stable operation of smart grids of SCADA systems that analyzed the scope of blockchain application
Feld et al. (2014)	2014	Focused on collecting network distribution, size of the network, and number of clients to reduce novel insights related to P2P network
Fujimura et al. (2015)	2015	Proposed in terms of the development of a management system that is decentralized for an application of blockchain technology
Anish Dev et al. (2014)	2014	Proposed an idea that would result in faster mining by mining bitcoin on non-customer hardware
Zyskind et al. (2015)	2015	Suggested implementation of protocols that transform blockchain into a control manager
Zhang and Wen (2015) (Begam et al. 2020)	2015	Proposed to observe the paid data on IoT with the help of P2P trade and transaction of a small property in IoT
Barkatullah and Hanke (2015) (Thanh et al. 2020)	2015	Analyzed that Coin Terra's first-generation Bitcoin mining processor's implementation and architecture were used as a precursor
Decker and Wattenhofer (2013) (Nguyen et al. 2020)	2013	Analyzed that through network and ledger replicas, it was possible to propagate transactions in Bitcoin
Di Battista et al. (2015) (Jha et al. 2019)	2015	Suggested when and how the Bitcoin's flow mixes well with other flows for high level analysis in a transaction graph
Giaglis (2015) (Sharma et al. 2019)	2015	Analyzed the concept of smart money and its various potential uses highlighting M2M money and smart contracts

(continued)

Table 12.2 (continued)

Reference	Year	Major contribution
Lee et al. (2014) (Sharma et al. 2020a)	2014	Suggested that to achieve productivity and transparency, transform the manufacturing sector in the fourth industrial revolution using Blockchain and Big Data
Kong et al. (2021) (Dansana et al. 2020)	2021	Suggested exploiting a Blockchain with the help of proof-of-stake consensus to achieve a profitable mechanism
Allian et al. (2021) (Malik et al. 2021)	2021	Proposed that a trustworthy interoperability requires a set of essential requirements in the fourth industrial revolution
Faz-Mendoza et al. (2020) (Sharma et al. 2020b)	2020	Proposed a study that constructs a bibliometric and conceptual result of quantified production in Knowledge Intelligence and Management
King et al. (2020) (Dansana et al. 2021)	2020	Highlighted current literature regarding the fourth Industrial revolution when considered from a business model perspective

Conclusion and Future Research Directions

In conclusion, since the launch of Bitcoin to today's date, the concept and use of Blockchain have only evolved along with the industrial revolution in Industry. A system that implements the concepts of keys introduced to us by Diffie and Hellman provides a tool to strictly prevent intruders from changing, hacking and cheating recorded information is essential. However, it is not only essential but important to evaluate every time another revolution in the industry occurs. The security of such companies like Bitcoin is still standing only because of the barrier created by Blockchain to stop an illegal or unusual activity from occurring. An algorithm that consists of public and private keys to implement Blockchain cannot be easily encountered by intruders. However, it may not be possible with such a revolution in the industry. Especially with changes from the third industrial revolution to the fourth comes with many new technologies and methods. The Blockchain or chain of blocks is attributed with different components that all work together to output a functional system helped to block intruders. Though these components can be enhanced or replaced as another industrial revolution takes place with the introduction of more enhanced and capable technologies. Role of Industry 4.0 is not only to give it a new name every often, but to initialize a checkpoint that points to another industrial revolution that brings many new technologies. The role of such technologies comes into place enhancing previous barriers or introducing new barriers that are much more efficient and secure than previous approaches.

Transparency of Blockchain deployment and runtime, Security of smart contracts, and Reliability of BaaS infrastructure are the three different aspects that the research can be extended towards in the future. Firstly, a new service paradigm is needed for NutBaas that helps in the transparency of blockchain to reduce the damage of NutBaaS platform to the decentralization of blockchain. Therefore, increasing the transparency of blockchain runtime and deployment via new service paradigm. Secondly, the Reliability of BaaS infrastructure, to seek more versatile and detailed evaluation for BaaS infrastructure. Therefore, the service users or service providers can take corresponding preventive measures or optimize the relevant components. Finally, regarding the security of smart contracts, conducting research on smart contracts' performance that includes the reduction of gas consumption of contracts, and existing machine learning models will be beneficial.

Future research can be done on both methodological and theoretical aspects. The digitalization process of society and organizations which are triggered by blockchain would show a result in a change to management practice that B&M disciplines naturally face the challenge of a particular question that arises. To whether the logic of an existing theory is still applicable in the new context a theory was proposed about B&M.

References

Abuturab MR (2014) An asymmetric color image cryptosystem based on Schur decomposition in gyrator transform domain. Opt Lasers Eng 58:39–47

Allian AP, Schnicke F, Antonino PO, Rombach D, Nakagawa EY (2021) Architecture drivers for trustworthy interoperability in Industry 4.0. IEEE Syst J 15(4):5454–5463. https://doi.org/10.1109/JSYST.2020.3041259

Anish Dev J (2014)Bitcoin mining acceleration and performance quantification. In: 2014 IEEE 27th Canadian conference on electrical and computer engineering (CCECE), pp 1–6. https://doi.org/10.1109/CCECE.2014.6900989

Azaria A, Ekblaw A, Vieira T, Lippman A (2016) Medrec: using blockchain for medical data access and permission management. In: 2016 2nd international conference on open and big data (OBD), IEEE, pp 25–30

Baliga A (2017) Understanding blockchain consensus models. Persistent 2017 (4)

Banerjee S, Odelu V, Das AK, Chattopadhyay S, Rodrigues JJPC, Park Y (2019) Physically secure lightweight anonymous user authentication protocol for Internet of Things using physically unclonable functions. IEEE Access 7:85627–85644

Barkatullah J, Hanke T (2015) Goldstrike 1: CoinTerra's first-generation cryptocurrency mining processor for bitcoin. IEEE Micro 35(2):68–76. https://doi.org/10.1109/MM.2015.13

Begam SS, V J, Selvachandran G, Ngan TT, Sharma R (2020) Similarity measure of lattice ordered multi-fuzzy soft sets based on set theoretic approach and its application in decision making. Mathematics 8:1255

Bhatt PC, Kumar V, Lu T-C (2021) Identifying technology trends for blockchain applications in industry 4.0 domain: a patent perspective. In: 2021 IEEE international conference on social sciences and intelligent management (SSIM), pp 1–5. https://doi.org/10.1109/SSIM49526.2021.9555213

Bhushan B, Sharma N (2020) Transaction privacy preservations for blockchain technology. In: Advances in intelligent systems and computing international conference on innovative computing and communications, pp 377–393.https://doi.org/10.1007/978-981-15-5148-2_34

Bhushan B, Sinha P, Sagayam KM, JA (2021). Untangling blockchain technology: a survey on state of the art, security threats, privacy services, applications and future research directions. Comput Electr Eng 90:106897. https://doi.org/10.1016/j.compeleceng.2020.106897

Bhushan B, Kadam K, Parashar R, Kumar S, Thakur AK (2022a) Leveraging blockchain technology in sustainable supply chain management and logistics. In: Muthu SS (eds) Blockchain technologies for sustainability. environmental footprints and eco-design of products and processes. Springer, Singapore. https://doi.org/10.1007/978-981-16-6301-7_9

Bhushan B, Anushka KA, Katiyar L (2022b) Security magnification in supply chain management using Blockchain technology. In: Muthu SS (eds) Blockchain technologies for sustainability. Environmental footprints and eco-design of products and processes. Springer, Singapore. https://doi.org/10.1007/978-981-16-6301-7_3

Biswal A, Bhushan B (2019) Blockchain for Internet of Things: architecture, consensus advancements, challenges and application areas. In: 2019 5th international conference on computing, communication, control and automation (ICCUBEA). https://doi.org/10.1109/iccubea47591.2019.9129181

Bodkhe U et al (2020) Blockchain for industry 4.0: a comprehensive review. IEEE Access 8:79764–79800. https://doi.org/10.1109/ACCESS.2020.2988579

Bonneau J, Miller A, Clark J, Narayanan A, Kroll JA, Felten EW (2015) SoK: research perspectives and challenges for Bitcoin and cryptocurrencies. In: Proceedings of IEEE symposium security privacy, pp 104–121

Calders T, Goethals B (2007) Non-derivable itemset mining. Data Mining Knowl Discov 14(1):171–206

Chenaghlu MA, Jamali S, Khasmakhi NN (2016) A novel keyed parallel hashing scheme based on a new chaotic system. Chaos, Solitons Fractals 87:216–225

Chen B, Wan J, Shu L, Li P, Mukherjee M, Yin B (2018) Smart factory of industry 4.0: key technologies, application case, and challenges. IEEE Access 6:6505–6519

Cheng Y, Shaoqin H (2020)Research on blockchain technology in cryptographic exploration. In: 2020 international conference on big data & artificial intelligence & software engineering (ICBASE), pp 120–123.https://doi.org/10.1109/ICBASE51474.2020.00033

Dallasega P, Rauch E, Linder C (2018) Industry 4.0 as an enabler of proximity for construction supply chains: a systematic literature review. Comput Ind 99:205–225

Dansana D, Kumar R, Das Adhikari J, Mohapatra M, Sharma R, Priyadarshini I and Le D-N (2020) Global forecasting confirmed and fatal cases of COVID-19 outbreak using autoregressive integrated moving average model. Front Public Health 8:580327. https://doi.org/10.3389/fpubh.2020.580327

Dansana D, Kumar R, Parida A, Sharma R, Adhikari JD et al (2021) Using susceptible-exposed-infectious-recovered model to forecast coronavirus outbreak. Comput, Mater Continua 67(2):1595–1612

Decker C, Wattenhofer R (2013) Information propagation in the Bitcoin network. In: IEEE P2P 2013 proceedings, pp 1–10. https://doi.org/10.1109/P2P.2013.6688704

Di Battista G, Di Donato V, Patrignani M, Pizzonia M, Roselli V, Tamassia R (2015) Bitconeview: visualization of flows in the bitcoin transaction graph. In: 2015 IEEE symposium on visualization for cyber security (VizSec), pp 1–8. https://doi.org/10.1109/VIZSEC.2015.7312773

Erboz G (2017) How to define industry 4.0: the main pillars of industry 4.0. In: Managerial trends in the development of enterprises in globalization Era, pp 761–766

Faz-Mendoza A, Gamboa-Rosales NK, Castorena-Robles A, Cobo MJ, Castañeda-Miranda R, López-Robles JR (2020) Strategic intelligence and knowledge management as drivers of decision-making in mining industry: An analysis of the literature. In: 2020 international conference on decision aid sciences and application (DASA), pp 536–540. https://doi.org/10.1109/DASA51403.2020.9317053

Feld S, Schönfeld M, Werner M (2014) Analyzing the deployment of Bitcoin's P2P network under an AS-level perspective. Procedia Comput Sci 32:1121–1126. https://doi.org/10.1016/j.procs.2014.05.542

Fujimura S, Watanabe H, Nakadaira A, Yamada T, Akutsu A, Kishigami JJ (2015)BRIGHT: a concept for a decentralized rights management system based on blockchain. In: 2015 IEEE 5th international conference on consumer electronics—Berlin (ICCE-Berlin), pp 345–346. https:// doi.org/10.1109/ICCE-Berlin.2015.7391275

Gan Y, Wang L, Wang L, Pan P, Yang Y (2013) Efficient construction of CCA-secure threshold PKE based on Hashed Diffie-Hellman assumption. Comput J 56(10):1249–1257. https://doi.org/ 10.1093/comjnl/bxs167

Garrocho CTB, Oliveira KN, Sena DJ, da Cunha Cavalcanti CFM, Oliveira RAR (2021) BACE: Blockchain-based access control at the edge for industrial control devices of industry 4.0. In: 2021 XI Brazilian symposium on computing systems engineering (SBESC), pp 1–8. https://doi. org/10.1109/SBESC53686.2021.9628291

Giaglis G (2015) Money-over-IP from Bitcoin to smart contracts and M2M money. In: 2015 international conference on evaluation of novel approaches to software engineering (ENASE), pp IS-5-IS-5

Hasan MK et al (2022) Evolution of industry and blockchain era: monitoring price hike and corruption using BIoT for smart government and industry 4.0. IEEE Trans Ind Inf 18(12):9153–9161. https://doi.org/10.1109/TII.2022.3164066

Hossain MT, Badsha S, Shen H (2020) PoRCH: a novel consensus mechanism for blockchain-enabled future SCADA systems in smart grids and industry 4.0. In: 2020 IEEE international IOT, electronics and mechatronics conference (IEMTRONICS), pp 1–7https://doi.org/10.1109/IEM TRONICS51293.2020.9216438

Jha S et al (2019) Deep learning approach for software maintainability metrics prediction. IEEE Access 7:61840–61855

Jogunola O, Hammoudeh M, Adebisi B, Anoh K (2019) Demonstrating blockchain-enabled Peer-to-Peer energy trading and sharing. In: Proceedings of IEEE Canadian conference on electrical computer engineering (CCECE), pp 1–4

King S, Grobbelaar SS (2020) Industry 4.0 and business model innovation: a scoping review. In: 2020 IEEE international conference on engineering, technology and innovation (ICE/ITMC), pp 1–8. https://doi.org/10.1109/ICE/ITMC49519.2020.9198424

Kong Q, Lu R, Yin F, Cui S (2021) Blockchain-based privacy-preserving driver monitoring for MaaS in the vehicular IoT. IEEE Trans Veh Technol 70(4):3788–3799. https://doi.org/10.1109/ TVT.2021.3064834

Kuperberg M (2020) Towards enabling deletion in append-only blockchains to support data growth management and GDPR compliance. In: 2020 IEEE international conference on blockchain (Blockchain), pp 393–400.https://doi.org/10.1109/Blockchain50366.2020.00057

Kurtulmus AB, Daniel K (2018) Trustless machine learning contracts; evaluating and exchanging machine learning models on the ethereum blockchain, arXiv preprint arXiv:1802.10185

Lahbib A, Toumi K, Laouiti A, Martin S (2021) Blockchain based privacy aware distributed access management framework for industry 4.0. In: 2021 IEEE 30th international conference on enabling technologies: infrastructure for collaborative enterprises (WETICE), pp 51–56. https://doi.org/ 10.1109/WETICE53228.2021.00021

Lee J, Kao H, Yang S (2014) Service innovation and smart analytics for industry 4.0 and big data environment. Procedia CIRP 16:3–8. https://doi.org/10.1016/j.procir.2014.02.001

Leng J, Ye SD, Zhou M et al (2021) Blockchain-secured smart manufacturing in industry 4.0: a survey. IEEE Trans Syst Man, Cybernetics: Systems 51(1):237–252. https://doi.org/10.1109/ tsmc.2020.3040789

Li Z, Kang J, Yu R, Ye D, Deng Q, Zhang Y (2017) Consortium blockchain for secure energy trading in industrial internet of things. IEEE Trans Ind Inf 14(8):3690–3700

Lu Y (2018) Blockchain and the related issues: a review of current research topics. J Manag Anal 5(4):231–255

Malik PK, Sharma R, Singh R, Gehlot A, Chandra Satapathy S, Alnumay WS, Pelusi D, Ghosh U, Nayak J (2021) Industrial internet of things and its applications in industry 4.0: state of the art. Comput Commun 166:125–139. ISSN 0140-3664. https://doi.org/10.1016/j.comcom.2020.11.016

Moschou K et al (2020) Performance evaluation of different Hyperledger Sawtooth transaction processors for blockchain log storage with varying workloads. In: 2020 IEEE international conference on blockchain (Blockchain), pp 476–481. https://doi.org/10.1109/Blockchain50366.2020.00069

Nakamoto S (2008) Bitcoin: a peer-to-peer electronic cash system. http://Bitcoin.org/Bitcoin. Accessed Jan 2017

Nguyen PT, Ha DH, Avand M, Jaafari A, Nguyen HD, Al-Ansari N, Van Phong T, Sharma R, Kumar R, Le HV, Ho LS, Prakash I, Pham BT (2020) Soft computing ensemble models based on logistic regression for groundwater potential mapping. Appl Sci 10:2469

Plos T, Hutter M, Feldhofer M, Stiglic M, Cavaliere F (2013) Securityenabled near-field communication tag with flexible architecture supporting asymmetric cryptography. IEEE Trans Very Large Scale Integr (VLSI) Syst 21(11):1965–1974

Qin R, Yuan Y, Wang F (2018) Research on the selection strategies of blockchain mining pools. IEEE Trans Comput Soc Syst 5(3):748–757

Qu Y, Pokhrel SR, Garg S, Gao L, Xiang Y (2021) A Blockchained federated learning framework for cognitive computing in industry 4.0 networks. IEEE Trans Ind Inf 17(4):2964–2973. https://doi.org/10.1109/TII.2020.3007817

Sajid S, Haleem A, Bahl S et al (2021) Data science applications for predictive maintenance and materials science in context to industry 4.0. Mater Today: Proc 45(6):4898–4905

Saxena S, Bhushan B, Ahad MA (2021) Blockchain based solutions to Secure Iot: background, integration trends and a way forward. J Netw Comput Appl 103050. https://doi.org/10.1016/j.jnca.2021.103050

Sharma R, Kumar R, Kumar Sharma D, Hoang Son L, Priyadarshini I, Thai Pham B, Tien Bui D, Rai S (2019) Inferring air pollution from air quality index by different geographical areas: case study in India. Air Qual Atmos Health 12:1347–1357

Sethi R, Bhushan B, Sharma N, Kumar R, Kaushik I (2020) Applicability of industrial IoT in diversified sectors: evolution, applications and challenges. In: Studies in big data multimedia technologies in the internet of things environment, pp 45–67. https://doi.org/10.1007/978-981-15-7965-3_4

Sharma R, Kumar R, Singh PK, Raboaca MS, Felseghi R-A (2020a) A systematic study on the analysis of the emission of CO, CO_2 and HC for four-wheelers and its impact on the sustainable ecosystem. Sustainability 12:6707

Sharma R, Kumar R, Satapathy SC, Al-Ansari N, Singh KK, Mahapatra RP, Agarwal AK, Le HV, Pham BT (2020b) Analysis of water pollution using different physicochemical parameters: a study of yamuna river. Front Environ Sci 8:581591. https://doi.org/10.3389/fenvs.2020.581591

Shukla A, Pansuriya Y, Tanwar S, Kumar N, Piran MJ (2021)Digital Twin-based prediction for CNC machines inspection using Blockchain for industry 4.0. In: ICC 2021—IEEE international conference on communications, pp 1–6. https://doi.org/10.1109/ICC42927.2021.9500498

Tang CB, Yang Z, Zheng ZL, Cheng ZY (2017) 'Analysis and optimization of game dilemma in PoW consensus algorithm.' Acta Automatica Sinica 43(9):1520–1531

Thanh V, Rohit S, Raghvendra K, Le Hoang S, Binh Thai P, Bui Dieu T, Ishaani P, Manash S, Tuong L (2020) Crime rate detection using social media of different crime locations and Twitter Part-of-speech Tagger with Brown Clustering: 4287–4299

Vishakha BS, Sharma N, Bhushan B, Kaushik I (2021) Blockchain-based cultivating ideas for growth: a new agronomics perspective. Adv Comput Commun Inf 195–219. https://doi.org/10.2174/9781681088624121010012

Vukolic´ M (2015) The quest for scalable blockchain fabric: Proof-of-work vs. BFT replication. In: International workshop on open problems in network security. Springer, 112–125

Vukolic´ M (2017) Rethinking permissioned blockchains. In: Proceedings of the ACM workshop on blockchain, cryptocurrencies and contracts, pp 3–7

Wang TT, Yu SY, Xu BM (2019) Research on PoW mining dilemma based on policy gradient algorithm. J Comput Appl 39(5):1336–1442. https://doi.org/10.11772/j.issn.1001-9081.201810 2197

Wu Y, Dai H-N, Wang H (2021) Convergence of blockchain and edge computing for secure and scalable IIoT critical infrastructures in industry 4.0. In: IEEE Internet of Things Journal 8(4):2300–2317. https://doi.org/10.1109/JIOT.2020.3025916

Zhang Y, Wen J (2015) An IoT electric business model based on the protocol of bitcoin. In 2015 18th international conference on intelligence in next generation networks, pp 184–191. https://doi.org/10.1109/ICIN.2015.7073830

Zhang S, Lee J-H (2019) Double-spending with a sybil attack in the bitcoin decentralized network. IEEE Trans Ind Inf 15(10):5715–5722. https://doi.org/10.1109/TII.2019.2921566

Zhou L, Su C, Yeh K-H (2019) A lightweight cryptographic protocol with certificateless signature for the Internet of Things. ACM Trans Embedd Comput Syst 18(3):1–10

Zyskind G, Nathan O, Pentland A (2015) Decentralizing privacy: using blockchain to protect personal data. In: 2015 IEEE security and privacy workshops, pp 180–184. https://doi.org/10.1109/SPW.2015.27

Chapter 13
Decentralized Blockchain Technology for the Development of IoT-Based Smart City Applications

Shashank Kumar, Pratik Jadon, Lakshya Sharma, Bharat Bhushan, and Ahmed J. Obaid

Introduction

For the past few years, blockchain has been surfacing in the headline as one of the most prominent technologies used for gathering data that draw the attention of several researchers and industries (Casino et al. 2019). Cryptocurrency is the first implementation of blockchain which is called Blockchain 1.0. Its successor emerged with the idea of a smart contract which is considered as a block of code that is defined, then executed, and then recorded in the distributed ledger and was called Blockchain 2.0. It was then succeeded by new Blockchain technology called Blockchain3.0 (Sunny et al. 2022). Blockchain 3.0 resolved around sectors like health care, financial, privacy, and security of important data and financial transactions (Li et al. 2022).

S. Kumar · P. Jadon (✉) · L. Sharma · B. Bhushan · A. J. Obaid
School of Engineering and Technology, Sharda University, Greater Noida, India
e-mail: 2020544538.pratik@ug.sharda.ac.in

S. Kumar
e-mail: 2020565265.shashank@ug.sharda.ac.in

L. Sharma
e-mail: 2020544570.lakshya@ug.sharda.ac.in

B. Bhushan
e-mail: bharat.bhushan@sharda.ac.in

A. J. Obaid
e-mail: ahmedj.aljanaby@uokufa.edu.iq

University of Kufa, Najaf, Iraq

© The Author(s), under exclusive license to Springer Nature Singapore Pte Ltd. 2023
D. K. Sharma et al. (eds.), *Low Power Architectures for IoT Applications*, Springer Tracts in Electrical and Electronics Engineering, https://doi.org/10.1007/978-981-99-0639-0_13

Data is continuously generated by all smart applications from heterogeneous sources. Still, recent technologies present for databases do not have the potential to handle, store and secure huge amounts of data (Liu et al. 2021). Devices such as sensors, smartphones, vehicles, etc. that are connected through the internet possess privacy risks and security issues (Jiang et al. 2019). Upcoming technologies have found a way for various opportunities for extra value creation, but progress regarding smart cities is still troubled by numerous challenges. Smart cities facing difficulty should improve the quality of life of their people by improving privacy protection, data sharing, data security, efficient decision-making, and good-quality services.

The most attractive part of using blockchain technology is that it provides privacy (Du et al. 2023). Blockchain periodically self-audits its network's digital value (between every 10 min approx) of its ecosystem through which it coordinates transition, one set of this transition is known as a block and this process leads to having two properties: transparency and impossible to corrupt (Bhutta et al. 2021). In the blockchain, the user's identity is kept safe as it's hidden through a powerful cipher, as one has to link 5 difficult-to-link public addresses to individual users to access its identity (Ahmad et al. 2022). Blockchain is nowadays already considered a powerful technology. It organizes its interaction in a way by which it vastly improves its reliability as well as also greatly eliminates the business and political risks regarding the handling of processes by central entities, thus lowering the requirement of trust. Blockchain is a network that creates a platform that can simultaneously run many different applications from many different companies, allowing seamless and effective dialogue and creating examining trails by which everyone verifies that all the processes are being processed correctly.

Markets of blockchain in health sectors are expected to be around 500 million dollars in 2022 (Sinha et al. 2022). Blockchain is used by the health sector for maintaining the audit of the material used in pharmaceutical products. Blockchain ensures the privacy of the record of patients during the development of their medical history of patients. It also helps in the development of important medicine. For the past few years, HIT (Health Information Technology) is the point of attraction of various studies (Pavel et al. 2013). Researchers have developed a variety of technologies like HMIS (Health management information system), EHR (electronic health record), HIoT (Health IoT) which is a segment of HIT and EMR (electronic medical record) (Bahalul Haque et al. 2022). Blockchain is used in the Internet of Things (IoT) by integrating different technologies. Developers are using blockchain for healthcare with the support of IoT and devices which can be carried easily by patients to keep the records of patients' sensitive data. This helps doctors to keep real-time records of patients who are at high risk. These wearable devices have various sensors like pulse sensors, blood pressure sensors, oxygen level sensors, etc. (Barvik et al. 2022; Goyal et al. 2020; Swain et al. 2022). The purpose of this paper is to discuss and explore the potential of blockchain in the development, and enhancement of various sectors in smart cities. It also discusses the development of blockchain technologies by integrating with IoT (Sadawi et al. 2021). The major contributions of this work can be enumerated as below.

- This paper presents the workings of blockchain and types of blockchain.
- This paper directed blockchain-enabled healthcare applications.
- This paper presents recent research onthe implementation of blockchain in smart cities.
- This paper also presented future advances of blockchain for smart cities.

The remainder of this paper is organized as follows. Section 13.2 presents an overview of the blockchain and the working of blockchain. Section 13.3 elaborates on the application of blockchain in various sectors of healthcare. Section 13.4 highlights the recent advances of blockchain. Finally, the paper concludes itself in Sect. 13.5 highlighting the major open research directions and future discussions.

Overview of Blockchain

The history, working, types of blockchain and application of blockchain in healthcare and transactions are discussed in the subsections below.

What is Blockchain?

Blockchain is a peer-to-peer network and decentralized that is made of nodes that stores data. Decentralization, anonymization, and persistence are the main characteristics of blockchain. Bitcoin is the first implementation of blockchain in 2008. It can be defined as a distributed ledger that logs data. Blockchain runs on a peer-to-peer network of computers (Lv et al. 2002). By using blockchain interaction of entities can be done without the central party. Each node in the network stores the data. It is a technology that is mainly used for protecting the sensitive data of a system. It is a collection of nodes that are interlinked to each other and nodes keep a record of past and recent changes. As it keeps a record of changes it allows collaboration between networks. These features protect the data from any hacking attempts. Due to the distributed ledger, it is impossible to delete entries which are accepted into the blockchain. Each User in the network has their own private key. Records in the blockchain are shielded by cryptography encryption. If anyone tries to alter the record or data, the signature will become invalid and the related network is going to be aware of the situation that one of the signatures is no longer valid (Anusha et al. 2022; Soni and Bhushan 2019). Due to these features blockchain gains so much attention in various sectors for data transmission or handling.

Types of Blockchain

Blockchain technology is used in exchanges of sensitive information and for safe transactions by a secured and safe network. Two technologies i.e. Blockchain and distributed ledger are being used parallel to each other for cryptocurrency. Experts divided Blockchain technology into four categories namely public, private, hybrid, and consortium blockchain (Das and Ammari 2009). Figure 13.1 presents the different types of blockchains.

Private Blockchain

Private blockchain is the one of blockchain technology which is restrictive and not so open, these types of blockchain also have features to access. In this blockchain, transaction permission is given under the control of the system administrator. Private blockchain develops things with advantages such as High efficiency, quicker transaction of data, improved scalability, and improved data privacy. Blockchain of this type works only on systems and networks that are closed. These blockchains have proper authorization, accessibility, security, and permissions. These blockchains are for voting on the management of supply chain, finding and handling digital identity, and so on. Various popular examples of this private blockchain type are like Hyperledger projects, Corda etc. These blockchains run with secured nodes which need authorization, thus no one apart from the one having the authorization to access it is able to access information like information of transactions between two different nodes (Buterin 2014).

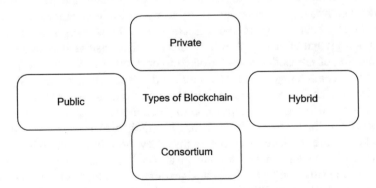

Fig. 13.1 Types of blockchain

Public Blockchain

Public blockchain is one of the biggest types of Blockchain, which is a decentralized as well as an open network and transactions access is available to everyone in this type of network of Blockchain technology. This blockchain technology is based on validation, the person which is validated is given a transaction reward, and furthermore, in this type, there are two types of models being used that are Proof-of-stake and Proof-of-work. It is the type of blockchain that is even a non-restrictive and ledger system that is distributed and anyone can be authorized if having access and can get the data or any part of the blockchain. However, these security protocols can be risky. A few examples of this type are Bitcoin, Ethereum, and Litecoin (Du et al. 2023).

Hybrid Blockchain

Hybrid Blockchain is a type of blockchain technology that is a combination of both private blockchain and public blockchain (Wu et al. 2017). This type of blockchain is required for improved and more access to the data. This blockchain deals with both centralized, as well as decentralized network systems, and it, is not open, but it still has various features in it like features of security as well as transparency. This type of blockchain considers maximum customization as most beneficial with both private permission-based network systems as well as permission-less public-based systems. These blockchains are flexible thus all new users can easily join it like a private blockchain and this blockchain has enabled us in improving the transparency and security of the network of blockchain.

Consortium Blockchain

Consortium Blockchains are a sub-part of Blockchain technology. These networks possess access controls and consist of present nodes. In this network, it has lesser nodes in comparison to other blockchain types such as public blockchain but as a result, it is far more scalable and secure in itself than others (Bai et al. 2022).

Working of Blockchain

Blockchain is a decentralized and peer-to-peer network without using any third parties to manage it. For instance, Bitcoin introduced a peer-to-peer (P2P) financial value transfer system in which no bank or other financial institution is required to share a financial data transaction with another institution or user on the Bitcoin blockchain network (Haleem et al. 2021). Such an agreement is within the shape of verifiable mathematical evidence; the provision of this agreement mechanism permits friends of a P2P community to transact with each other without necessarily trusting one another. Sometimes that is known as the trustless assets of blockchain. This lack of trust also means that a party interested in doing business with another blockchain entity does not necessarily know its true identity. This allows users of public blockchains the transaction of virtual currencies like bitcoin, Ethereum, etc. By hashing each block/node record or data is kept secure. This is mostly due to the fact that the mathematical hash function always generates hash codes of the same length for each block, regardless of the size of the data. Therefore, trying to alter a block of data would result in a brand-new hash value. Blockchain decentralizes the block which stores the record/data. This digital store of value enables peer-to-peer transactions over the Internet without the involvement of third parties (Saxena et al. 2021). A Blockchain network is a decentralized system made up of dispersed nodes (computers) that examine and confirm the legitimacy of any brand-new transactions to be made. The mining method is used to achieve this combined agreement using a number of consensus models. Each of the nodes is trying to attach the recent transaction that has worked hard to solve the intricate computational problem and is entitled to compensation for their efforts (Bhushan et al. 2021). Figure 13.2 presents the working steps of blockchain.

The management of health data, which might be enhanced by the capacity for disparate system integration and for enhancing the accuracy and privacy of EHR, it had to be given priority in the effort to change healthcare. EMR and EHR are two different things, they have different meanings (Adere 2022). An EMR basically contain the treatment, medical and operational history of the individual. On another side, EMR basically contain the patients overall medical report, dataset from the doctors related to the patients and it puts more effort on the patients care and how recovery of the patients can be done. According to the mapping study, blockchain technology helps manage EHRs. To handle authorization, permissions, and data exchange across healthcare stakeholders describe MedRec, an EHR-related implementation that suggests a decentralized method. The Ethereum platform is used by MedRec to give patients information about who have the permission to access the medical and health records of the patients. FHIRChain, a second programme that incorporates EHR, is available (Dubovitskaya et al. 2017; Jiang et al. 2018). Its healthcare record management-focused platform is based on blockchain for

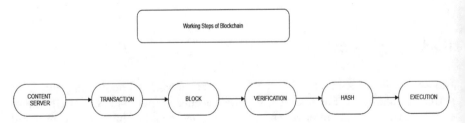

Fig. 13.2 Working steps of blockchain

exchanging health data that is developed using Ethereum. Patients can get solutions from FHIRChain that satisfy the ONC's standards.

Blockchain-Enabled HIoT Systems—A Case Study from a Smart City Perspective

Different types of applications of blockchain in healthcare like proper data handling of the patient's data, and integrating blockchain technology with IoT. Figure 13.3 presents a blockchain-enabled application in healthcare. The blockchain-enabled application in healthcare is discussed in the subsection below.

Storing Medical Data of Patients

After the completion of clinical study, huge amounts of data are generated. Healthcare uses the blockchain to check the validity of data and to store data. Blockchain has the framework for the cryptography of data that is shared and stored (Tulkinbekov and Kim 2021). All the details like the name of the patient, admission date, birth date, and all the treatment given to the patients are stored in the EHR format (Tulkinbekov and Kim 2021).

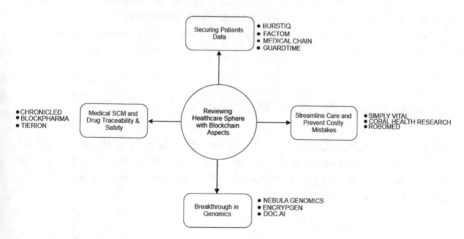

Fig. 13.3 Blockchain enabled HIoT systems

Examine the Effect of Procedure

Researchers analyse the effect of a particular treatment done on a large number of people after some period of time. Blockchain helps healthcare companies to collect real-time data for delivering the accurate prescription of medicine (Garcia and Kleinschmidt Jun 2020). They can take the procedure and the right amount to take a particular medicine. This real-time data also helps in alerting the patients during any type of emergency.

Alert During a Clinical Trial

During clinical time if any data that does not match the objective of the clinical trial or any false data that comes up during the trial will be addressed with the help of blockchain. This helps in increasing the accuracy of the results of a clinical trial (Seshadri et al. 2020).

Transparency, Safety, and Privacy

High levels of transparency and privacy are one of the main features of blockchain (Guidi et al. 2021). Precision diagnosis can be possible because of the safety provided by blockchain during an exchange of health data (Casey et al. 2018). It creates an ecosystem where health organization keeps in touch with each other and exchanges data with each other.

Hospitals Annual Financial Report

Doing clinical trials, research, and development requires lots of money, so it is necessary to maintain the financial update and it should be accurate. Researchers have developed technology using blockchain that can streamline the annual financial report (Casey et al. 2018).

Monitoring of Patient

Access control, data sharing, and monitoring an audit trail of medical activities are all possible with the use of blockchain technology (Hao 2022). Doctors can see the real-time data of patients, especially high-risk patients. Doctors can react immediately if any emergency comes (Muniasamy and Tabassam 2019).

Recognizing the Fake Records

Blockchain technology will give greater clarity and identify forgeries tenors and content of data. It offers more secure access to patients past medical records. Blockchain technologies first made it possible for common people to see what happened in clinical trials (Chen et al. 2020).

Research and Development

Blockchain can provide sensitive and valuable data. By exchanging affected person information, Blockchains might also additionally mobilize new and innovative studies initiatives (Hur 2011). Further, the trade of affected person findings in extra intensity will catalyze new and innovative studies.

Reduce the Transaction Cost

Blockchain networks reduce data conversion time and cost. In a Blockchain network issues and errors are resolved quickly and effectively with the confirmation of medical certificates. Blockchain network guarantees transaction guarantee and security. Blockchain is a dispersed network figuring innovation that permits putting away exchange history and every hub in this network processes checks and records every information input (Tai et al. 2017; Schmidt and Wagner 2019).

Blockchain-Based Solutions for IoT and Smart City Applications

Zhang et al. (2016) proposed a fully protected system for healthcare which is based on PSN. There are two protocols here. The first one is an improved and upgraded version of the system that is present in the IEEE 802.15.16 authenticated system. The second one is a protocol that uses blockchain technology for the transaction of data between nodes. Rahman et al. (2018) proposed an in-home management framework therapy that supports lower latency, anonymous and secure. It is sharing scenarios by utilizing nodes of IoT and the decentralized MEC paradigm built on blockchain technology. Ferraro et al. (2018) presented a set of delay differential equations to characterize the dynamical behavior of the Tangle, a directed acyclic network created for the cryptocurrency IOTA and inspired by the Internet of Things. The application of DLTs as a method for dynamic deposit pricing is proposed in the second section. Guo et al. (2018) analysed a method which is based on signature characterizes with various authorities to ensure the authenticity of EHR which is integrated with blockchain. A patient writes information without revealing its identity and another information accepts that it is attested. Wang et al. (2018) presented a framework based on the artificial systems + computational experiments + parallel execution (ACP) method for parallel healthcare systems (PHSs) in order to increase the precision of diagnosis and the efficacy of therapy.

Xie et al. (2019) proposed a comprehensive review of the literature on the application of blockchain technology in smart cities. Sharma et al. (2019) proposed an algorithm for blockchain selection nodes that are decentralized. They presented a model based on the platform of Ethereum that gathered the data mined from Litecoin pool. Ismail et al. (2019) analysed a lightweight architecture that reduces the computational and communication overhead compared to the Bitcoin network for healthcare data management by dividing the network participants into different clusters and maintaining one copy of the ledger per cluster.

Abou Jaoude and George Saade (2019) proposed a systematic literature review on blockchain technology and trace its growing popularity in relation to cryptocurrencies and similar technologies such as Bitcoin. The purpose of this white paper is to establish the current state of blockchain technology in the literature and to identify key research areas and applications where blockchain offers valuable solutions. Li et al. (2020) proposed the framework of ChainSDI that works with the blockchain technique. It computes the resources to manage secure data sharing and computing on sensitive patient data. They basically execute the programmable ChainSDI application to help home-based healthcare. Omar et al. (Begam et al. 2020) analysed blockchain technology with the use of smart contracts to computerize the GPO contract process. Yazdinejad et al. (Thanh et al. 2020) represented decentralized authentication of data of patients. It also proposed a detailed comparison between the model without blockchain and the model with blockchain to show the effectiveness of the model.

(Nguyen et al. 2020) proposed the analysis of blockchain technology that can be used in different smart cities. the features of blockchain that could be considered in the development of smart cities. (Jha ct al. 2019) highlight a responsive management system based on blockchain technology for the management of the power overall load of the industrial, residential and commercial places. (Sharma et al. 2019) explore the critical role of blockchain technology in smart city waste management. Blockchain technology can provide traceability, immutability, transparency, and auditability in a decentralized, trustworthy and secure way. (Sharma et al. 2020a) propose four forms of smart contracts: user authentication, access authorization, fraud detection, and access blocking. (Dansana et al. 2020) endorse blockchain-primarily based totally energy trading (B-ET) surroundings and layout clever contracts to make certain that transactions are carried out in a stable and straightforward manner.

(Malik et al. 2021) proposed a decentralized system for patient-centric healthcare management with a blockchain-based EHR using JavaScript-based smart contracts. To ensure the security of the proposed model a working prototype based on Hyperledger Fabric and Composer technologies has also been implemented. (Sharma et al. 2020b) presented a scope of blockchain technology related to incorporating blockchain in various sectors of society. Awareness about the application of blockchain technology in cities. (Dansana et al. 2021) analysed a healthcare system that has private, secure and reliable data sharing and exchange between users. To provide secure sharing of data they proposed a dynamic framework with LDP (Local Differential Privacy).

(Cunha et al. 2022) presented an overview of blockchain technology in healthcare. The business analytics of blockchain. It discusses the application of blockchains like EMRs, drugs supply chains etc. (Alzahrani et al. 2022) proposed a framework that recognizes the factors that help in securing the exchange of user data using blockchain technology. It has basically three factors: security, health care system, and blockchain. (Ming et al. Dec. 2022) presented a platform based on blockchain technology to secure patients' sensitive data. They propose a new data-processing framework that combines distributed and edge servers with a blockchain to facilitate frequent data processing. (Bawany et al. 2022) proposed a patient-centric mathematical data model and a healthcare digital twin system based on Blockchain. To collect the patient-sensitive data they proposed the mathematical data model.

Future Research Direction

This block bestows the recent advances of the blockchain which are perceived from the review paper. Infrastructure is a major part of smart cities along with the data of the people living in it which is being transmitted from multiple CPSs to the security operations center (SOC) through the internet, this gives rise to a huge threat to security. Smart cities need to build robust mechanisms to tackle this, a few of the advances are mentioned below.

Blockchain-As-A-Service (BaaS)

Blockchain architecture provides the addition of a BC layer to the general smart city architecture layer. In blockchain-enabled CPSs IoT-enabled, smart devices are integrated. The blockchain-enabled architecture of smart cities can be classified into four different layers and it supports robust security mechanisms. Out of these four layers

Sensing layer, Application layer, physical layer and blockchain layer the blockchain layer shows a huge importance as it offers Blockchain as a service (BaaS).

Non-Fungible Tokens (NFTs)

One of the most popular crypto-tokens uses the guidelines of the ERC-721 standards on developing (NFTS) by utilizing smart contracts on the Ethereum blockchain. NFTs appear for the ownership of digital or physical assets such as virtual collectibles, physical property or negative assets. It is believed that these tokens can be utilized to access, identify and authenticate assets in a smart city's infrastructure where devices and users can be identified by a public key and transact uniquely only via identified tokens.

Conclusion

Blockchain technology can help in multiple ways in the development of smart cities and healthcare facilities because of the properties like decentralization and inherent encryption. It promotes the monetization of health information, improves interoperability among healthcare organizations, and aids in the fight against counterfeit medicines. Precision diagnosis will be possible because of the safety guaranteed by blockchain during an exchange of health records and test data. It creates an ecosystem where health organizations keep in touch with each other and exchange data with each other. Blockchain technology integrated with IoT devices to keep track of real-time data of crucial patients. It also increases the security of patients' EMR. This includes proper management of the transaction of data. Records in the blockchain are shielded by cryptography encryption. If anyone tries to alter the record or data; the signature will no longer be valid and the peer network will immediately become aware of the situation (Table 13.1).

Table 13.1 The major advances in blockchain-based applications in healthcare

References	Year	Major Contribution
Zhang et al. (2016)	2016	Secured system for PSN-based healthcare
Rahman et al. (2018)	2018	Home therapy management system with low-latency, secure, anonymous
Ferraro et al. (2018)	2018	Set of delay differential equations to characterize the dynamical behavior of the Tangle
Guo et al. (2018)	2018	Analysed attribute-based signature method for the authenticity of EHRs
Wang et al. (2018)	2018	Framework for (PHS) with ACP method to increase diagnosis precision
Xie et al. (2019)	2019	Comprehensive review of the information on the blockchain technology application in smart cities
Sharma et al. (2019)	2019	Framework for novel algorithm miner node selection for decentralized network architectures of blockchain-based
Ismail et al. (2019)	2019	Analysed a lightweight architecture that reduces the computational and communication overhead compared to the Bitcoin network for healthcare data management
Abou Jaoude and George Saade (2019)	2019	Systematic literature review of blockchain technology and traces its growing popularity in relation to cryptocurrencies and similar technologies such as Bitcoin
Li et al. (2020)	2020	Framework of ChainSDI that works with the blockchain technique
(Begam et al. 2020)	2021	Analysed blockchain technology with the use of smart contracts to computerize the GPO contract process
(Thanh et al. 2020)	2020	Represented decentralized authentication of data. It also proposed a detailed comparison between the model with and without blockchain to show their effectiveness
(Nguyen et al. 2020)	2020	Analysis of blockchain technology that can be used in different smart cities
(Jha et al. 2019)	2020	Responsive management technique based on blockchain technology for the management of the power overall load
(Sharma et al. 2019)	2021	Explored various features of blockchain technology can provide as well as critical roles in smart cities that can be achieved via blockchain

(continued)

Table 13.1 (continued)

References	Year	Major Contribution
(Sharma et al. 2020a)	2021	Gave four different forms for smart contracts: Accessing by the user, fraud detection, authorization, and access blocking
(Dansana et al. 2020)	2021	Blockchain energy trading (B-ET) surroundings and layout of clever contracts to make those transactions are carried out in a stable and straightforward manner
(Malik et al. 2021)	2021	Blockchain-based EHR Decentralized healthcare management system using JavaScript-based smart contracts
(Sharma et al. 2020b)	2021	Presented the scope of blockchain in various sectors of society
(Dansana et al. 2021)	2022	LDP framework for a private, secure and reliable data sharing system for users
Cunha et al. (2022)	2022	Overview and business analytics of blockchain in healthcare
Alzahrani et al. (2022)	2022	Recognize the factors that help in securing the exchange of user data
Ming et al. (2022)	2022	Platform to secure patient-sensitive data using blockchain technology
Bawany et al. (2022)	2022	Patient-centric data model and a healthcare digital twin system

References

Abou Jaoude J, George Saade R (2019) Blockchain applications – usage in different domains. IEEE Access 7:45360–45381. doi:https://doi.org/10.1109/ACCESS.2019.2902501

Adere EM (2022) Blockchain in healthcare and IoT: a systematic literature review. Array 14:100139. https://doi.org/10.1016/j.array.2022.100139

Ahmad A, Saad M, Al Ghamdi M, Nyang D, Mohaisen D, BlockTrail: a service for secure and transparent blockchain-driven audit trails. IEEE Syst J 16(1):1367–1378. doi: https://doi.org/10.1109/JSYST.2021.3097744

Alzahrani AG, Alhomoud A, Wills G (2022) A framework of the critical factors for healthcare providers to share data securely using blockchain. IEEE Access 10:41064–41077. https://doi.org/10.1109/ACCESS.2022.3162218

Anusha R, Yousuff M, Bhushan B, Deepa J, Vijayashree J, Jayashree J (2022) Connecting blockchain with IoT—a review. In: Sharma DK, Peng SL, Sharma R, Zaitsev DA (eds) Micro-electronics and telecommunication engineering. lecture notes in networks and systems, vol 373. Springer, Singapore. https://doi.org/10.1007/978-981-16-8721-1_14

Bahalul Haque AKM, Bhushan B, Nawar A, Talha KR, Ayesha SJ (2022) Attacks and countermeasures in IoT based smart healthcare applications. In: Balas VE, Solanki VK, Kumar R (eds) Recent advances in internet of things and machine learning. intelligent systems reference library, vol 215. Springer, Cham. https://doi.org/10.1007/978-3-030-90119-6_6

Bai Y, Hu Q, Seo SH, Kang K, Lee JJ (2022) Public participation consortium blockchain for smart city governance. IEEE Internet Things J 9(3):2094–2108. doi:https://doi.org/10.1109/JIOT.2021.3091151

Barvik D, Cerny M, Penhaker M, Noury N (2022) Noninvasive continuous blood pressure estimation from pulse transit time: a review of the calibration models. IEEE Rev Biomed Eng 15:138–151. https://doi.org/10.1109/RBME.2021.3109643

Bawany NZ, Qamar T, Tariq H, Adnan S (2022) Integrating healthcare services using blockchain-based telehealth framework. IEEE Access 10:36505–36517. https://doi.org/10.1109/ACCESS.2022.3161944

Begam SS, JV, Selvachandran G, Ngan TT, Sharma R (2020) Similarity measure of lattice ordered multi-fuzzy soft sets based on set theoretic approach and its application in decision making. Mathematics 8:1255

Bhushan B, Sinha P, Sagayam KM, J, A. (2021) Untangling blockchain technology: a survey on state of the art, security threats, privacy services, applications and future research directions. Comput Electr Eng 90:106897. https://doi.org/10.1016/j.compeleceng.2020.106897

Bhutta MNM et al (2021) A survey on blockchain technology: evolution, architecture and security. IEEE Access 9:61048–61073. https://doi.org/10.1109/ACCESS.2021.3072849

Buterin VJwp, A Next-generation Smart Contract and Decentralized Application Platform, (2014)

Casey M, Crane J, Gensler G, Johnson S, Narula N (2018) The impact of blockchain technology on finance: a catalyst for change. Int. Center Monetary Banking Stud., London, U.K., 2018. [Online]. Available: https://www.sipotra.it/old/wp-content/uploads/2018/07/The-Impactof-Blockchain-Technology-on-Finance-A-Catalyst-for-Change.pdf

Casino F, Dasaklis TK, Patsakis C (2019) A systematic literature review of blockchain-based applications: Current status classification and open issues. Telematics Informat 36:55–81

Chen C, Wang C, Qiu T, Lv N, Pei Q (2020) A secure content sharing scheme based on blockchain in vehicular named data networks. IEEE Trans Industr Inf 16(5):3278–3289. https://doi.org/10.1109/TII.2019.2954345

Cunha J, Duarte R, Guimarães T, Quintas C, Santos MF (2022) Blockchain analytics in healthcare: an Overview. Proc Comput Sci 201:708–713

Dansana D, Kumar R, Das Adhikari J, Mohapatra M, Sharma R, Priyadarshini I, Le D-N (2020) Global forecasting confirmed and fatal cases of COVID-19 outbreak using autoregressive integrated moving average model. Front Public Health 8:580327. https://doi.org/10.3389/fpubh.2020.580327

Dansana D, Kumar R, Parida A, Sharma R, Adhikari JD et al (2021) Using susceptible-exposed-infectious-recovered model to forecast coronavirus outbreak. Comput Mater Continua 67(2):1595–1612

Das SK, Ammari HM. Routing and data dissemination. In: Zheng J, Jamalipour A (eds). Wireless Sensor Networks. Hoboken, NJ, USA: John Wiley & Sons, Inc.; 2009. p. 67–143. https://doi.org/10.1002/9780470443521.ch4

Du R, Ma C, Li M (2023) Privacy-preserving searchable encryption scheme based on public and private blockchains. Tsinghua Sci Technol 28(1):13–26. https://doi.org/10.26599/TST.2021.9010070

Dubovitskaya A, Xu Z, Ryu S, Schumacher M, Wang F (2017) Secure and trustable electronic medical records sharing using blockchain. Proc. AMIA Annu. Symp. pp. 650–659, 2017

Ferraro P, King C, Shorten R (2018) Distributed ledger technology for smart cities, the sharing economy, and social compliance. IEEE Access 6:62728–62746. https://doi.org/10.1109/ACCESS.2018.2876766

Garcia PSR, Kleinschmidt JH (2020) Sharing health and wellness data with blockchain and smart contracts. IEEE Lat Am Trans 18(06):1026–1033. https://doi.org/10.1109/TLA.2020.9099679

Goyal S, Sharma N, Bhushan B, Shankar A, Sagayam M (2020) Iot enabled technology in secured healthcare: Applications, challenges and future directions. Cogn Internet Med Things Smart Healthc 25–48. https://doi.org/10.1007/978-3-030-55833-8_2

Guidi B, Michienzi A, Ricci L (2021) Data persistence in decentralized social applications: the IPFS approach. In: 2021 IEEE 18th Annual Consumer Communications & Networking Conference (CCNC) |©2021 IEEE

Guo R, Shi H, Zhao Q, Zheng D (2018) Secure attribute-based signature scheme with multiple authorities for blockchain in electronic health records systems. IEEE Access 6:11676–11686. https://doi.org/10.1109/ACCESS.2018.2801266

Haleem A, Javaid M, Singh RP, Suman R, Rab S (2021) Blockchain technology applications in healthcare: an overview. Int J Intell Netw 2:130–139. https://doi.org/10.1016/j.ijin.2021.09.005

Hao I, Tang W, Huang C, Liu J, Wang H, Xian M (2022) Secure data sharing with flexible user access privilege update in cloud-assisted IoMT. IEEE Trans Emerg Top Comput 10(2):933–947

Hur J (2011) Improving security and efficiency in attribute-based data sharing. IEEE Trans Knowl Data Eng 25(10):2271–2282

Ismail L, Materwala H, Zeadally S (2019) Lightweight blockchain for healthcare. IEEE Access 7:149935–149951. https://doi.org/10.1109/ACCESS.2019.2947613

Jha S et al (2019) Deep learning approach for software maintainability metrics prediction. IEEE Access 7:61840–61855

Jiang R, Shi M, Zhou W (2019) A privacy security risk analysis method for medical big data in urban computing. IEEE Access 7:143841–143854. https://doi.org/10.1109/ACCESS.2019.2943547

Jiang S, Cao J, Wu H, Yang Y, Ma M, He J (2018) BlocHIE: A blockchain-based platform for healthcare information exchange. In: Proc. IEEE Int. Conf. Smart Comput. (SMARTCOMP), pp. 49–56

Li T, Wang H, He D, Yu J (2022) Blockchain-based privacy-preserving and rewarding private data sharing for IoT. IEEE Internet Things J 9(16):15138–15149. doi:https://doi.org/10.1109/JIOT.2022.3147925

Li P et al (2020) ChainSDI: a software-defined infrastructure for regulation-compliant home-based healthcare services secured by blockchains. IEEE Syst J 14(2):2042–2053. https://doi.org/10.1109/JSYST.2019.2937930

Liu L, Zhou S, Huang H, Zheng Z (2021) From technology to society: an overview of blockchain-based DAO. IEEE Open J Comput Soc 2:204–215. https://doi.org/10.1109/OJCS.2021.3072661

Lv Q, Cao P, Cohen E, Li K, Shenker S (2002) Search and replication in unstructured peer-to-peer networks. In: Proceedings of the 16th international conference on Supercomputing – ICS '02, p. 84. https://doi.org/10.1145/514191.514206. New York, New York, USA

Malik PK, Sharma R, Singh R, Gehlot A, Satapathy SC, Alnumay WS, Pelusi D, Ghosh U, Nayak J (2021) Industrial internet of things and its applications in industry 4.0: state of the art, Comput Commun 166:125–139. ISSN 0140–3664, https://doi.org/10.1016/j.comcom.2020.11.016

Ming Z, Zhou M, Cui L, Yang S (2022) FAITH: a fast blockchain-assisted edge computing platform for healthcare applications. IEEE Trans Industr Inf 18(12):9217–9226. https://doi.org/10.1109/TII.2022.3166813

Muniasamy A, Tabassam S (2019) Deep learning for predictive analytics in healthcare. Conference Paper, March 2019. DOI: https://doi.org/10.1007/978-3-030-14118-9

Nguyen PT, Ha DH, Avand M, Jaafari A, Nguyen HD, Al-Ansari N, Van Phong T, Sharma R, Kumar R, Le HV, Ho LS, Prakash I, Pham BT (2020) Soft computing ensemble models based on logistic regression for groundwater potential mapping. Appl Sci 10:2469

Pavel et al (2013) The role of technology and engineering models in transforming healthcare. IEEE Rev Biomed Eng 6:156–177. https://doi.org/10.1109/RBME.2012.2222636

Peltokangas M, Vehkaoja A, Verho J, Huotari M, Röning J, Lekkala J (2014)Monitoring arterial pulse waves with synchronous body sensor network. IEEE J Biomed Health Inform 18(6) 1781–1787. doi: https://doi.org/10.1109/JBHI.2014.2328788

Rahman MA et al (2018) Blockchain-based mobile edge computing framework for secure therapy applications. IEEE Access 6:72469–72478. https://doi.org/10.1109/ACCESS.2018.2881246

Sadawi AA, Hassan MS, Ndiaye M (2021) A survey on the integration of blockchain with IoT to enhance performance and eliminate challenges. IEEE Access 9:54478–54497. https://doi.org/10.1109/ACCESS.2021.3070555

Saxena S, Bhushan B, Ahad MA (2021) Blockchain based solutions to Secure Iot: Background, integration trends and a way forward. J Netw Comput Appl 103050. https://doi.org/10.1016/j. jnca.2021.103050

Schmidt CG, Wagner SM (2019) Blockchain and supply chain relations: a transaction cost theory perspective. J Purchasing Supply Manage 25(4):100552

Seshadri RD, Evan V, Davies, Ethan RH, Jeffrey JH, Shanina C, Knighton C, Timothy AW, James EV, Colin KD (2020) Wearable sensors for COVID-19: A call to action to harness our digital infrastructure for remote patient monitoring and virtual assessments. Front Digit Health 2(2020):8

Sharma PK, Kumar N, Park JH (2019) Blockchain-based distributed framework for automotive industry in a smart city. IEEE Trans Industr Inf 15(7):4197–4205. https://doi.org/10.1109/TII. 2018.2887101

Sharma R, Kumar R, Singh PK, Raboaca MS, Felseghi R-A (2020a) A systematic study on the analysis of the emission of CO, CO_2 and HC for four-wheelers and its impact on the sustainable ecosystem. Sustainability 12:6707

Sharma R, Kumar R, Satapathy SC, Al-Ansari N, Singh KK, Mahapatra RP, Agarwal AK, Le HV, Pham BT (2020b) Analysis of water pollution using different physicochemical parameters: a study of Yamuna River. Front Environ Sci 8:581591. https://doi.org/10.3389/fenvs.2020.581591

Sharma R, Kumar R, Sharma DK, Son LH, Priyadarshini I, Pham BT, Bui DT, Rai S (2019) Inferring air pollution from air quality index by different geographical areas: case study in India. Air Qual Atmos Health 12, 1347–1357 (2019)

Sinha A, Patel A, Jagdish M (2022)Application of Blockchain in Healthcare. In: 2022 First International Conference on Artificial Intelligence Trends and Pattern Recognition (ICAITPR), 2022, pp. 1–4. doi:https://doi.org/10.1109/ICAITPR51569.2022.9844186

Soni S, Bhushan B (2019) A Comprehensive survey on Blockchain: Working, security analysis, privacy threats and potential applications. In: 2019 2nd international conference on intelligent computing, instrumentation and control technologies (ICICICT). DOI: https://doi.org/10.1109/ icicict46008.2019.8993210.

Sunny FA et al (2022) A systematic review of blockchain applications. IEEE Access 10:59155–59177. https://doi.org/10.1109/ACCESS.2022.3179690

Swain S, Bhushan , Dhiman, G. et al. (2020) Appositeness of optimized and reliable machine learning for healthcare: a survey. Arch Computat Methods Eng 29:3981–4003. https://doi.org/ 10.1007/s11831-022-09733-8

Tai X, Sun H, Guo Q (2017) Transaction efficiency analysis of blockchain applied to energy Internet. Power Syst. Technol. 41(10):3400–3406

Thanh V, Rohit S, Raghvendra K, Hoang SL, Thai PB, Dieu TB, Ishaani P, Manash S, Tuong L (2020) Crime rate detection using social media of different crime locations and twitter part-of-speech tagger with brown clustering 4287–4299

Tulkinbekov K, Kim D-H (2021) Storing blockchain data in public storage. Twelfth International Conference on Ubiquitous and Future Networks (ICUFN) 2021:299–301. https://doi.org/10.1109/ ICUFN49451.2021.9528568

Wang S et al (2018) Blockchain-powered parallel healthcare systems based on the ACP approach. IEEE Trans Comput Soc Syst 5(4):942–950. https://doi.org/10.1109/TCSS.2018.2865526

Wu L, Meng K, Xu S, Li S, Ding M, Suo Y (2017) Democratic centralism: a hybrid blockchain architecture and its applications in energy Internet. Proc. IEEE Int. Conf. Energy Internet (ICEI), pp. 176–181, Apr. 2017

Xie J, et al. (2019) A survey of blockchain technology applied to smart cities: research issues and challenges. IEEE Commun Surv & Tutor 21(3):2794–2830, third quarter 2019. doi:https://doi. org/10.1109/COMST.2019.2899617

Zhang J, Xue N, Huang X (2016) A secure system for pervasive social network-based healthcare. IEEE Access 4:9239–9250. https://doi.org/10.1109/ACCESS.2016.2645904

Chapter 14
Nullifying the Prevalent Threats in IoT Based Applications and Smart Cities Using Blockchain Technology

Lokesh Yadav, Milan Mitra, Akash Kumar, Bharat Bhushan, and Mustafa A. Al-Asadi

Introduction

The revolutionary population expansion in urban areas has been witnessed in the past few decades. Only 45% of the population is living in rural areas which will further reduce to 30% in the next 3 decades and 25% of the population would shift to urban cities (Department of Economic and Social Affairs 2014). This eruptive population growth would make it impossible for current methods to deal with economic, social, educational and other sorts of problems. To cope up with these inescapable problems, officials and chairpersons are moreover interested in implementing the smart cum sustainable methods to tackle both tangible and intangible (various sources of capital) assets (Bibri and Krogstie 2017). Thus, the idea of a smart city comes into play. A Smart city is a combination of various systems designed to deal with problems mentioned above by evolving and adapting to the changes and needs of the environment and other sorts of commodities with the help of data analysis thus reducing human involvement. Decentralization, transparency, privacy, security, and this interconnection are the main features of blockchain which could be tools to manage, develop, maintain and run smart cities. The elimination of mediators i.e. decentralization is the main objective of achieving sustainability (Makrushin and Dashchenko 2016).

While considering the security aspect, the major enhancement in IoT and wireless transmission has made it simple and easy for a range of devices to get interconnected

L. Yadav (✉) · M. Mitra · A. Kumar · B. Bhushan
School of Engineering and Technology, Sharda University, Greater Noida, India
e-mail: lokeshyadav4703@gmail.com

B. Bhushan
e-mail: bharat.bhushan@sharda.ac.in

M. A. Al-Asadi
Department of Computer Engineering, Selçuk University, Konyo, Turkey
e-mail: masadi@lisansustu.selcuk.edu.tr

© The Author(s), under exclusive license to Springer Nature Singapore Pte Ltd. 2023
D. K. Sharma et al. (eds.), *Low Power Architectures for IoT Applications*, Springer Tracts in Electrical and Electronics Engineering, https://doi.org/10.1007/978-981-99-0639-0_14

and even share data from distinct locations. However, the data which is open may contain sensitive information like financial, personal and other private information thus increasing the chances of security attacks and hence they must be able to repel these deadly attacks. As shown by Kaspersky Labs, smart terminals like self-service machines, bicycle rental terminals and information kiosks have many security gaps (Bhushan et al. 2020). Cybercriminals could target these devices and can further get access to the private and financial information of any user. It is important to note that the old security mechanism has failed to make the city's critical infrastructure smart. Thus, alternative and new solutions should be developed which provide data privacy, confidentiality and integrity which is based on the data type i.e. public or private. This article conceptualizes a security framework based on blockchain which would let the communication between entities of smart city to communicate without compromising the cost of privacy and security.

Due to variegated types of resources constrained in devices smart cities are vulnerable to many data security attacks. Therefore, identification of these kinds of important threats and their further leading consequences need to be identified to design a relevant solution. Numerous studies and research have been carried out in this area like Computer Emergency Response Teams (CERT) which provides graphical information about potential risks, Open Web Application Security Project (OWASP) mobilize common security attacks, G-Cloud which shows a collection of Cloud Computer Service Provider (CCSP) needs (OWASP Foundation 2013; Goyal et al. 2021; HMGovernment 2011). Major threats to smart cities are as follows- Integrity threats-this includes manipulation and alteration of critical data and information through unauthorized means. Authenticity threats—Access of resources and critical information by unauthorized means. Availability threats—Upholding of resources by unauthorized means. Accountability threats—Refusal of acceptance or transmission of messages by co-related entities. Confidentiality threats—Disclosure of critical information by unauthorized access (Biswas and Muthukkumarasamy 2016). The main contributions of this work are enumerated below.

- This paper presents the dimensions of smart cities, security framework and major cyberattacks launched in the realm of smart cities.
- This paper explores the working of blockchain, its type, its consensus protocols and motivation for its widespread deployment in smart cities.
- This paper presents the major recent advancements dedicated towards blockchain enabled secure smart cities.
- This paper also presents future advancements in securing smart cities with or without blockchain.

The remainder of this article is organized as follows: Sect. 14.2 presents an overview of the smart city dimension of smart cities, the security of the frameworks and layers involved in it. Section 14.3 highlights major cyberattacks on smart cities. Section 14.4 elaborates on the workings of blockchain, its types, its consensus protocols, and the motivation for its widespread deployment in smart cities. Section 14.5 highlights the recent advances in securing smart cities with blockchain. Finally, the paper concludes itself in Sect. 14.6, highlighting the major open research directions and future discussion.

Overview of Smart City

Smart city includes various reliable frameworks and designs with the top most priority of user convenience according to primary needs compromising security, privacy, all shorts of solution to Urban problems along with secure transactions and other data monitoring features. The main reason for bringing up the smart city concept is to provide the most reliable and quality efficient development of infrastructure with the utilization of fore technologies like IoT and Machine Learning (ML) with Artificial Intelligence in order to develop a user-friendly ecosystem that provides interaction and deployment of digital services and devices interaction to uplift the quality of living of peoples. This integration provides a secure network that does not compromise security; moreover, as we further proceed with automation, the above-mentioned components should hold cyber security as one of the primary components (Alnahari and Ariaratnam 2022).

Smart Cities Dimensions

The four major pillars involved in the planning of smart cities are economic, social, physical, and institutional infrastructures. The main motive for the dimensions of smart cities is to support the above-mentioned pillars (Silva et al. 2018).

Smart Economy

Apostol et al. (2020) researched about smart economy projects and talked about strategies and suggestions that motivates creative vision along with scientific research, leading-edge technology, and the idea of sustainable development with regard to the environment. Zahi et al. (2016) described a smart economy as creative, full of statistics figures and data with the determination of competition and transmission technologies about the economy and its resources. Kumar (Bhushan and Sahoo 2017) studied smart economies and addressed the understanding of economies based on research in all factors, including heritage, industry, business, development, construction planning, and science. The smart economy has various forms in smart cities, along with different features, challenges, and remedies.

Smart Governance

Silva et al. (2018) explored the different dimensions of smart cities and their challenges and further showed that the governance of smart cities collaborated with offerings to various services, including public and social services, managing decisions along with governance with full transparency. The author defines governance as cooperation between institutions of administration and citizens. Also, maximum gain in the aspects of greater dependability, planning, and productiveness of services could be achieved with governance by a combination of public, and civil governing systems. Addressing governance with technology is critical because it makes sure to represent every service of the city via high-tech solutions. On the basis of a study on smart city features, he classifies different methods for expanding smart cities' creative potential (Silva et al. 2018). Nilssen focuses mostly on collective governance to upgrade creative transformation (Nilssen 2019). Collective governance can be achieved directly through e-governance. E-governance can be intensified by artificial intelligence (AI) and 5G technology. Collaborative governance with the help of information based on cloud services aids in the contribution, involvement, and splitting of information (Ismagilova et al. 2019).

Smart Living

The important components for smart living observed by the OECD which is a Better-Life Initiative framework called are the evolution and maintenance of natural, profitable, human capitals. Medical management can be achieved completely by actual time tracking of the requirements of care, and urgent sustenance activated by the ICT (Ismagilova et al. 2019; Mehta et al. 2022; Nižetić et al. 2020). Another important factor for smart living is the upshot of the smart economy. ICT is considered as a helping guide in smart living via automatic connectivity network-enabled living space processing, and merging security systems (Ande et al. 2020; Bhowmik et al. 2022). Author states that smart homes consist of applications that are linked to smart assistance and these applications grab individual information about their users even then no harm is done to any security system or privacy. Elahi et al. (2019) did research on the lucidity of products available in smart cities and labeled that provisions for smart applications along with setting standards are important to discover the probability of risks connected with these products.

Smart Mobility

Smart mobility centralizes majorly on the foundation of infrastructure and transport networks. The author discusses common issues such as overcrowding, long chain queues and hindrances which led to delays (Appio et al. 2019). They put forward the idea that the system should divert attention from the operation of private vehicles and come up with interrelated alternatives for people to relieve their travel schedule.

Actual real-time data on roads and time travelers' analysis is compiled using IoT (Silva et al. 2018). With the help of IoT, there is a linking of information in automobile means of transport and IOV helps in the functioning of traffic safety to reach smart mobility (Ismagilova et al. 2019). The universal operation of IoT and IOV maximizes the effectiveness needed to attain smart mobility. It also came up with a superior transport system (Porru et al. 2020). For the sanction of smart mobility, there is a need to allow technologies like AI, IoT, big data, and blockchain along with their developments and answers (Paiva et al. 2021).

Smart People

The main role in smart cities development is played by two important elements-social capital and human capital. The potentiality and skill of an individual or a mass are defined as Human Capital on the other side Social Capital points towards the caliber and numeral amount of relation linking in between social organizations. There is a high requirement for efficient human and social capital for fruitfulness and creativity in building smart cities. Human capital can only be developed by implementing the role of higher education in schools and universities. To become a wiser and smarter individual, one needs knowledge and understanding, which can only be gained through high educational institutes (Ismagilova et al. 2019). Smart applications such as AI and big data help to lift up the learning and teaching proficiency to upgrade a better grip on knowledge gaining (Radu 2020).

Security Framework

A data security framework is a defined approach to making data processing free from data security risks and data protection threats. Security frameworks in four different layers are discussed below.

Physical Layer

Devices used in the smart city come with sensors and actuators which accumulate and send data further to higher or upper levels. A few of such devices Acer Fitbit and Nest thermostat are more likely to have cyberattacks because of poor encryption and maybe access control structures. And then, there are no standards available for smart devices which can share and integrate data which is generated by the smart devices to bring forth cross functionality (Topal et al. 2020).

Communication Layer

Different types of communication mechanisms are used by smart city networks. For ex-Ethernet, Bluetooth, 4G and 3G to pass information between various systems. This layer must be integrated with blockchain protocols to bring forth the security and privacy of data (Arsh et al. 2021).

Database Layer

One after another, a decentralized database stores records, known as distributed ledger. Unique cryptographic signatures and timestamps are included in each record in the ledger. Any authorized user may verify and audit the ledger's whole transaction history. Distributed ledgers can be either permissionless as well as permissioned. The main advantages of a permissionless ledger are transparency and censorship resistance. However, compared to the private ledger, the public ledger takes a longer time to attain agreement and requires more maintenance of complex records. In addition, anonymous attackers may target public ledgers. Thus, to provide security, scalability, and speed in real-time applications like traffic systems in a smart city, it is advised to use private ledgers (Yu et al. 2018).

Interface Layer

This layer contains several intelligent applications that work together to make effective decisions. For instance, to turn on the air conditioner a few minutes before you arrive home, a smartphone application can deliver location to a smart home system. Although, vulnerabilities and bugs in one application might provide anonymous attackers access to dependent operations. So, the app should be carefully integrated (Hussain et al. 2018).

Attacks in IoT Enabled Smart City Applications

Nowadays, Cyber Attacks in smart cities are very common and exponentially increasing day by day. There are several types of cyberattacks, some of them are listed below in this section.

Data and Identity Theft

Unsecured smart city data facilitates vile behavior with an abundance of targeted sensitive data that can ultimately be used for suspicious transactions. An identity thief that obtains a victim's credit or debit card or national insurance number may use it to make transactions or create accounts in the victim's name. Financial gain is the main purpose of the attack, a poll also revealed that a big majority of respondents place the greatest importance on their passwords. It may also be performed with an account that almost all people don't mind giving out like email (Burnes et al. 2020).

Distributed Denial-of-Service Attack (DDoS)

DDoS issue addressed in this study is that one or more devices transmit unusually enormous amounts of data in order to overwhelm a network. DDoS assaults are effective because they use several computer servers to attack web traffic. Personal computers that were potentially compromised are made up of networks which allows the attacker to manage them remotely. Once a botnet is created, delivering remote commands to each bot the attacker may conduct the attack (Khalaf et al. 2019).

Permanent Denial of Service (PDoS)

PDoS, also known colloquially as Phlashing, in this necessitating hardware replacement or reinstallation is required as this attack causes significant damage to the device (Bhushan and Sahoo 2017). An attacker bricks a device or damages firmware during such an attack, leaving the device or an entire network inoperable. Because the attacks are permanent, the attackers also couldn't demand a monetary payment to terminate the attack, but this generates problems for the victim.

Device Hijacking

The attacker controls the device or hijacks it by seizing control over everything. Because the attacker does not affect the basic functions of the device, these attacks can be more difficult to detect. Hackers may use browser security holes to induce victims to download their malware, commonly known as hijackware (Flynn et al. 2020). Various cyberattacks rely on some form of kidnapping, as well as other kidnappings such as B. Criminals hijacking planes or hijacking invulnerable transport vehicles.

Man-In-The-Middle (MITM)

In order to eavesdrop or impersonate one of the participants, the perpetrator puts themselves together into a dialogue between a user and a software. MITM is about the certain data flowing between endpoints and the furtiveness and rectitude of the data itself (Al-shareeda et al. 2020). This attack is based on multiple parameters, including the attacker's location within the network, the nature of the conversation channel, and enactment techniques. Then, based on our taxonomy of pose techniques, we provide electrocution instructions for each MITM class.

Eclipse Attack

Controlling a victim's local Internet connection is part of the eclipse. To begin, the attacker obscures the merchant's view of the blockchain. Seemingly legitimate transaction H including payment for a good is sent to the merchant, and then a defective transaction F to the miners is transmitted which shifts the cash elsewhere. The attacker floods the network with rogue nodes and communicates with infected nodes (Liu et al. 2020).

Sybil Attack

Sybil's attack attacks the entire network, trying to affect the network by flooding it by including a large number of nodes with fictitious IDs. In this, Sybil nodes are closely connected with other Sybil nodes. The ability to interact with authentic nodes is not strong in a Sybil attack. There are a limited number of social connections between Sybil and honest nodes. The main goal is to wield popular options or reputation (Bhushan and Sahoo 2020). For example, in an online voting system, SA-1 can illegally impersonate many identities to act as a regular user and vote on partisan options.

Double Spending

The double-spend is a basic Bitcoin assault attack. In this, an attacker makes a transaction that moves money to a business's address. After the transaction is shown in the most recent block, the attacker gets ownership of the purchased goods. After that the attacker immediately releases two blocks, the first of which contains a transaction that sends the money to a second address owned by himself (Begum et al. 2020).

Race Attack

The attacker sends an unusual exchange to a victim while concurrently sending another transaction to the network. This gives the merchant the impression thinking his transaction might be the first, but the attacker never submits it to the blockchain network. First, the user logs out and requests a transaction through the user's wallet (Aggarwal and Kumar 2021). This unjustifiable transaction takes place in a pool of unjustifiable transactions, from which a miner selects his transactions, solves a complex numerical problem through the POW consensus, obtains a unique hash output, and sends it to Add blocks to the blockchain. Blocks are added only if other miners verify these hashes.

51% Attack

51% attack is a smart blockchain attack in which fifty percent of the total of the network's mining hash rate is dominated by a team of hackers, and these ruling parties have the power to modify the blockchain by owning 51% of the whole network's nodes (Ye et al. 2018). This attack begins by privately accomplishing a chain of blocks that is completely separate from any version of the chain. Later, the decoupled chains are granted to the network and built as real chains. This allows for double-spending attacks.

Blockchain Enabled Smart Cities

Smart cities offer various unique benefits including privacy, reliability, better scalability, efficiency and fault tolerance. Blockchain integrated Smart city provides more resistance to threats. Thus, integration of blockchain on all the available smart devices would create a web that would provide better reliable and secure communication.

Motivation for Deployment of Blockchain in IoT Based Smart Cities

Currently, popularity is gained by smart city projects, and many nations and cities such as Manchester, Amsterdam, Madrid, Singapore, Barcelona, etc. are actively planning and making strategies to convert normal cities into smart cities (Xie et al. 2019). Also, a variety of smart city testbeds were developed to evaluate and simulate the proposed solutions for smart cities (Lanza et al. 2015). Some of them are listed below:

- SmartSantander is a well known testbed in which RFID tag labels/2000 popular QR codes, 200 GPRS modules, and 2000 IoT devices are successfully deployed in Santander, Spain (Latre et al. 2016). Additionally, eight use cases are implemented, including free parking, traffic monitoring, augmented reality, mobile perimeter monitoring, perimeter monitoring, outdoor parking management and participatory sensing.
- A new smart city testbed called City of Things is in Antwerp, Belgium (https://www.ibm.com/in-en/topics/what-is-blockchain#:~:text=Blockchain%20defi ned%3A%20Blockchain%20is%20a,patents%2C%20copyrights%2C%20bran ding). It arranges validation of advanced experiments of smart cities at the two users along with the technology level.
- NYUAD is developed by Abu Dhabi Center for Cyber Security (CCS-AD), a smart city test bed that aims to give a realistic and real-time environment of a smart city (Biswas and Muthukkumarasamy 2016). These environments further can be used by researchers or developers to study and rate the models they provide.

Blockchain Technology Overview

Blockchain ledger which is shared and records transactions, tracks assets (tangible and intangible), agreements, and contracts (Qiu et al. 2018). Originally developed to guide cryptocurrency transactions, but can also be used in all short-term transactions except the mediator. The major convenience of the blockchain is that to give up the hash power of the network, 51% of the system must be compromised. Hence, concluding the impracticality of succeeding in an attack over the blockchain network. Whenever any transaction happens over a blockchain network it is categorized as a block containing proof of work, record of transactions, number of the block, and also previous block's number to each and every entity involved in this network. The block gets cross checked by the entities and when 50% plus of them approve the transaction then it becomes successful and hence gets included in the current chain.

Types of Blockchain

The four major categories of blockchains are described in subsections below.

Public Blockchain

Public blockchains do not need any permissions and further allow any random person to join, they are also 100% decentralized. In these types of blockchain access rights, node creation rights, as well as validation rights are the same for every node. Till date, all sorts of transactions including mining and exchange of cryptocurrencies are done over the public blockchain. By computing hard cryptographic equations the nodes over the public blockchain mine crypto over most familiar coins like Bitcoin, In exchange these nodes are rewarded with small amounts of cryptocurrencies, where they act as bank tellers who get the reward for transaction formulation.

Private Blockchains

Private blockchains also known to be managed blockchains are called so because a single organization controls them and they also require specific permissions. A node to be part of the blockchain is totally determined by the central authority, and the functional rights may not be necessarily same for each and every node. Since public access is restricted over managed blockchains they are not fully decentralized. Many B2B digital currency exchanges like ripple are examples of private blockchains. Private and public blockchain have their own disadvantages—private blockchains are more likely to be scams whereas public blockchains are time taking for the validation of any new data.

Consortium Blockchains

Consortium blockchains are similar in terms of requiring permissions like private blockchains. They also differ from private blockchains as they are in control by a group of organizations, rather than any individual entity. Thus, making it more decentralized and further increasing the security. The involvement of a number of groups makes it challenging to operate since every group may not have all the required infrastructure as well as technology required to implement blockchain and also it creates a trust risk.

Working of Blockchain

In recent years, we may have recorded that many companies around the world have integrated blockchain technology in late new years. But how does it work? Is it one major change or a simple extension? Blockchain progress is just beginning and has revolutionary potential in the future. So let's start debunking this technology. Figure 14.1 shows the Process of transaction in a blockchain.

Blockchain is a solution of three main technologies: A Peer-to-Peer network with shared ledger, Cryptographic keys, and a computing device that stores network transactions and records.

Cryptography keys consist of two keys—a public key and a private key. These keys make every transaction between two parties successful. Everyone carries the above-mentioned two keys for creating a secure digital identity reference. This aspect of Blockchain is the most critical secured identity. In the cryptocurrency world, this identification is known as a "virtual signature" and is used to authorize and manage transactions. Digital signatures are integrated in peer-to-peer networks. Various

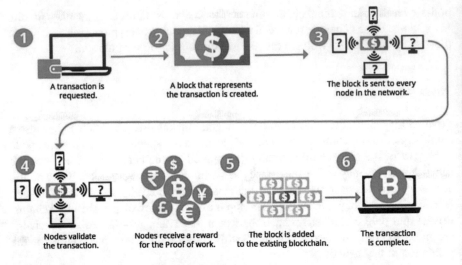

Fig. 14.1 Process of transaction in a blockchain

people assist as high-level advisors create agreements on transactions using digital signatures. Once they authorize the transaction, the numerical checks prove it and the transaction is acknowledged and protected between two parties associated with the network. In short, blockchain users practice cryptographic keys to conduct various kinds of digital communications over peer-to-peer networks. In summary, blockchain users use cryptographic keys to conduct various kinds of digital intercommunication over peer-to-peer networks.

Whenever a blockchain is included in a new blockchain transaction or a new block needs to be added to the blockchain, typically multiple nodes in the same blockchain implementation are required to run algorithms for evaluation, testing, and processing. Blockchain block history: A new block of a blockchain transaction is added to the ledger and a new block of all-inclusive data is combined with the blockchain once most nodes have authenticated the history and signature of the block. Blocks will be rejected for addition to the blockchain if consensus is not reached. This dispersed consensus model allows the blockchain to act as a distributed ledger without the need for a central authority or unified authorization to approve the blockchain transactions as shown in Fig. 14.1. Blockchain transactions are therefore very secure.

Consensus Protocols

The blockchain consensus protocol can be found in several definitive goals, such as achieving consensus, working together, collaboration, equal rights of all nodes, and compulsory participation of all nodes in the consensus process. Different types of Consensus protocols are described in further sections below.

PoS (Proof of Stake)

In this, the stake that is held determines which node is selected to build each new block, not the computational power. The major difference between PoW and PoS is that the simple way to find the solution is to find out the stake amount instead of adjusting the nonce several times. Hence, we can say that PoS uses energy efficiently. Similarly to PoW, this is also called as probabilistic-finality consensus protocol.

DPoS (Delegated Proof of Stake)

DPoS works on the basic principle of letting the nodes holding a stake vote on the choice of block validators. With this type of voting, stakeholders get the right to create blocks for the representatives they support and not create blocks themselves, thus reducing consumption power to 0. In comparison to PoS and PoW, this consensus protocol is low-cost and provides high efficiency.

PoW (Proof of Work)

Bitcoin and Ethereum have adopted PoW etc. In each consensus round, PoW selects a node and builds a different block using competition for computational power. The nodes which take part in the competition have to decode the cryptographic puzzle. Permission to create new blocks is only given to all nodes that tackle the puzzle first. Solving a PoW puzzle is very complex. A Higher level of computational power is required by the nodes to auto-adjust the value to find the right answer.

Ripple

Ripple is an open source based payment protocol[i]. In this, with the help of tracking or validating nodes clients initiate the transactions which are then broadcasted in the entire network, node validation performs the consensus process, and each node has a list of trusted nodes known as the Unique Node List (UNL). Votes for transactions are awarded to delegates backed by UNL nodes.

PoI (Point of Importance)

In PoS, the users who have more coins have higher chances that they will mine the next block. Similarly in PoW, to increase the computational power, parallel AISCs (application specific integrated circuits) chips are deployed by the miners. Whereas in PoI to overcome these limitations, the users which have a high number of transactions and the users who have high net stakes are rewarded. In this, an important value is assigned to every node. The node with the higher important value has higher priority to mine the next block even if the stake value of that node is lower than the other nodes.

PoET (Proof of Elapsed Time)

PoET is an improvement over the PoW protocol where the selection of the mining node depends on the node which has the lowest waiting time. The same can be achieved by assigning a random timer value to each node. The earliest node (whose timer runs out earliest) generates a signed certificate which allows the node that in the current iteration this node will be the block leader.

PoC (Proof of Capacity)

The mechanism of PoC is such that based on the availability of the free memory capacity of HDD (external) a minor node is chosen. More possible solutions to nonce problems can be stored in the node which has a large capacity, before the beginning of the mining. The overall complexity and the difficulties in managing the nodes in PoW can be improved with the help of PoC.

PoB (Proof of Burn)

In PoB protocol, to access the mining rights to the authorized source the virtual cryptocurrency is burned by the nodes. This is quite similar to the PoW but the difference is that the assets in PoB are in terms of cryptocurrency. Whereas in PoW, the assets are in terms of the computing power of nodes. Here the burning coins shows us the node's commitment to be honest in the entire network as to gain the mining rights it has burned the original coins.

PoP (Proof of Proof)

To protect Sybil and attacks in blockchain a modification in PoS is made which is known as PoP. In standard PoS a recently developed mechanism is introduced, which states that after every successful transaction, every node in the entire network should get incentives. This reward policy is an incentive based which depends on the quality of work, amount of work and chain performance. The nodes can use the earned rewards as stakes to mine the new blocks.

FRChain (Fault Resilient Chain)

These types of algorithms are highly used in case of permissioned blockchains. This algorithm tries its best to make the network irrepressible from failures. These are scalable. It replaces faulty or malicious nodes with the good nodes after crashes with high efficiency. The security is provided to the network with the help of collective signing which is based on routing of oral messages over multicast trees. After a root is selected, validation and block propagation is conducted in the blockchain.

Recent Advancements in Blockchain Assisted IoT and Smart City Applications

Liang et al. (2018) proposed a framework of security that integrates smart devices with blockchain technology to make smart cities a secure communication platform. Noh and Kwon (2019) presented a use case where Blockchain promises to balance security and privacy. Montes et al. (2019) discussed how the integration of healthcare and smart cities will use information and technology in healthcare and medical practice around the world. Al-Abbasi and El-Medany (2019) examined potential security issues in integrating blockchain technology into smart city infrastructure and provided blockchain-based solutions ensuring the security and resilience of smart cities. Yetis and Sahingoz (2019) intended to look into the institutional and technical frameworks for the adoption of safe urban living using blockchain technology. In this project, Majdoubi et al. (2020) focused on the Supply-He-Chain Operational Oriented Document of Understanding (DOU) contract, which serves as a framework for interaction between consumers of services and their suppliers.

Begam et al. (2020) examined the architecture of blockchain technology platforms, the security stability and vulnerability of the technology, and how it addresses the critical areas of information security integrity, availability, and confidentiality. Thanh et al. (2020) proposed an allocated node structure for blockchain systems and attempted to set up an authentication system for IoT devices using the blocks stored in these nodes. Nguyen et al. (2020) proposed measures to comply with the requirements of major data protection laws and regulations, in particular the European Union's General Data Protection Regulation. Finally, he proposed a Proof of Reputation (PoR) consensus scheme based on a multidimensional trust model. Jha et al. (2019) proposed a consensus-based decentralized blockchain solution to address e-FIR data integrity and registration errors related to police stations in a constitutional database as a key component of smart city environments.

Sharma et al. (2019) offered an innovative and efficient security protection architecture that uses digital video on the Blockchain network to conceal sensitive information. It has been demonstrated that the suggested framework could safeguard digital video content with high accuracy and efficiency. Sharma et al. (2020a) established a secure communication platform in smart cities. The purpose of this article is to combine blockchain and IoT. This will be done by creating a secure decentralized architecture. Dansana et al. (2020) proposed the Temporal Pattern Attention-Based LSTM (TPA-LSTM) natural gas performance prediction illustrative to enable the system to detect changes in natural gas supply capacity. Malik et al. (2021) studied a case for how the creation and growth of smart cities will alter both the way that cities are created today and how people live in future. Smart cities have grown to be an inevitable fashion of world development.

Sharma et al. 2020b) proposed a way to combine IoT and blockchain along the Consensus Algorithm Framework (BCIoT-CAF) to address the problem and ensure riskless data exchange in smart cities. Dansana et al. (2021) used a machine learning (ML) method in our proposed consensus protocol to accomplish effective leader election, and a novel dynamic block construction mechanism was created as a result. Each transaction's hash value is initially generated using the Merkle hash tree (Table 14.1).

Future Research Directions

On the basis of the review of this paper, few research could be carried out on smart city, a few similar concepts are mentioned below. Sharma et al. (2020b) came up

Table 14.1 Summary of recent advancements

Reference	Year	Major Contribution
Liang et al. (2018)	2016	Proposed security framework that integrates smart devices with blockchain
Noh and Kwon (2019)	2018	Presents a use case where Blockchain promises to balance security and privacy
Montes et al. (2019)	2018	Discussed how the integration of healthcare and smart cities will use information and technology in healthcare
Al-Abbasi and El-Medany (2019)	2018	Examined potential security issues in integrating blockchain technology into smart city infrastructure and provided blockchain-based solutions
Yetis and Sahingoz (2019)	2019	Intended to look into the institutional and technical frameworks for the adoption of safe urban living
Majdoubi et al. (2020)	2019	Focused on the Supply-He-Chain Operational Oriented Document of Understanding (DOU) contract
Begam et al. (2020)	2019	Examined the architecture of blockchain technology platforms, the security stability and vulnerability of the technology

(continued)

Table 14.1 (continued)

Reference	Year	Major Contribution
Thanh et al. (2020)	2019	Proposed an allocated node structure for blockchain systems and attempted to set up an authentication system
Nguyen et al. (2020)	2020	Proposed measures to comply with the requirements of major data protection laws and regulations
Jha et al. (2019)	2020	Proposed a consensus-based decentralized blockchain solution to address e-FIR data integrity and registration errors related to police stations
Sharma et al. (2019)	2020	Offered innovative and efficient security protection architecture that uses digital video
Sharma et al. (2020a)	2020	Established a secure communication platform in smart cities. The purpose of this article is to combine blockchain and IoT
Dansana et al. (2020)	2020	Proposed the Temporal Pattern Attention-Based LSTM (TPA-LSTM) natural gas performance prediction illustrative
Malik et al. (2021)	2021	Studied a case for how the creation and growth of smart cities will alter both the way cities are created today
Sharma et al. (2020b)	2021	Proposed a way to combine IoT and blockchain along the Consensus Algorithm Framework (BCIoT-CAF) to address the problem and ensure riskless data exchange
Dansana et al. (2021)	2022	Proposed consensus protocol to accomplish effective leader election

with few tools and techniques in order to evaluate smart cities on the basis of their management sustainability and smartness to operate. Sharma et al. (2020b) conducted a comparison of different tools and further pointed out the lackings and strengths. According to these authors, better development of smart cities assessment tools could be the main focus of further research and also the assessing the measures which would increase their performance. IoT is a leading tech used to apply smart cities in various dimensions. Scientists such as Sharma et al. (2020b) noted his use of IoT in areas such as transportation, waste management, healthcare and power transmission.

What is still lacking, however, is the integration of IoT across multiple dimensions and the further use of blockchain technology and AI to improve multiple dimensions of smart cities. This kind of research could help to eliminate the problems of cyber threats and security issues in smart cities. Dansana et al. (2021), highlighted that available risk assessment and management approaches are not comprehensive. Available tools do not appropriately consider non-technology-associated uncertainty. His research emphasized assessing technology-associated uncertainty without looking at non-technology-associated risks. In addition, it is important to consider all aspects and their interrelationships, as these aspects are not practically separate in reality. Therefore, in-depth research into the risk landscape, proprietary assessment methodologies, and non-technology and technology-based risk management are critical. Such approaches can leverage AI technology and blockchain to predict and identify triggers to resolve manual disruptions, semi-autonomous, or autonomous. Since smart cities are bottom-up businesses, they adopt the enterprise architecture approach proposed by Helfert and Singh et al. can be considered for further analysis. Such advances will help advance a burgeoning program risk management pathway that can be deployed in a variety of smart city domains by taking a few precautions.

Conclusion

In this paper, we propose a security framework that uses blockchain technology to ensure reliable intercommunication between smart cities and ensure their security. Along with various unique benefits including privacy, reliability, better scalability, efficiency and fault tolerance. Blockchain integrated Smart city provides more resistance to threats. Thus, integration of blockchain on all the available smart devices would create a web which would provide better reliable and secure communication. Further work on this technology aims at designing the system model, authenticating its operability, and testing.

References

Aggarwal S, Kumar N (2021) Attacks on blockchain. In: Advances in computers, vol 121, pp 399–410. Elsevier
Al-Abbasi L, El-Medany W (2019) Blockchain security architecture: a review technology platform, security strength and weakness. In: 2nd smart cities symposium (SCS 2019), pp 1–5. https://doi.org/10.1049/cp.2019.0190
Alnahari MS, Ariaratnam ST (2022) The application of blockchain technology to smart city infrastructure. Smart Cities 5(3):979–993
Al-shareeda MA, Anbar M, Manickam S, Hasbullah IH (2020) Review of prevention schemes for man-in-the-middle (MITM) attack in vehicular ad hoc networks. Int J Eng Manag Res 10
Ande R, Adebisi B, Hammoudeh M, Saleem J (2020) IoT: evolution and technologies from a security perspective. Sustain Cities Soc 54(February 2019):101728. https://doi.org/10.1016/j.scs.2019.101728
Appio FP, Lima M, Paroutis S (2019) Understanding smart cities: innovation ecosystems, technological advancements, and societal challenges. Technol Forecast Soc Chang 142(1–14):2018. https://doi.org/10.1016/j.techfore.2018.12.018
Apostol D, Balaceanu C, Constantinescu EM (2015) Smart—Economy concept—Facts and perspectives. HOLISTICA J Bus Public Admin 6(3):67–77
Arroub A, Zahi B, Sabir E, Sadik M (2016) A literature review on smart cities: paradigms, opportunities and open problems. In: Proceedings—2016 international conference on wireless networks and

mobile communications, WINCOM 2016: green communications and networking, pp 180–186. https://doi.org/10.1109/WINCOM.2016.7777211

Arsh M, Bhushan B, Uppal M (2021) Internet of Things (IoT) toward 5G NETWORK: design requirements, integration trends, and future research directions. In: Advances in intelligent systems and computing, pp 887–899.https://doi.org/10.1007/978-981-15-9927-9_85

Begam SS, JV, Selvachandran G, Ngan TT, Sharma R (2020) Similarity measure of lattice ordered multi-fuzzy soft sets based on set theoretic approach and its application in decision making. Mathematics 8:1255

Begum A, Tareq A, Sultana M, Sohel M, Rahman T, Sarwar A (2020) Blockchain attacks analysis and a model to solve double spending attacks. Int J Mach Learn Comput 10(2):352–357

Biswas K, Muthukkumarasamy V (2016)Securing smart cities using blockchain technology. In: 2016 IEEE 18th international conference on high performance computing and communications; IEEE 14th international conference on smart city; IEEE 2nd international conference on data science and systems (HPCC/SmartCity/DSS), pp 1392–1393. https://doi.org/10.1109/HPCC-SmartCity-DSS.2016.0198

Bhowmik T, Bhadwaj A, Kumar A, Bhushan B (2022) Machine learning and deep learning models for privacy management and data analysis in smart cities. In: Balas VE, Solanki VK, Kumar R (eds) Recent advances in Internet of Things and machine learning. intelligent systems reference library, vol 215. Springer, Cham. https://doi.org/10.1007/978-3-030-90119-6_13

Bhushan B, Sahoo G (2020) Requirements, protocols, and security challenges in wireless sensor networks: an industrial perspective. In: Handbook of computer networks and cyber security, pp 683–713.https://doi.org/10.1007/978-3-030-22277-2_27

Bibri SE, Krogstie J (2017) Smart sustainable cities of the future: an extensive interdisciplinary literature review. Sustain Cities Soc 31:183–212. https://doi.org/10.1016/j.scs.2017.02.016

Burnes D, DeLiema M, Langton L (2020) Risk and protective factors of identity theft victimization in the United States. Prevent Med Rep 17:101058

Biswas K, Muthukkumarasamy V (2016) Securing smart cities using blockchain technology. https://doi.org/10.1109/HPCC-SmartCity-DSS.2016.0198

Bhushan B, Sahoo C, Sinha P, Khamparia A (2020) Unification of Blockchain and Internet of Things (BIoT): requirements, working model, challenges and future directions. Wirel Netw. https://doi.org/10.1007/s11276-020-02445-6

Bhushan B, Sahoo G (2017) Recent advances in attacks, technical challenges, vulnerabilities and their countermeasures in wireless sensor networks. Wirel Pers Commun 98(2):2037–2077. https://doi.org/10.1007/s11277-017-4962-0

Dansana D, Kumar R, Das Adhikari J, Mohapatra M, Sharma R, Priyadarshini I, Le D-N (2020) Global forecasting confirmed and fatal cases of COVID-19 outbreak using autoregressive integrated moving average model. Front Public Health 8:580327. https://doi.org/10.3389/fpubh.2020.580327

Dansana D, Kumar R, Parida A, Sharma R, Adhikari JD et al (2021) Using susceptible-exposed-infectious-recovered model to forecast coronavirus outbreak. Comput, Mater Continua 67(2):1595–1612

Department of Economic and Social Affairs (2014) World urbanization prospects: The 2014 revision, highlights (ST/ESA/SER.A/352). United Nations: Department of Economic and Social Affairs, Population Division, Tech. Rep. https://esa.un.org/unpd/wup/Publications/Files/WUP 2014-Highlights.pdf

Elahi H, Wang G, Peng T, Chen J (2019) On transparency and accountability of smart assistants in smart cities. Appl Sci (Switzerland) (24):9. https://doi.org/10.3390/app9245344

Flynn T, Grispos G, Glisson W, Mahoney W (2020) Knock! Knock! Who is there? Investigating data leakage from a medical IoT hijacking attack. In: Proceedings of the 53rd Hawaii international conference on system sciences

Goyal S, Sharma N, Kaushik I, Bhushan B (2021) Blockchain as a solution for security attacks in named data networking of things. In: Security and privacy issues in IoT devices and sensor networks, pp 211–243.https://doi.org/10.1016/b978-0-12-821255-4.00010-9

HMGovernment (2011) Government cloud strategy, pp 1–24

Hussain M, Al-Haiqi A, Zaidan AA, Zaidan BB, Kiah M, Iqbal S, Iqbal S, Abdulnabi M (2018) A security framework for mHealth apps on Android platform. Comput Secur 75:191–217

https://www.ibm.com/in-en/topics/what-is-blockchain#:~:text=Blockchain%20defined%3A%20B lockchain%20is%20a,patents%2C%20copyrights%2C%20branding

Ismagilova E, Hughes L, Dwivedi YK, Raman KR (2019) Smart cities: advances in research—An information systems perspective. Int J Inf Manag 47(88–100):2018. https://doi.org/10.1016/j.iji nfomgt.2019.01.004

Jha S et al (2019) Deep learning approach for software maintainability metrics prediction. IEEE Access 7:61840–61855

Khalaf BA, Mostafa SA, Mustapha A, Mohammed MA, Abduallah WM (2019) Comprehensive review of artificial intelligence and statistical approaches in distributed denial of service attack and defense methods. IEEE Access 7:51691–51713. https://doi.org/10.1109/ACCESS.2019.290 8998

Lanza J, Sánchez L, Muñoz L, Galache JA, Sotres P, Santana JR, Gutiérrez V (2015) Large-scale mobile sensing enabled internet-of-Things testbed for smart city services. Int J Distribut Sensor Netw 11(8). Article 785061. https://doi.org/10.1155/2015/785061

Latre S, Leroux P, Coenen T, Braem B, Ballon P, Demeester P (2016) City of things: an integrated and multi-technology testbed for IoT smart city experiments. In: 2016 IEEE International Smart Cities Conference (ISC2). https://doi.org/10.1109/isc2.2016.7580875

Liang X, Shetty S, Tosh D (2018)Exploring the attack surfaces in blockchain enabled smart cities. In: 2018 IEEE international smart cities conference (ISC2), pp 1–8. https://doi.org/10.1109/ISC2. 2018.8656852

Liu Y, Hei Y, Xu T, Liu J (2020) An evaluation of uncle block mechanism effect on ethereum selfish and stubborn mining combined with an eclipse attack. IEEE Access 8:17489–17499

Majdoubi DE, El Bakkali H, Sadki S (2020) Towards smart blockchain-based system for privacy and security in a smart city environment. In: 2020 5th international conference on cloud computing and artificial intelligence: technologies and applications (CloudTech), pp 1–7. https://doi.org/10. 1109/CloudTech49835.2020.9365905

Makrushin D, Dashchenko V (2016) Fooling the 'Smart City.' Technical Report, Kaspersky Lab, pp 1–22

Malik PK, Sharma R, Singh R, Gehlot A, Chandra Satapathy S, Alnumay WS, Pelusi D, Ghosh U, Nayak J (2021) Industrial Internet of Things and its applications in industry 4.0: state of the art. Comput Commun 166:125–139. ISSN 0140-3664. https://doi.org/10.1016/j.comcom.2020. 11.016

Mehta S, Bhushan B, Kumar R (2022) Machine learning approaches for smart city applications: emergence, challenges and opportunities. In: Balas VE, Solanki VK, Kumar R (eds) Recent advances in internet of things and machine learning. Intelligent Systems Reference Library, vol 215. Springer, Cham. https://doi.org/10.1007/978-3-030-90119-6_12

Montes JM, Ramirez CE, Gutierrez MC, Larios VM (2019) Smart contracts for supply chain applicable to smart cities daily operations. In: 2019 IEEE international smart cities conference (ISC2), pp 565–570. https://doi.org/10.1109/ISC246665.2019.9071650

Nguyen PT, Ha DH, Avand M, Jaafari A, Nguyen HD, Al-Ansari N, Van Phong T, Sharma R, Kumar R, Le HV, Ho LS, Prakash I, Pham BT (2020) Soft computing ensemble models based on logistic regression for groundwater potential mapping. Appl Sci 10:2469

Nilssen M (2019) To the smart city and beyond? Developing a typology of smart urban innovation. Technol Forecast Soc Change 142:98–104. https://doi.org/10.1016/j.techfore.2018.07.060. July 2018

Nižetić S, Solić, P, Lopez-de-Ipi´na˜ Gonzalez-de-Artaza´ D, Patrono L (2020) IoT (IoT): opportunities, issues and challenges towards a smart and sustainable future. J Clean Prod 274.https:// doi.org/10.1016/j.jclepro.2020.122877

Noh Jh, Kwon Hy (2019) A Study on smart city security policy based on blockchain in 5G Age. In: 2019 international conference on platform technology and service (PlatCon), pp 1–4. https://doi.org/10.1109/PlatCon.2019.8669406

OWASP Foundation (2013) OWASP top 10-2013: the most critical web application security risks

Paiva S, Ahad MA, Tripathi G, Feroz N, Casalino G (2021) Enabling technologies for urban smart mobility: recent trends, opportunities and challenges. Sensors 21(6):1–45. https://doi.org/10.3390/s21062143

Porru S, Misso FE, Pani FE, Repetto C (2020) Smart mobility and public transport: opportunities and challenges in rural and urban areas. J Traffic Transp Eng (English Edition) 7(1):88–97. https://doi.org/10.1016/j.jtte.2019.10.002

Qiu J, Liang X, Shetty S, Bowden D (2018)Towards secure and smart healthcare in smart cities using blockchain. In: 2018 IEEE international smart cities conference (ISC2), pp 1–4. https://doi.org/10.1109/ISC2.2018.8656914

Radu LD (2020) Disruptive technologies in smart cities: a survey on current trends and challenges. Smart Cities 3(3):1022–1038. https://doi.org/10.3390/smartcities3030051

Sharma R, Kumar R, Kumar Sharma D, Hoang Son L, Priyadarshini I, Thai Pham B, Tien Bui D, Rai S (2019) Inferring air pollution from air quality index by different geographical areas: case study in India. Air Qual Atmos Health 12:1347–1357 (2019)

Sharma R, Kumar R, Singh PK, Raboaca MS, Felseghi R-A (2020a) A systematic study on the analysis of the emission of CO, CO_2 and HC for four-wheelers and its impact on the sustainable ecosystem. Sustainability 12:6707

Sharma R, Kumar R, Satapathy SC, Al-Ansari N, Singh KK, Mahapatra RP, Agarwal AK, Le HV, Pham BT (2020b) Analysis of water pollution using different physicochemical parameters: a study of Yamuna River. Front Environ Sci 8:581591. https://doi.org/10.3389/fenvs.2020.581591

Silva BN, Khan M, Han K (2018) Towards sustainable smart cities: a review of trends, architectures, components, and open challenges in smart cities. Sustain Cities Soc 38(697–713):2017. https://doi.org/10.1016/j.scs.2018.01.053

Thanh V, Rohit S, Raghvendra K, Le Hoang S, Binh Thai P, Bui Dieu T, Ishaani P, Manash S, Tuong L (2020) Crime rate detection using social media of different crime locations and twitter part-of-speech tagger with brown clustering. 1 Jan. 2020:4287–4299

Topal OA, Demir MO, Liang Z, Pusane AE, Dartmann G, Ascheid G, Kur GK (2020) A physical layer security framework for cognitive cyber-physical systems. IEEE Wirel Commun 27(4):32–39

Xie J, Tang H, Huang T, Yu FR, Xie R, Liu J, Liu Y (2019) A survey of blockchain technology applied to smart cities: research issues and challenges. IEEE Commun Surv Tutor 21(3):2794–2830. https://doi.org/10.1109/comst.2019.2899617

Ye C, Li G, Cai H, Gu Y, Fukuda A (2018). Analysis of security in blockchain: case study in 51%-attack detecting. In: 2018 5th international conference on dependable systems and their applications (DSA). IEEE, September, pp 15–24

Yetis R, Sahingoz OK (2019)Blockchain based secure communication for IoT devices in smart cities. In: 2019 7th international Istanbul smart grids and cities congress and fair (ICSG), pp 134–138. https://doi.org/10.1109/SGCF.2019.8782285

Yu Y, Li Y, Tian J, Liu J (2018) Blockchain-based solutions to security and privacy issues in the IoT. IEEE Wirel Commun 25(6):12–18

Correction to: A Shared Patch MIMO Antenna for NB-IoT Applications

Sneha, Praveen Kumar Malik, and Ahmed Alkhayyat

Correction to:
Chapter 9 in: D. K. Sharma et al. (eds.), *Low Power Architectures for IoT Applications*, Springer Tracts in Electrical and Electronics Engineering,
https://doi.org/10.1007/978-981-99-0639-0_9

In the original version of the chapter, the following belated correction has been incorporated: The affiliation for author "Praveen Kumar Malik" has been changed from "College of Technical Engineering, The Islamic University, Najaf, Iraq" to "Department of Electronics and Communication, Lovely Professional University, Phagwara, India".

The correction chapter and the book have been updated with the changes.

The updated version of this chapter can be found at
https://doi.org/10.1007/978-981-99-0639-0_9

Printed in the United States
by Baker & Taylor Publisher Services